PORT IN A STORM

The Air Attacks on Liverpool and its Shipping in the Second World War

JOHN HUGHES

NATIONAL MUSEUMS & GALLERIES
· ON MERSEYSIDE ·

First published in 1993 by Merseyside Port Folios.
1 & 3 Grove Road, Rock Ferry, Birkenhead, Wirral, Merseyside L42 3XS.

Merseyside Port Folios is the joint publishing imprint of the National Museums and Galleries on Merseyside and Countyvise Limited.

ISBN 0 9516129 5 6 (Hardback)
ISBN 0 9516129 6 4 (Paperback)

Typesetting by Milepost Research, 41 Fountain Street, Accrington, Lancashire BB5 0QR.

Printed by Birkenhead Press Limited, 1 & 3 Grove Road, Rock Ferry, Birkenhead, Wirral, Merseyside L42 3XS.

CONTENTS

TO THE MEMORY OF MY FATHER

Charles D. Hughes

AFS

8.3.1939 to 17.8.1941

NFS

18.8.1941 to 13.12.1945

ACKNOWLEDGEMENTS

Crown Copyright material in the Public Record office is reproduced by permission of the Controller of Her Majesty's Stationery Office, as is the quotation from ***The Emergency Medical Services.***

Grateful acknowledgement is also made to the following for their kind permission to reproduce passages of copyright material: The Trustees of the Mass-Observation Archive, University of Sussex; Ocean Transport & Trading plc; Lloyd's Maritime Information Services Ltd; the Littlewoods Organisation; L. S. Dixon Group Ltd; BBC Written Archives Centre, Caversham Park; The Liverpool Daily Post and Echo Ltd; Merseyside Fire and Civil Defence Authority; Mrs Ann Monsarrat; Angus and Robertson, the publishers of ***Softly Tread the Brave*** by Ivan Southall; Edith Pargeter.

The reseach for this book has added significantly to the work-load in various archives around the country. In paricular, I should like to thank the staff at the following for their unfailing courtesy and helpfulness: The Public Record Office, Kew; The Maritime Records Centre, Merseyside Maritime Museum; The Liverpool Record Office and the Microfilm Section, Liverpool Central Library.

I should also like to express my gratitude to the following, who provided information - with apologies to many others who went to some trouble searching without success or who supplied information that I have not used: Captain H. G. Allan, Gillingham; Mr W. L. Barber, Stockport; The Belgian Embassy, London; City of Birmingham Public Libraries Department; James Boyce, Hythe; British Telecom; Jim Burke, Kirkby; Mr D. L. Campbell, Liverpool; William Clarke, Liverpool; Mrs Margaret Cullen, Huyton; The East Asiatic Company Ltd. A/S; Denis Foss, Yeovil; Fred Olsen & Co; Glaxo Pharmaceuticals Ltd; Mr J. Green, Walkden; Fred Heyworth, Middleton; John H. Hindley, Queensland, Australia; Mr A.W. J. Holland, Moreton; Sam Holt, Liverpool; Dennis H Johnzon, Filey; Frank B. Jones, Hull; Joe Kinsella, Liverpool; Mr D.W.Large, Plymouth; Fred Lester, Greasby; Mr H.B. Lodewijks, Hilversum; Nedlloyd Group; Mr C. A. Neil, Hightown; The Post Office; Mrs Hilda Roberts, St Helens; Mr J. D. Robertson, Hon. Archivist, Merseyside Fire and Civil Defence Authority; Alan Stanley, Aintree; Mr M.W. W ebster, Godalming; Mr C.W.White, Huyton; Robert Wright, Haskayne.

Photographs are mainly from the Stewart Bale Collection held by the National Museums and Galleries on Merseyside. Those on pages 151, 153 and 162 are from the photographic collection of the North West Sound Archive.

Producing an academic book whose subject is tightly drawn in both time and space during a recession is not easy, and I would like to thank John Emmerson of Countyvise and Adrian Jarvis of Merseyside Maritime Museum for their determination that it should happen. That too would have come to nought without the support, financial, practical and moral of the Trustees of the National Museums and Galleries on Merseyside.

FOREWORD

This book has been published to coincide with the commemoration of the fiftieth anniversary of the Battle of the Atlantic and with the opening of Merseyside Maritime Museum's display which forms a part of that commemoration.

The attacks on Liverpool, as on Glasgow, Bristol, Belfast and Plymouth, were not aimed at the destruction of military targets, of production of war materials or of civilian morale, though some damage was demonstrably done to each of those 'targets'. They were a concerted campaign whose objective was exactly the same as that of the U-Boat campaign, namely to hinder, and if possible prevent, the supply of foodstuffs and material to Britain across the North Atlantic.

The method had a compelling logic. The objective for the side on the defensive in naval warfare - as plainly merchant shipping was - is often to rely on being somewhere else when the enemy is looking for you. There is an awful lot of 'somewhere else' in the Atlantic Ocean for U-boats to search. However, the ships must eventually make port, and finding them there is an altogether easier matter. If they are to fulfil their supply role, then there is no alternative to tying up in eminently predictable places for days at a time, presenting a sitting target. Even getting that far involved navigating approach channels which presented relatively easy targets for minelaying aircraft.

The tonnage of shipping sunk in the Mersey, its approaches and its docks seems modest alongside that sunk in the open ocean, but the comparison of simple tonnage figures does not tell the whole story. One ship sunk in mid-Atlantic meant the loss of one ship, one cargo and usually some of its crew. As John Hughes graphically explains, one ship set on fire in the Docks could destroy the cargoes of many others, cause damage to dock installations which slowed down the turn-round of every vessel using the Port, possibly ignite other vessels, and usually provide thousands of man-hours of grinding toil for fire-fighters, salvage teams and ship-repairers. In the record book, it is just one ship damaged in Port: in real life the loss was far greater than had it simply been sunk in open water.

There have been many books about the Blitz. The Trustees of the National Museums and Galleries on Merseyside have chosen to support the publication of this one because it follows the leading principle of their own publications on port history, which is to distrust previous work, and to start from contemporary source material. Here, as elsewhere, the result has been the laying to rest of some venerable stories which had passed uncritically from author to author until they had come to resemble folk tradition more than history.

The fundamental myth, however, was that a book such as this could not be written. It is still commonly believed that so much was 'hushed up' at the time, in the interests of preserving civilian morale, that the information simply does not exist. John Hughes has not only shown that it does, but he has deployed it in a way which explains in minute detail what was happening, laying bare causes and effects previously obscure. He may well be right when he modestly suggests that more might yet emerge, but I am confident that this book sets a new standard for its subject.

On a lighter note, I will close this preface by re-iterating John Hughes' appeal. Among the older readers of this book there may be someone who broke the law in 1941 by poking the lens of their camera through a gap in the blackout curtains and taking photographs by the light of the fires or who has other information. If this is so, then please write to John Hughes, c/o Merseyside Maritime Museum.

Adrian Jarvis
Curator of Port History
Merseyside Maritime Museum

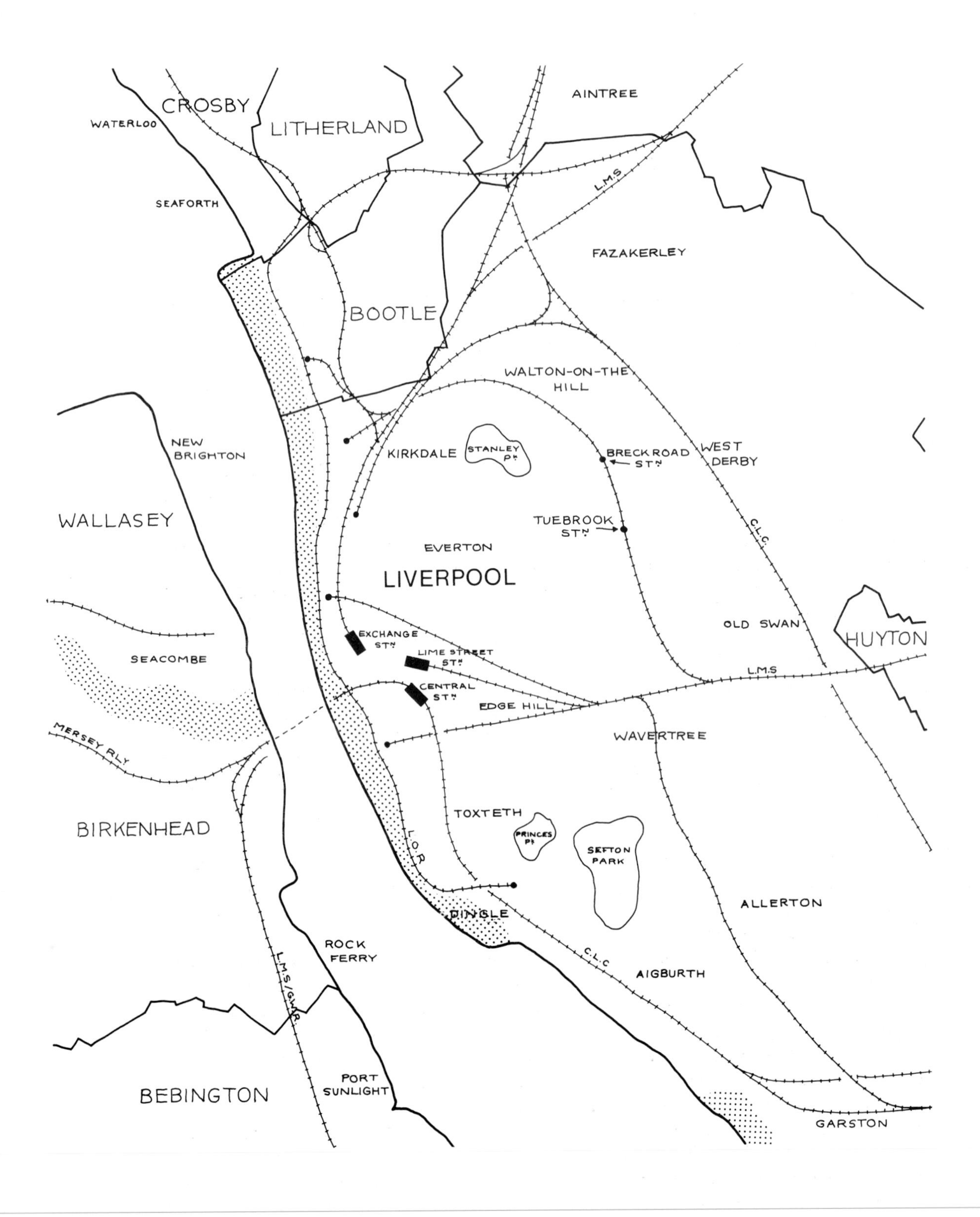

Merseyside and its main railways. The tinted area shows the position of the docks.

PREFACE

This book is principally concerned with the 'May Blitz', earlier events being included only to set the scene and to make it clear in what way the raids of May 1941 differed from what had gone before. The towns on the Cheshire bank of the Mersey were only slightly affected in May, and although they had been badly hit in earlier raids there was relatively little of the industrial damage and matters relevant to May that will take up much of the introduction.

The general outline of life in England at this time is familiar and there seems to be no need to recount all the details of preparation for war or the activities of the various organisations engaged in civil defence.

The story of the May Blitz has been told several times before; usually briefly, with the emphasis on domestic troubles, and based heavily on information that it was thought fit to release during the war. (The last two are not unconnected.) The story of the raids as they affected the port rather than the city has never been told except in the most general outline.

I have not attempted a detailed exploration of the effects of the raids on the home life of Merseysiders. In this respect the experience of any heavily-bombed area will be much the same and the subject has been well covered. For similar reasons I have made no attempt to cover the German side. The Luftwaffe's night attacks on the United Kingdom and the efforts made to combat them form a separate story in which the events of one week, over one area, mean little when taken out of context.

It should be said that I was not born at the time these events took place and have not generally thought it proper to criticise those who faced difficulties that I can only imagine. Critical comment made at the time, or since by people who were there, is another matter – though it may still be unfair. If the bare recitation of facts sometimes suggests shortcomings in the organisation and management of the defences, which it does, I hope this will not cause undue offence. Ordinary, decent men and women who sought a career in local government or services such as the Fire Brigade did not do so with total war in mind and ought not to be condemned for weaknesses exposed by trials they never expected to have to face. Those who volunteered for the new or expanded wartime services – often putting in long hours without pay – deserve similar consideration.

On the other hand, the Merseyside blitz has given rise to one or two outrageous myths, the overdue exposure of which requires no apology.

The main problem in putting this account together has been the tracing of sources – especially frustrating in cases (such as the ***Malakand*** incident) where previous accounts make it clear that much of what happened has been omitted or positively suppressed.

Liverpool's civil defence records are hidden or – more likely – destroyed. A few Incident Officer's Record Sheets survive at the Imperial War Museum, and the Liverpool City Engineer's list of certain categories of incident for the first six nights of May are in the Liverpool Record Office. Another potentially invaluable source is the 'bomb census' – a careful record of every bomb dropped, maintained for a few selected places, of which Liverpool was one. This record survives at the Public Record Office – except for the first week of May 1941. The work done on the first few nights was destroyed by enemy action and it was not possible to resume the survey until the raids that concern us had ended. The minutes of Liverpool's Civil Defence Emergency Committee contain the Chief Constable's reports on all raids up to, but excluding, those of May.

There are many other fragmentary sources: general reports on limited aspects of the raids, accounts of specific incidents, lists of ships sunk and damaged. Some of the most graphic contemporary accounts appeared in the local press, some months after the event, in connection with the award of medals for bravery. However, these generally do not give details of the times and locations of the incidents, nor are such details given in the *London Gazette.* With the exception of incidents involving the Liverpool Police Force and a few others that have been singled out for attention since, it is infuriatingly difficult to establish these facts.[1]

Another source, now fast failing, is the personal recollections of survivors, and I am grateful to those who have helped in this way – whether or not their contributions are visible in the finished work. It is fifty years now and, while some memories remain vivid, details of times, dates, and the order in which events occurred tend to be less certain. To be told as a fact that one major incident happened at one o'clock in the morning and at mid-day when official records place it definitely at 7.30 a.m. (as well as 9.00) requires thoughtful treatment.

To the uninitiated, it may seem that a live survivor is better than a dusty contemporary report in that one can ask the former to explain any doubtful points and add fresh detail: unfortunately, people tend to remember the story as they have told it over the years; information they could have added with ease the day after is now beyond recall. The ideal, of course, is to have the report *and* one or two people who were there.

One must not forget the local press, particularly the ***Liverpool Daily Post***, the ***Liverpool Echo*** and the ***Bootle Times***. The accounts of the Merseyside blitz published by the first two at various times form the base camp for any research into this subject and include much information that is not to be found elsewhere. Even the contemporary news reports of raids contain more useful information than one might expect at first sight.

I have undoubtedly missed some sources that *are* available – some good ones have come to light by mere chance. There must be others not yet available for public scrutiny; in particular, the Liverpool Record Office holds a considerable store of Council records that have not yet been catalogued. What follows is thus by no means the last word more an interim report. It is bound to contain errors and omissions, some having been discovered and corrected perilously late. It is impossible to guarantee accuracy when so many of the incidents recounted depend on a single source, and I have assuredly contributed errors of my own for which I can only beg the indulgence due to one sailing uncharted waters. To be fair, I have corrected some previously-published errors and, I hope, thrown fresh light on a surprisingly obscure period of Merseyside's recent history.

A good deal has been left to the imagination. A heavy air raid was a hell of noise, smoke and dust – the lights of fires, flares and searchlights – alarm bells, gunfire, the cries of the injured. Where this is not reflected in my sources I have not felt it proper to add imaginative, and probably inaccurate, trimmings of my own. Likewise, the effects of high-explosive, fire, and falling buildings on mere flesh and blood were not infrequently horrific, but this aspect of things hardly surfaces in the records of this particular period. Even now, one still catches the occasional flash of terror or irredeemable loss when talking to those who were there, but it is only a rare and faint echo of the truth. The reader will thus find very little as chilling as an early minute referring to the City Engineer's provision of "a special vehicle with bins to deal with dismembered bodies."[2] I think the thoughtful reader will have some conception of the unpleasantness lying behind the statistics without the help of novelist's trimmings on my part.

INTRODUCTION

Liverpool and Bootle had a combined population of over 900,000 in 1939. Within their bounds there were some farms, one or two quarries, and a limited range of manufacturing industry – much of the last enticed onto new industrial estates since 1918. Women who in other parts of Lancashire would have worked in the mills here found work with pools and mail-order companies. Otherwise, most employment was connected directly or indirectly with the port. This prompts the question: what did they all do?

Thousands went to sea, and thousands more worked on the docks – then bustling with grey ships, often two or more abreast at the quays. There were 231 sea-going merchant ships in the port at the beginning of May 1941; mostly British, with a substantial contingent from the allies past and present – Belgium, Denmark, France, Greece, Holland, Norway – and a few neutrals. There were also 48 tugs; 292 barges, flats, elevators and other small craft; plus the Royal Navy's contribution – destroyers, corvettes, minesweepers, sloops...

There was a multitude of more or less directly related occupations: ship repairing; lighterage; the manufacture and maintenance of nautical instruments, lifeboats and a hundred other items down to seamen's clothing. Ship-building had been pushed to the other side of the river through the expansion of the docks. Goods in transit had to be stored in warehouses – from modest eighteenth-century buildings to nineteenth-century monsters – though these contributed more to architecture than to employment. There were also vast cold-stores and extensive timber yards.

Transport engaged more thousands – by road and canal, but then mostly by rail. A dozen major goods stations as well as several smaller ones clustered along the dock road, through which goods passed to and from the marshalling yards further inland. The LMS (London Midland & Scottish) was the principal company on Merseyside; all lines and stations mentioned belonged to them unless otherwise specified. The CLC (Cheshire Lines Committee) was partly owned by the LMS, which also shared the main line to Birkenhead with the GWR (Great Western). There were also two small independent companies – the Mersey Railway, an underground line connecting the two sides of the river, and the LOR (Liverpool Overhead Railway) running along the Liverpool docks. Both these were all-electric passenger lines.

The LOR was unique in this country. It was opened in 1893 to facilitate movement along the docks and ran the whole length of them on a steel and iron viaduct. For most of the way this spanned the main line of the dock goods railway. Although, for various reasons, an impecunious concern, it came into its own when there was a war on and was carrying over 200,000 passengers a week when in full running order: dockers, seamen – all who had work to do in the docks or the related industries that clung to them. Unfortunately, it was also one of only three lines in Liverpool that were seriously vulnerable to attack on account of their exposed position. From the 1st September 1940 to the 26th March 1941 only sections of the railway were workable, although damage was made good as soon as possible in view of the LOR's importance to the working of the port.

There were a number of industries based on the processing of raw materials off the ships: tobacco, tanning, sugar-refining, flour-milling, paper-making (and printing), seed-crushing – the last leading to the production of edible oils and 'fats', margarine, animal feedstuffs and soap. Crackers and jam come under the same heading, hence the presence of firms such as Jacob's, Crawford's and Hartley's.

Liverpool's commercial heart still contained the head offices of some of the world's major shipping companies and was a national centre for insurance – historically founded, as in London, on marine insurance. A multitude of merchants and agents clustered round the Cotton, Corn and Royal exchanges.

The war brought a variety of new occupations, from a major aircraft factory at Speke and ordnance factories at Kirkby down to the production of parachutes and rubber dinghies, as well as adding munitions to the usual run of cargoes in and out. The concentration of legitimate military targets in the area was ominous.

It takes an effort of the imagination to picture the city as it was then, with the docks crowded and the industrial districts inland teeming with life; the tightly-packed terraces to the west and the Victorian villas and suburban semis in the greener east, all bound together by gleaming tram tracks and the cat's cradle of overhead wires. Then there was the smoke – from ships, factories, railway engines, and steam wagons on the dock road. The prevailing architectural textures were grimy red brick, blackened stone, and grey slate.

There were also the purely wartime features: the sandbagged buildings, the wardens' posts, the square, ugly surface shelters in the side streets – the balloons, searchlight sites, and AA guns.

It was not pretty, but – with the possible exception of the twentieth-century housing estates – it was endlessly fascinating. The war was only the first and least of the blows that were to destroy so much of this.

After a hectic night in May 1941, Captain Ruytenschildt of the ***Moena*** thought to relax by having a quiet smoke on the quayside. When a policeman called his attention to a notice forbidding smoking there, the captain looked around at the reeking ruin of burnt out sheds and smiled, assuming that he was joking. "But I had forgotten that I was in England – the man was in full earnest."[3]

When I first heard this story I shared the Dutch captain's amusement though when someone suggested that the policeman's eccentric behaviour might be attributable to shock I thought he might have a point. However, I now realise that the man was simply doing his job. Smoking had been forbidden on the quays of the Mersey Docks & Harbour Board (MDHB) for many years past, even in places where no conceivable fire risk was visible. There was no earthly reason to relax the rules in the circumstances prevailing on that May morning.

The Dock Board's fear of fire seems to the casual observer to verge on paranoia – for instance, they managed to almost completely exclude steam locomotives from the dock estate until 1895 when competition from more progressive ports forced a change of heart. In fact, there were sound reasons for the Board's attitude; in spite of the early use of fireproof construction, there had over the years been some spectacularly expensive fires in the docks and the warehouse districts inland.

In the 1940's only a few of the smaller vessels on the Mersey were still composed mostly of wood, hemp and tar, but modern ships had timber and inflammable insulating material under their steel skins – not to mention bunkers full of coal or oil. As in the past, most of the cargoes passing through the port were more or less inflammable, and now they included large quantities of rubber, petrol, and explosives.

In an area where a carelessly discarded cigarette could start a fire that might burn for days, the prospect of deliberate fire-raising attacks on a large scale was frightening; and when the real test came it was the fire service that proved to be the weak link in the chain of defence. In view of these facts, special attention is given to the development of fire precautions in what follows.

In July 1939 the Chief Officer of the Liverpool Fire Brigade (LFB) was seconded to the Home Office to examine emergency fire brigade schemes. He was succeeded, on a temporary basis at first, by Inspector H. R. Owen, who had joined the LFB as an 'engineer fireman' when demobbed after the previous war. Owen's appointment was confirmed in September 1940 when his predecessor formally retired from the LFB.

With the German invasion of Poland on the 1st September 1939, the country was put on a war footing; Liverpool's Civil Defence Emergency Committee sat for the first time on that day. It comprised three aldermen who had been appointed for this purpose in April: Sir Sydney Jones (the Lord Mayor), Luke Hogan, and A. E. Shennan, representing the Liberal, Labour and Conservative parties respectively. This committee would act on behalf of the Council in civil defence matters and effectively run the city in times of crisis – their main task at first was to supervise the frantic construction of air raid shelters. Mr. W. H. Baines, the Town Clerk, took up his post as ARP Controller at the same time – he was frequently referred to as the Air Raid Controller, which would seem to exaggerate his powers somewhat. (The Chief Constable was in executive control of all ARP functions during raids.) Although these men held positions of great importance in Liverpool, being given powers unthinkable in peacetime, their actions and decisions in May 1941 are so ill-recorded that a more generous introduction to them would be of little value.

On the evening of the following day several balloons of the defensive barrage that had already been raised about the city were struck by lightning and broke away from their moorings; one at least came down into the river in flames and another was later seen passing over Preston. One of the RAF balloon handlers was killed – it is debatable whether this can be counted as Merseyside's first fatality.[4] Earlier that day the ***Athenia*** had sailed from Liverpool, to become famous on the 3rd as the first British ship sunk in the war.

On the 6th a number of unidentified aircraft swept in low from the Irish Sea and flew up the river. AA batteries on either bank opened fire. None of the shells hit the intended targets, but some from the Cheshire side caused damage to property in

Lancashire and *vice versa*. Luckily, no-one was hurt. The planes turned out to be 'ours'.[5]

A lone aircraft that flew over Lancashire, Cheshire and North Wales on the 17th November set the sirens wailing on Merseyside for the first time – there would be over 500 more alerts in this area. This time it *was* the enemy, but only on a reconnaissance mission.

In January 1940 the approaches to the Mersey were mined. The tanker ***El Oso*** (7,267), sunk on the 11th, was the first local casualty from this cause. (Unless otherwise specified, numbers in brackets after ships' names are gross tonnage – a measure of volume rather than weight. Before the days of enormous tankers, seven or eight thousand tons was a good size for a freighter.) The salvage-men of the Dock Board's Marine Department were to spend much of the next eighteen months going to the aid of such vessels and were frequently able to bring them into port for repair.

At 1930 hours on the 21st January fire was discovered in one of the after holds of the Blue Funnel steamer ***Diomedes*** in Gladstone Dock;[6] she was carrying copra, palm kernels and sago meal. The Bootle Fire Brigade was called. It soon became clear that it was a serious blaze and smoke helmets were issued as a dense pall spread over the docks. Six AFS pumps assisted the regulars, gaining priceless experience.

At 2130, with the fire now in two holds, Alfred Holt & Co's Marine Superintendent rang the Liverpool Brigade to seek their attendance – without success as Gladstone Dock was not in the LFB's territory. Half an hour later the man rang again. This time he spoke to the Acting Chief Officer, Mr Owen, who explained that he could not send pumps into Bootle without a request from Bootle's Chief Officer, Mr Collins. Attempts were being made to get in touch with him when Lawrence Holt rang Owen at 2235. Mr. Holt evidently had little confidence in the Bootle Brigade's handling of the situation and pressed Owen to send help – Liverpool would be paid for their services. On these terms Owen ordered a pump out at once. He was leaving for the scene himself when Collins rang to say that he had plenty of pumps in reserve and no help was required. Owen explained that it was coming anyway at the request of the ship's owners.

When the Liverpool men arrived they found the ***Diomedes*** well alight at the stern, with fire in Nos. 7 and 8 holds and spreading to 9. After taking in the situation Owen called for Liverpool's special appliance van, containing breathing apparatus and cutting equipment, and then had two revolving nozzles lowered into No. 8 hold to spray water into the far corners. The fire spread forward to the coal bunkers, where it was tackled by the Bootle Brigade, but by 0300 on the 22nd it was just about out everywhere else and Owen left the Bootle Brigade to it with Collins' agreement.

This incident led to strained relations between Bootle and Liverpool. Either would gladly have sent assistance to the other on request; to do so uninvited was plainly a breach of fire service etiquette on Liverpool's part, though the ship's owners were presumably at liberty to seek help from any quarter. (The fact that these owners included Liverpool's Lord Mayor is unlikely to have influenced events.) The difficulty experienced with this single fire attended personally by Liverpool's Chief Fire Officer and with up to twenty-five branches (hoses) in use – helps us to understand events in May 1941 when five or six branches manned by the AFS would have counted as a good turn-out.

On the 12th February, a small convoy of four ships ran onto Taylor's Spit, flanking the Queen's Channel. This gave rise to the memorable signal: "The Whole Bloody Convoy has gone ashore." All were refloated without serious damage.[7]

THE FIRE SERVICE

On the 16th April 1940 the Liverpool Watch Committee considered a report on the state of the fire service.[8] This was now far stronger than the LFB had been a couple of years earlier – mostly through the formation of the Auxiliary Fire Service – though there was still room for improvement.

WATER SUPPLY: In an emergency, Liverpool could count on a variety of sources in addition to the usual mains supply: the Leeds and Liverpool Canal (level for thirty miles to its Liverpool terminus), park lakes, swimming baths (including those in schools), reservoirs – and, of course, the River Mersey. Fifty-two 5,000-gallon steel dams (tanks) had been placed around the city with more to come, and there were over a hundred smaller, canvas dams that could be moved quickly to areas where the mains had failed. Twenty-five tank wagons were also planned. There were a couple of salt-water mains to swimming baths, to which hydrants had been added. had been noted eight months earlier that the one running along Victoria Street "affords an adequate alternative supply for Lord Street and Dale Street.")[9] Additional 'stop-planks' were provided at intervals along the canal in Liverpool and Bootle to ensure that in the event of a breach the water would drain from only a short section.

These provisions must have seemed reasonably adequate before the raids started. The national planners had grossly over-estimated the likely number of casualties from bombing while under-estimating the danger of fire, so no particular blame attaches to the Liverpool authorities for failing to see into the future more accurately.

EQUIPMENT: In addition to the LFB's peace-time equipment, the Home Office (now the Ministry of Home Security) had supplied 200 'first-line' pumps (to be manned at all times) and another 245 'second-line' pumps (to be manned on receipt of an air-raid warning). The former included 185 trailer pumps (mostly large) and ten self-propelled pumps; the second-line pumps were all light trailers. In April there were only 174 motor cars available to tow the first-line trailers, of which a number would be under repair at any given moment; the Watch Committee were well aware of the need to obtain more, but this was not easy. There were also twenty tenders to carry equipment, hoses and personnel.

Some of the equipment to hand was not of the best; for instance, Liverpool had two turntable escapes dating from 1907 and 1910 that were now positively unsafe and were only retained in case of emergency.[10] My father, Charles Hughes, had dealings with two self-propelled pumps that were less than perfect. One had the irritating habit (for a fire engine) of catching fire itself while in motion. The other was not good at hill-climbing; on one occasion, when going up William Brown Street on the way to a call, the crew were so embarrassed at being overtaken by a pedal-cyclist that they thought it best to stop ringing the bell till they had reached more level ground.

Five of the first-line pumps, all heavy, were allocated to Liverpool's four fire-floats (presumably one of these carried two pumps as a spare would hardly qualify as first-line). Two life-boats had been acquired for use on the canal and two motor launches, the ***Silver Foam*** and ***Morag***, for the docks.[11] (Bootle had one, the ***James Spence***, in the docks. Another, the ***Simon Mahon***, was added by the beginning of 1941.) In case of fire aboard ships in the river, the LFB had a long-standing agreement allowing them to put pumps on one of the luggage ferries (of which a few had survived the opening of the Mersey Road Tunnel), but access to the landing stage was limited and might be blocked during a raid. There were also the Dock Board's salvage boats, ***Vigilant*** and ***Salvor***, which were fitted with fire hoses, but this was not their primary function and they might well be unavailable when needed. It was generally agreed that a fire-boat suitable for use in the river was needed and attempts were being made to obtain one, without success as yet.[12]

FIRE STATIONS: There were eight regular fire stations in Liverpool, the headquarters station being that at Hatton Garden in the city centre. The original plan for the AFS was to have the pumps distributed around 350 'sector stations', each responsible for its own small area, but after second thoughts most were now concentrated at forty-seven auxiliary stations. Eighty-four sector posts survived, notably in the docks where there were twenty-five in addition to four auxiliary stations.

PERSONNEL: The regular Fire Brigade, somewhat expanded, could call on 250 men including fifty policemen trained to act as auxiliary firemen in an emergency. (This arose from the LFB still being a police brigade under the Chief Constable, so that even the full-time firemen had police ranks and numbers.) These were greatly outnumbered by the AFS – now 2,009 full-time paid firemen and 2,825 unpaid part-timers. The numbers were not considered adequate and recruitment continued, bringing the number of part-time volunteers to 3,268 in July. (Before the war there had been talk of a need for 10,000 men, but this was probably in the expectation that all would be part-time. It is worth noting that while a smaller number of full-time men could keep the pumps manned there would not be the same local resources to call on in an emergency, when part-timers could work full shifts with the rest.)

As from the 1st May 1940 Herbert Winstanley, OBE, was appointed Chief Constable of Liverpool and Director of the Fire Brigade. He had been in the Liverpool Police Force for thirty-three years.

In May and June the war began to go wrong; soon the Luftwaffe had air fields in France and Norway and was ready to make the opening moves in the Battle of Britain. On the night of 23/24th July 1940 an enemy aircraft machine-gunned searchlight sites at New Brighton in what seems to have been the first actual attack on Merseyside.[13] Five nights later the first bombs were dropped on the area. On the night of 8/9th August the first civilian death occurred, at Prenton, Birkenhead. On the following night six more were killed in Wallasey, the fact that bombs were falling and that searchlights and AA guns were in action before the sirens were heard leading to some adverse comment.[14]

The night of 17/18th August saw the first bombs on Liverpool as well as the first significant damage in the docks. The Dock Board's dredger ***Lyster*** (619) began taking in water after a near miss at the north end of Brunswick Dock. Six hours later the fire service was called in but, before a start could be made on pumping her out, the ***Lyster*** suddenly turned over and sank, wrecking the wooden jetty at which she was moored.[15] Salvage operations – always more difficult with a vessel on her side – were started at once.

Up to this point the Germans had merely been indulging in 'armed reconnaissance'. On the four nights between the 28th August and 1st September they made what were intended to be their first heavy raids on any British city. If the 455 tons of HE bombs and 37,000 incendiaries that were dispatched had all been delivered on target the effects would doubtless have been serious, bearing in mind the fact that the defences had hardly been blooded as yet. Fortunately, the enemy were inexperienced as well when it came to long-distance night-flying and many failed to arrive; on the first night it was not even apparent from the ground that Liverpool had been the main target.

In the last and most effective of these raids (during which General De Gaulle sailed from the Mersey with half of the forces for the ill-fated Dakar expedition) some damage was done in the dock areas and Foster's Custom House was badly damaged by fire, one bomb scoring a direct hit on the dome.

There were twenty-three raids in September, few of them heavy. The one that started at 1930 hours on the 21st was worst in Bootle where serious fires began to break out from 2300, largely because the provision of fire-watchers was not as good as it became later. Fires started in at least nine timber yards, and one was only saved by some boys who climbed an 'unclimbable' fence to tackle incendiaries. A paper store and a jute sack works also burned, but the most damaging fire was the one that destroyed the large, five-storey warehouse at the LMS Alexandra Dock Goods Station. Three passenger coaches had to be brought in to replace the offices lost.

Bootle is not a large town and it is no surprise that a call for reinforcements was sent out twenty-nine minutes after the first bad fire was reported. Pumps came from Liverpool, Crosby, Litherland, Southport, St. Helens and Bolton. The LMS also brought in their own fire train from Horwich Works.

The first raid to stretch Liverpool's resources came on the night of 26/27th September[16] (starting in daylight) though it was Birkenhead that was hit first. Most incidents there occurred in the town, but some bombs fell on the docks and a serious situation developed when incendiaries fell on the GWR goods station between Morpeth and Wallasey Docks, setting light to buildings and wagons. One of the wagons contained ammunition fuses in cases, which had to be extracted at considerable risk.

Also in the yard, with the flames encroaching on it, was a train imaginatively loaded with a combination of HE bombs and petrol in tins. An engine manned by Driver Ivor Davies and Fireman Frank Newns was attached and drew the wagons clear of the fires, halting in a cutting (near Cleveland Street bridge) on the goods line leading out of the docks. Shunter Norman Tunna then saw a fire in one of the wagons. He ran to the engine for a bucket of water to throw on it and then acquired a stirrup pump and suppressed the fire with the help of the engine crew. Seeing flames coming from another wagon, Tunna climbed onto it, pulled away the tarpaulin, and found two incendiaries burning on top of a layer of 250-lb bombs. He quickly threw one of the incendiaries clear, but the other was jammed between two HE bombs. Davies passed Tunna his shunting pole, with which he prised the bombs apart until he could pull the incendiary out. He then sprayed water on the hot bombs to cool them. For this action, which certainly prevented considerable destruction in the dock area of Birkenhead, Davies and Newns received the George Medal and Tunna the George Cross.[17]

Reinforcements were sent to Birkenhead from Liverpool and Bootle, but were returned before midnight. In Liverpool it was mostly the south docks and the warehouses inland of them that got it. At King's Dock two sheds containing rubber and tobacco for export were burnt and a flat with a hundred tons of copra aboard was hit by fire-bombs and sunk. (I make no excuse for the frequent references to cargoes on ships and ashore. The main reason for Liverpool being bombed so heavily and often was the enemy's desire to destroy such cargoes or prevent their movement from place to place. The destruction of ships, buildings and people was incidental to this.) On the east side – called Wapping Dock for historical reasons – the upper section of the very large warehouse was burnt out, causing the collapse of walls on either side.

To the east, the rubble fell onto the Overhead Railway, buckling some of the girders. The wall that fell on the dock side of the Wapping warehouse sank a flat loaded with 250 tons of caustic soda in drums. The tug ***Wellington*** was moored at the knuckle opposite, between King's 1 and 2. A wall of the blazing shed there fell on her deck and she had to be towed out and beached in a sinking condition with her superstructure destroyed. At South Queen's 2 the upper halves of two sheds containing palm kernels, grain, meal and clothing were destroyed by fire. About fifteen warehouses burned in the streets inland of these docks, most of them full of cotton.

The situation around Brunswick Dock, a little further to the south, was worse. In the Dock Yard (the Board's maintenance department) most of an array of small buildings was destroyed along with piles of timber and various assemblies connected with work in progress. The fires here extended to part of a shed at South Coburg Dock and 500 yards of the sheds at West Brunswick, containing large quantities of cereals and oil. Two ships in Brunswick were damaged by fire and salvage gear assembled for the recovery of the ***Lyster*** was destroyed – with other distractions, the work was not taken up again until June 1942.

On the east side of Brunswick Dock a section of shed containing timber and wood pulp was burnt out. To the north of this was Grain Silo No. 2, connected to Silo No. 1 at the east end of Coburg by an overhead conveyor. This conveyor and the south-west corner of No. 1 Silo were set alight and there was serious danger of the fire spreading, but things were brought under control before the Navy arrived with demolition charges. On the east side of Silo No. 2, still on the dock estate, were some railway sidings on which 35 wagons loaded with coal and

The Custom House Dome seen from the roof after suffering damage in 1940. It was patched up in time for the May raids.

general goods were burnt, the intense heat buckling more girders of the Overhead Railway.

Across the dock road from the sidings all but a small part of two complete blocks was completely gutted. These included a small LMS goods station and sheds containing preserved food, 500 tons of oil and tallow, a thousand tons of nuts, 4,500 tons of palm kernels, 4,500 tons of rice meal, and 8,000 tons of cattle cereals.

Plainly, the situation east and west of Brunswick Dock had got out of hand – again, there is more than a hint that it was a shortage of fire-watchers that allowed many of the fires to gain a hold. Now it was Liverpool's turn to call for reinforcements. Fifteen pumps and one turntable escape were called in from the nearer towns, including Bootle, while Regional HQ in Manchester sent another thirty pumps from Blackpool, Bolton, Manchester and Preston. (All returned by the evening of the 28th) For a few days ratings from HMS ***Wellesley*** – a Royal Navy shore training establishment – were called on by the LFB to travel around rolling up hoses and dealing with "small smouldering fires."[18] According to the Chief Constable fifty-five of Liverpool's own pumps were used during the night along with all five of the city's turntable escapes (including the two condemned ones) and the fire-float ***Silver Foam*** (pumping water from the docks for use inland).

A raid on the following night had little effect, but some of the fires from the 26/27th were still burning around King's Dock when the alert sounded at 2202 on the 29th. This too was not a particularly heavy raid, but fires were started inland (mostly in Aigburth) and at Duke's Dock, just north of King's, where warehouses full of oil cake, flax and grain

Cotton warehouses, Shaw's Alley, fired on the night of 26/27th September.

were set alight. There were fifty-five fires in all. This time only thirty-four Liverpool pumps and two turntable escapes were used, but reinforcements were called in again – four pumps from Bootle and ten from other towns as far as Wigan and Warrington, all returned on the 1st October. On Monday, the 30th September, the Chief Constable reported that the Duke's Dock fires, together with those at the Queen's Dock sheds and six cotton warehouses in Shaw's Alley outstanding from Thursday night, seemed likely to burn indefinitely unless steps were taken to remove the contents of the buildings.

It seems odd that outside help should have been sought when only a small proportion of Liverpool's own pumps was engaged, but there must have been good reasons for this. It may have been thought a good idea to test the procedures and give the AFS in outlying towns a taste of action, but that does not explain the need to call on the Navy to roll up hoses.

In the wake of these raids, which had made the inadequacy of the arrangements to counter incendiary attack painfully apparent, the Regional Commissioner issued fresh advice. The top floors of warehouses should be cleared, at least enough to give the fire-watchers room to get at fires and especially where inflammable or explosive materials were stored. Stocks should be dispersed wherever possible. Salvage arrangements should be improved.[19] With the quantities of goods now passing through the port, these suggestions were easier made than acted upon and it is doubtful whether much was achieved. Some restoration was done at the docks, with two-storey sheds repaired as single-storey and a Bellman hangar ordered to replace the lost sheds at Brunswick. Meanwhile, dock staff displayed the spirit of the time by hoisting Union Flags and Red Ensigns on the ruins.

There were about twenty-five raids between the 1st October and the 28th November; none of them was very heavy and the docks were hit on only a few occasions. Some fairly serious damage was done to sheds and dock gates and the Swedish steamer ***Bifrost*** (1,781) was sunk in Alfred Basin, but she was refloated within a couple of days.

From the 7th September to mid-November London had been the main target with Liverpool clearly second favourite. Even after allowing for its smaller size and population, Merseyside had not had as much to put up with as the capital, though 500 were killed in this period and there were raids on up to six nights in succession.

Starting with the raid of 14/15th November on Coventry, the enemy changed his tactics and switched to a series of heavy raids on provincial towns (or switched back if one counts the failed attempt of late August). Liverpool's turn for one of these major attacks came on the night of 28/29th November. Well over 300 aircraft were directed to Liverpool, but the night was moonless and cloudy and fifty or more failed to find the target. Even so, 324 claimed to have arrived and dropped 30,960 incendiaries and 356 tons HE, the latter figure including 151 'very heavy bombs'. This probably means parachute mines – the first time that these had been directed at land targets on Merseyside.

Parachute mines were popularly known as land mines – a misnomer as they were in fact ordinary sea mines. These, usually magnetic, had a short time fuse intended to destroy them if they fell on land or in shallow water. This was introduced to prevent their falling into the hands of British mine experts, but in mid-September 1940 the Germans realised that aircraft adapted to carry this weapon – two at a time – could just as well be used in the campaign against the British mainland. They came in two sizes – ton and half-ton – most of which was high-explosive as the casing was thinner than that of an ordinary bomb (hence the parachute). As the aircraft could not fly comfortably with only one aboard, they were generally dropped in pairs.

Being let down gently, they did not penetrate the ground; consequently the blast could cause devastating damage to property over a wide area, flattening houses and street shelters alike. They were genuine block-busters – the most hated and feared weapon in the German armoury at that time. The only good thing about them was the surprising number that failed to explode, sometimes in excess of fifty per cent. Even then they caused widespread disruption as the area within a radius of 400 yards had to be evacuated until the Royal Navy's mine-disposal experts from HMS ***Vernon***, Portsmouth, had dealt with them. A curious rumour to the effect that these were British mines left behind at Dunkirk is entirely without foundation.

Such was the threat. The reality was that the first three hours of desultory and scattered attacks left less than twenty dead on Merseyside and did little damage of military value. Then followed two hours in which nothing fell on the built-up area at all.[20] From a later German report it seems that, apart from scattering their loads over Cheshire, they had been lured into attacking decoy oil fires on the Dee. Now, though, they saw their mistake – possibly assisted by a mine that set light to Wavertree Gas Works at 0100.[21] At any rate, 1,500,000 cubic feet of gas burned away in a fire that was visible from Fleetwood and the last two hours of the raid were concentrated around Wavertree.

The raid is chiefly remembered for a particularly unpleasant incident involving the collapse of the Junior Instruction Centre, Durning Road. 164 bodies were recovered from the basement shelter here,[22] making it probably the worst single incident of the 1940-41 blitz anywhere in the country – it was the main reason for Liverpool's organising its first mass funeral of the war, after seeking advice from Coventry.

The mine that landed inside a gas holder at Garston Gas Works without exploding caused more trouble than many that did. In order to allow the Naval mine expert, Lieutenant Newgass, to deal with it, the holder had to be pumped clear of one and a quarter million gallons of water (over which the gas was stored) as well as lingering gas fumes. Newgass then had to tackle the mine, which was awkwardly placed, in the most unpleasant conditions imaginable. (His support team – also working in the face of sudden death – included gas workers. It is noticeable that among the roll of civilians awarded medals for bravery at this time the obvious categories of police, wardens, firemen and such are joined by two other large groups – gas workers and railwaymen.) This mine was not made safe until the evening of the 3rd December. Until then all access to the LMS Railway's Garston Docks was blocked and this small but important port was effectively closed.

Apart from this there was a fire at a sugar silo at Garston and some HE damage at Gladstone Dock in Bootle – both in the earlier part of the raid. Otherwise, the docks and industry came through practically unscathed and fires were not a serious problem. After the first five hours of misplaced activity, the Luftwaffe had succeeded in killing 250 people in under two hours, which gives an idea of what Liverpool would have been in for if the raid had been on target from the start.

The Watch Committee reviewed the resources of the fire service in Liverpool on the 17th December. The number of 5,000-gallon dams had risen from 52 to 87, with fourteen more to come. Local firms had promised to make 220 vehicles available to carry water or portable dams in an emergency. Twelve light trailers had been replaced by self-propelled pumps and a new hundred-foot turntable escape had been acquired. There were now 224 towing vehicles (58 of them under repair) for a total of 418 trailer pumps. Ten elderly single-decker buses had been converted to hose-laying vehicles.

The Chief Constable had asked the Home Office to allow Liverpool to take on more full-time auxiliary firemen and this had been granted – though not as many as he wanted. Winstanley had also been worried at the prospect of losing 250 firemen aged 28 and 29 whose call-up had only been deferred till November.[23] They were trained, experienced, and fitter than many of the older men. Evidently Winstanley won on this point and there were now 2,253 full-time men in the AFS and 2,997 part-time – the reduction from 3,268 part-timers in June would have been mostly due to men taking full-time posts.

The first of the major attacks on Merseyside actually to cause serious damage to the port followed a few days later. On the night of Friday the 20th December 205 aircraft were said to have arrived with 205 tons of HE (see Appendix I) and 27,396 incendiaries. 299 aircraft came the next night with 280 tons of HE and 33,840 incendiaries. There was a light attack on the third night. It being mid-winter, the raids were long, the alert on the Saturday night lasting for nearly eleven hours. The whole of Merseyside was affected, and casualties and damage were heavy.

Much of the damage occurred in residential areas – especially on the Cheshire side – but there was also more in the docks and industrial areas of Liverpool and Bootle than can be conveniently recorded here. Of warehouses not owned by the Dock Board, 135 were damaged and another 65 totally destroyed, usually by fire.[24] Those destroyed accounted for 90,000 tons of storage space out of a total 411,000 tons. About 78,000 tons of goods, mostly cotton, were actually lost.[25] On the first two nights the fire service was called to about 500 outbreaks in Liverpool alone, while many more were dealt with by the people on the spot.

On the Friday night bombs caused damage to the adjacent Canada and Bankfield Goods Stations and brought down two spans of the Overhead Railway where it passed the former. A 500-kg delayed-action bomb landed on the west side of the canal where it passed Canada Dock Station and exploded at 0515 with catastrophic results. Unfortunately, some of the stop-planks had been removed to allow the passage of the canal fire-floats and although the planks were then replaced, with some difficulty, a mile of the canal was drained and ten million gallons of water flowed into the railway yard through a breach eventually 120 feet wide. A number of barges were grounded and at least one ended up on the tracks. The yard was flooded up to three feet deep and a foot of mud remained when the water had gone. Bankfield Station on the north side and the distillery to the south were also affected to some extent by this. The scale of the torrent unleashed can be gauged from the fact that it not only crossed the dock road to pour into Canada Dock – No. 1 branch – but also flooded the sheds on the south side of the branch from end to end, causing damage to the goods inside. Until a new concrete retaining wall could be built the normal traffic on the canal – coal to various works and grain from docks to mills – was completely disrupted.[26]

Another 500-kg bomb hit the railway viaduct leading to Exchange Station. Three arches and two piers were destroyed, two more arches following after. The whole 56-foot width of the viaduct was wrecked for the space of five 30-foot spans although the four lines remained intact over the gap. Some of the arches had been sandbagged to provide shelter and forty-two bodies were eventually recovered. This lucky hit cut off all access to one of Liverpool's three main passenger termini and the goods station at Great Howard Street for months.

The worst fires broke out on the Friday night in the timber yards around Sandhills Lane, involving adjacent premises that included Huskisson (CLC) and Sandon goods stations. Thirty-five pumps and two fire-floats were used here and it took forty-eight hours to get all the fires out.

On the Saturday night much of the North Mersey Goods Station was destroyed, the main warehouse being gutted and all lines through the station blocked by debris and roof girders while many loaded wagons burned in the yard. At the same time the large warehouse at Canada Dock Station was utterly destroyed by fire.

A number of ships were caught in the river. The tanker ***John A. Brown*** (10,455) was at anchor opposite Canada Basin when, at midnight on the Friday, she was straddled by a stick of bombs of which one scored a direct hit. Seven hundred tons of her cargo of petrol, kerosene and gas oil escaped into the river. Luckily there was no fire and the salvage-boat ***Vigilant*** (344), which had been on her way to Gladstone, was able to give immediate assistance. At 0400 a mine exploded, causing further damage to the tanker, but she remained afloat and tugs got her to Dingle jetty to discharge her cargo before she went into Birkenhead Docks for repair.

On the afternoon of the next day, ships due out in the morning were seeking places to anchor in the river overnight. At 1640 the tanker ***Elax*** (7,403), bound for Trinidad in ballast, was approaching a convenient space off Canada Dock when the ***Innisfallen*** (3,071), bound for Dublin, cut across her bow and went full astern to grab the anchorage for herself. It was a mistake as she set off a mine. An attempt was made to beach her, but she sank near Egremont on the Cheshire side with only the tops of her two funnels showing at low water. In addition to her cargo she was carrying 42 crew, 6 cattlemen and 148 passengers. All but two crew and two cattlemen were saved by tugs after life-belts had been thrown out by the grateful crew of the ***Elax***.[27]

During the night, the ***Elax*** was shaken by near misses and then had her after lifeboat covers set on fire by incendiaries. While the crew were dealing with this, bombers homed in on the lighted ship and more near misses hurled pieces of old anchor chain from the bed of the river onto her deck. Next day there was some doubt about the condition of the engines, but it was resolved that they should be tested on the way to the Bar. The ***Elax*** had just passed the mouth of the river in the wake of six other vessels when a mine exploded under her engine room and she veered off course onto a sandbank. Luckily, she came to rest on a flat bottom and was back in dock by Christmas Eve.

On the same day, the tug ***Poolgarth*** was blown to bits – again off Canada Basin – and all seven men aboard were killed.

There was a good deal of damage in the docks. Several locks and dock gates were affected, the outer gates of the eighty-foot lock at Sandon being completely removed, leading to a loss of water from the North Docks that left a number of large vessels on the bottom – including Cunard White Star's ***Britannic*** and ***Samaria***. More sheds were burnt at Queen's and the north side of the Waterloo Dock grain warehouse was destroyed by a parachute mine.

On the north side of Huskisson No. 2 Branch was the ***Europa*** (10,224), a Danish liner requisitioned by the Canadian Government for troops and stores. She was a motor-ship, with two squat funnels set towards the rear of her central superstructure and cabins for only fifty-odd passengers in normal times – emphatically not to be confused with the much larger German ***Europa***, although she has been. She had just finished loading general cargo and aircraft and was due to sail on the 21st, but at about 2200 on the Friday night a bomb exploded between her and the barge ***Overdale*** lying alongside. The ***Overdale***, loaded with sand (for ballast), was sunk. A hole eighty feet by thirty was torn in the ***Europa's*** side, exposing Nos. 1 and 2 holds, and she was left with her bow on the bottom; most of the cargo was recoverable but she would be a long salvage job. At North Huskisson 3 the upper floors of the sheds, containing sugar, were completely gutted.

In South Alexandra 1 the ***Silvio*** (1,293) was sunk by a direct hit forward – she proved to be a hopeless case and no immediate action was taken to remove her. Two sections of the shed at West Alexandra were gutted, the fire spreading to the Dutch steamer ***Marisa*** (8,029). The men tried to move her away from the fire, apparently without success, and the stern was soon in flames. No. 5 hold was flooded in the hope of extinguishing the fire there, while No. 6 was damaged and making water anyway. The fire continued to spread in spite of efforts to bring it under control by cutting holes in the decks and sides so that hoses could be passed through. It was three days before it was finally killed and by that time there was water in all the holds. (A deep-seated fire in a large ship is the devil's own job to put out; a similar problem on Brocklebank's ***Mahronda*** was tackled – also without success – by filling the hold with steam. Such techniques must have been used on other occasions, but the records are scanty.)

Another twenty sea-going merchant ships were more or less seriously damaged in the docks. To take one example, the ***Eastern Prince*** (10,926) in Hornby Dock was hit by an HE bomb at about 2300 on the Friday night and set on fire – fires also started in nearby sheds. Parties were sent from

Silvio sunk in Alexandra 1

Wrecked sheds at West Alexandra. The debris includes some produce of South Africa.

several Naval vessels in Gladstone to assist. The Royal Navy's reports on this incident[28] are critical of the efforts of the ***Eastern Prince's*** crew to cope with the fire aboard, but omit to mention the important fact that most of the officers had been killed or injured when the bomb fell. The AFS (presumably Bootle's) arrived at midnight and had the shed fire under control by 0200 – the Naval fire parties were then gradually withdrawn. The ***Eastern Prince*** was saved.

Events in Gladstone Dock on the following night are worth going into in detail in view of the lessons learnt – and not learnt – that would be of great importance in May 1941. At 0200 a bomb landed on the massive, three-storey, concrete shed at South-west Gladstone 1, starting a fire that spread rapidly so as to threaten the ships moored there. The destroyers ***Chelsea*** and ***Vanquisher***, moored at West Gladstone, immediately sent parties to assist. On the way they were machine-gunned by low-flying aircraft, fortunately without any casualties resulting; several Naval vessels returned the fire. What followed is disputed.

Vanquisher's party of nineteen ratings was led by the Officer of the Day – a young sub-lieutenant. He boarded the first ship he came to – the ***Glenorchy*** – to find Chinese seamen milling about "frantically donning life-jackets." With some difficulty, he found the Chief Engineer and asked to be taken to the Chief Officer.* The Chief Engineer agreed to do so and led the sub-lieutenant down to the engine room, then turned on him and informed him with much abuse that the Chief Officer was up on deck. "He was obviously in a state of panic."

Undaunted, the sub-lieutenant made his way up again and found an officer. By this time the ship was on fire forward and "the crew were in a state of disorganisation." Accordingly, the sub-lieutenant brought some of his men in to man a life-boat and carry lines across the dock so that the ship could be hauled clear of the fire. Seeing that the small Naval crew was struggling to manage the heavy life-boat, a tug offered to assist but an officer on the ***Glenorchy*** rejected this for fear of a salvage claim. They then rowed to the bow and were told that it was too hot to get lines off from there only to see members of their own party doing just that.

Once the ***Glenorchy*** was away from the quay they turned to the next ship – the ***Eurybates*** – where they had more trouble with those on board – in particular, they were only given one manila line from the stern, which the sub-lieutenant did not think would be enough. He was not surprised, when the ***Eurybates*** had been hauled across, to see her stern swinging back to the burning shed. The tug moved in to help only to be rejected again, and it was only when the Navy returned that her services were accepted. Finally, naval ratings were sent to make fast the stern line only to have a ship's officer appear with some men and reject their services with further abuse, "accusing the Naval ratings of slipping lines and getting in the way."

When the Navy called for volunteers to help ashore the numbers that came forward were substantially greater than was needed – and many of them had only returned a few hours earlier from strenuous duty at sea. In view of this it is hardly surprising that the Royal Navy retired with hurt feelings and the sub-lieutenant resolved to write the stinging report that now lies in the Public Record Office.[29]

Nine times out of ten that would be the only information available unless one could trace a survivor from the incident – it has in fact been used, discreetly, by one writer. However, the records of the Ocean Transport & Trading Group are now available in the Maritime Records Centre of the Merseyside Maritime Museum.[30] These contain statements taken from a number of the men involved on the merchant ships in answer to the Royal Navy's complaints. They throw a rather different light on things. It is possible to be cynical about a parade of junior officers confirming that what their superiors have said is correct, and it is not improbable that this version errs a little on the creditable side, but it is in most respects a good deal more

* The officers of merchant ships ought properly to be designated mates and engineers or deck officers and engine-room officers. The widespread custom of calling them officers and engineers respectively is naturally irritating to the latter, but I have not presumed to correct the nautical terminology of my sources.

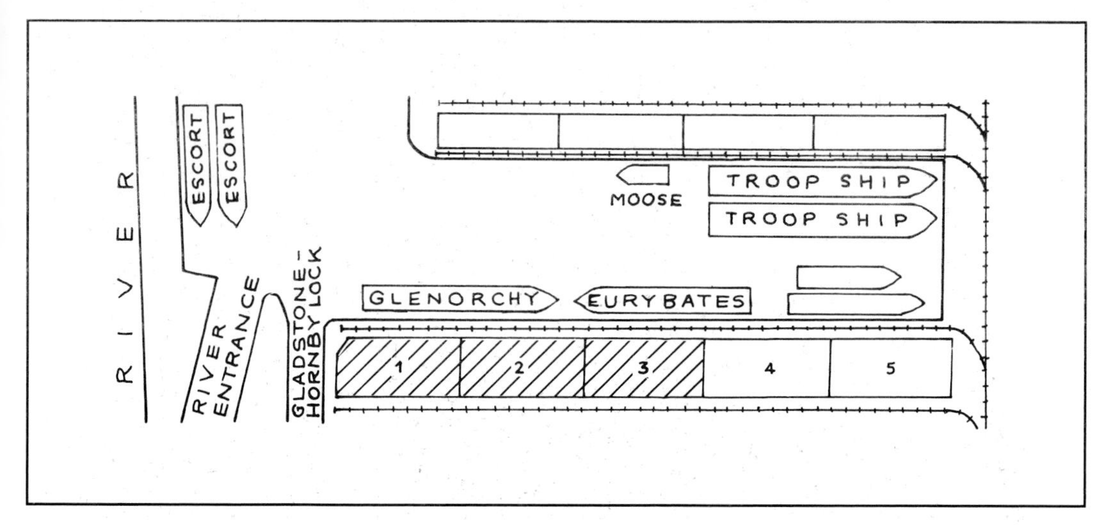

Gladstone Dock

plausible. Taken in conjunction with the Navy's account, it makes it possible to reconstruct the incident with reasonable confidence.

At the outset the ships in Gladstone 1 were arranged as shown in the plan – the troopships were Canadian Pacific's ***Empress of Australia*** and ***Duchess of Richmond.*** On the ***Glenorchy***, the Chinese crew had donned life-jackets as soon as the raid started – their usual procedure, as they believed that these offered some protection from flying splinters.

Leonard Eccles, assistant to the Company's dock superintendent, was on board when: "at about 2.00 a.m. a violent explosion occurred in the warehouse about abreast of our No. 3 hatch, which is just forward of our Bridge, and a big wooden door from the warehouse fell on our deck. Previous thereto all hands with the exception of a few of the engineers had been sheltering in or about the saloon, but the noise caused us to go on deck to see what was happening.

"When we got on deck flames were noticed coming through the warehouse door (top storey) and pieces of burning wood were falling on the quay. A crane opposite the burning door, which was about abreast of our No. 2 and 3 hatches caught fire in the driver's wooden cabin. The ship's gun crew consisting of 5 men mustered and manned the hoses and played them on the burning warehouse." (The sheds at South Gladstone were about forty feet back from the quayside.)

"It was by this time evident that the situation was dangerous and we then decided to shift the ship to the North side of the dock. The crew was split up, some being sent forward and some aft and the remainder preparing the port life boat for lowering, the intention being to take ropes to the opposite side and warp the ship across. So far as the stern moorings were concerned they were let go from the shore by members of the Chinese Crew who went on shore for the purpose. The forward lines could not be handled from the quay on account of falling burning debris from the warehouse. They had to be slacked off from the forecastle head."

Some of the blocks and guy-ropes for the forward derricks caught fire from the burning crane, but these were quickly doused using one of the ship's hoses. The Chief Officer, Mr Tyler, and Chief Engineer, Mr Threlfall, met for a moment abaft the saloon to discuss the possibility of using the main engines to move the ship. (The idea was rejected.)

Meanwhile, the sub-lieutenant from ***Vanquisher*** had arrived to find a scene of apparent confusion. (The ***Glenorchy's*** officers thought that he was simply unfamiliar with the Chinese temperament.) He asked the Chief Steward the way to the Officers' quarters and was pointed to a companion way. He went in with a rating to arrive abaft the saloon just as Tyler and Threlfall were going their separate ways.

Mr Threlfall: "The discussion ended and the Chief Officer, Mr. Tyler, started to leave by the port door of the alleyway which led out on to the centrecastle deck on the port side. As he was doing so a man wearing a tin hat and an oilskin coat but with no distinguishing rank badges entered the alleyway from the starboard side and asked me where the Chief Officer was. I pointed in the direction of the port door through which the Chief Officer was then leaving. I said nothing. I then proceeded to the engine room and when I had reached the bottom platform I found the man was still following me. He was accompanied by another man, similarly dressed. I went to open up the valve on one of the pumps and he came up behind me and said 'Where's the Chief Officer?' I said 'Up on deck somewhere.' He replied 'You said he was down here.' I said 'No, I didn't.' He replied 'You damned well did.' I replied 'Get to hell out of this' and he went without any further interchange of words. I then proceeded with my job of opening the pump up. I had no idea that he was a Naval Officer. I was certainly not in a state of panic."

On reaching the deck, the sub-lieutenant found Eccles and Tyler by the boat that was being lowered and offered assistance. This was accepted gratefully and it was suggested that he and his men should man the boat and take the lines across. The Third Officer was sent to bring half-a-dozen of the ratings – who were helping to move railway wagons on the far side of the shed – and soon they were pulling away with a rope from the after well-deck. As soon as this had been secured on the north side the winch was started and the ***Glenorchy*** was pulled out at the stern. (The intention was apparently to moor her round the corner of the 'knuckle' – it is unlikely that there was room for both her and the ***Eurybates*** at the north quay.)

The life-boat was returning when the tug ***Moose***, which had been moored on the north side, offered assistance. It was Eccles who rejected this; not only would a claim for salvage follow, but the ship was already being moved without the ***Moose's*** help. (The Merchant Marine was inclined to scoff at the Royal Navy's struggles with a simple boating job.) A second line was run across from the stern before the life-boat moved on to take one from the bow.

The men on the forecastle head – the Third Officer with about five Chinese crewmen and two or three ratings – were having problems in casting off as the heat from the burning shed was intense. A hose was played over the ship's starboard side to counter it. The ropes were not so bad, though one of the ratings contrived to "let go the topping lift of No. 1 port forward derrick which crashed on to the lower table of the foremast. Presumably he was under the impression he was letting go one of the moorings, but it was a silly thing to do and might have caused a serious accident." However, there was

Ravaged concrete sheds at South Gladstone 1, with a crane that threatened to spread the fire to the adjacent ships. Blue Funnel's *Perseus* (China Mutual) is at the quayside.

also a three-and-a-half-inch steel wire that could not be handled at all until it had been cooled by the hose and even then proved impossible to dislodge.

It seems that the sub-lieutenant's first request for a line from the bow was met by an explanation of this situation from the Third Officer that he may not have heard properly. Chief Officer Tyler then went to see what was happening forward and heard another plaintive cry from the life-boat – "Give us a line." "I called down 'Wait a minute while I get the line across from the other side'. The line had to be got from the starboard side being the only line not in use. The crew with the help of some naval ratings – 3 I think – passed the line across and paid it into the boat. This was done within 3 minutes at the very outside of the request from the boat to give them a line."

The rope was taken over and made fast. Tyler then had the winch started only to be told by the Third Officer about the recalcitrant wire. He decided that an attempt must be made to cut it with an axe. The heat was so great that Tyler, the Third Officer, the Chief Engineer and another Naval sub-lieutenant (possibly off ***Chelsea***) had to take it in turns until the wire parted at last and the bow started to move away from the quay.

Unlike the ***Glenorchy***, the ***Eurybates*** was short-handed. When the bomb hit the shed and the fire started, the relief Chief Officer, Mr Broad, ordered the men to hose down the decks and hatch-covers and prepare ropes on the starboard side for warping her off should this prove necessary.

"As the fire spread I came to the conclusion that the ship should be moved to the other side of the basin and gave orders to get out No. 1 lifeboat. This was being done by the Third Officer and the four ARP men. I went ashore and found a small punt tied to the ladder by our stern. I realised that this would be more useful and went back and stopped them lowering the lifeboat and sent away two ARP men in the punt with oars and rowlocks from the life-boat. They came round to the starboard bow and took off the mooring rope ready tied." It was a new seven-inch manila.

When they had nearly reached the north quay, the ***Glenorchy's*** boat came to their aid. Someone called out, "Heave away," and the winch was started. The line, which had apparently not been secured, came away and the ***Glenorchy's*** boat had to come across to pick it up again. When they arrived the Third Officer "told them off for letting the rope go. The language I used was not a bit stronger than the occasion warranted." Next time it was successfully tied up and, with the shore moorings already slipped, a start was made on pulling the bow out.

As soon as a line was got across from the stern, "the ship was breasted over bodily and brought starboard side to the other (North) wall." Another line was then thrown ashore from the bow. Now she was safe, but perhaps too close to the Canadian Pacific vessel next along. Broad: "I then had to heave-a-head a little bit to clear the C.P.R. boat moored there and the third officer instructed those on shore to move the stern rope up one bollard. Unfortunately whilst this was being done the rope slipped from the hands of the men on shore into the water. I did not hear any abusive language used from the ship at this stage but the circumstances would justify its use."

"The wind caught the ship and blew her stern back across the dock into a position of some danger again. By that time the 'Glenorchy' was in the middle of the basin having one bow rope ashore and had let go her port anchor. I could see a tug on the far side of her and I called out to Mr. Eccles, the Officer-in-Charge, asking him to engage the tug to push our stern back on the north side. The tug 'Moose' came up and did this. It took about 25 minutes. As the tug was pushing us back a rope was lowered from our poop and assistance was given in taking it by two boats – ours and another from the 'Glenorchy' – to the shore and made fast."

No doubt the Navy offered help again at this stage only to have some robust comment made on the dropping of ropes, though there is no evidence that this was their fault in either case. It was about 0430 before the two ships were safely tied up clear of the fire.

The three-storey sheds at South Gladstone 1 contained paint, sugar, hemp, and large quantities of rubber – and we have seen how quickly the fire started when the bomb hit. (The place was full of rubber boots and plimsolls, the material of which was soon "running down the stairs like lava from a volcano.") There were some firemen on hand at the outset, soon joined by Naval fire parties, but their first problem was that the doors of the shed were locked, causing delay in reaching the fire. When they had found a way in another bomb hit the shed, killing two auxiliary firemen and injuring three ratings from ***Chelsea.*** In the circumstances it is no discredit to the fire service that the blaze spread rapidly, till "the bitumastic roof resembled a moving mass of molten metal."[31] At 0500 the wind changed to blow a constant rain of burning debris across to the Naval vessels along the west quay.

There is a report in the Public Record Office[32] describing events in these same sheds – they are tentatively attributed to the raid of 4/5th May 1941, but the report was compiled a couple of years later and there seems to be no doubt that this was the fire referred to. In order to create a fire-break the Navy was called in to lash a 600-lb depth charge to the top of one of the reinforced-concrete pillars inside the shed. With goods on the floors above loaded at two hundredweight to the square foot there was no doubt that this would bring about the collapse of a section of the shed and limit the otherwise inexorable spread of the fire. The charge was detonated while everyone stood well back. The resulting explosion caused serious damage to sliding doors and shattered the concrete of the pillar, leaving the steel reinforcing bars inside exposed for a couple of feet and bowed out like a Chinese lantern. Other damage to the shed was negligible.

Unfortunately, everyone was so thrilled by this revelation of the strength of reinforced concrete that they omitted to report exactly how the fire *was* halted, which it was eventually. Of the five sections into which the shed was divided, Nos. 1 and 2 and the two upper storeys of No. 3 (containing the materials specified above) were completely gutted; timber stored on the ground floor of No. 3 suffered water damage only.

On the first night fifty-seven pumps were sent into Liverpool from outside and more were standing by as far away as Leeds and Cardiff – their first moves would have been to nearer towns to cover for pumps already sent to Liverpool. However, it was noted in London that the situation never looked like getting really out of hand and all fires were at least under control by 0415. 226 pumps were actually in use in Liverpool on this night.

The second night was worse and 82 pumps were sent to Liverpool, twelve of them passed on to Bootle. (Liverpool's Chief Fire Officer was responsible for the allocation of outside pumps to Bootle.) Thirty-six pumps and 180,000 feet of hose were used just to deliver water from the canal and docks, mostly for the Sandhills area.[33] Some difficulty was experienced with incompatible equipment; for instance, Manchester standpipes were bayonet fitting – Liverpool screw. One can quite see that this problem was not an easy one to solve in wartime conditions, but that it should still have been taking people by surprise as late as December 1940 seems odd. Firemen were brought into Liverpool by bus from such places as Lincoln, Chesterfield and Scunthorpe.[34] It was a bad few days for the fire service; of at least fifteen men killed in Liverpool and Bootle five were auxiliary firemen from Blackpool and Birmingham.

The amount of clearing up to be done after these raids was considerable. Most of the railway goods stations were functioning within three weeks, but temporary repairs to the Exchange Station viaduct were not completed till March. In the meantime a special express service was run from Southport, Lord Street, to Liverpool Central using the CLC route that made a complete detour round the east and south sides of Liverpool. Normal services on the Overhead Railway were not restored until the 26th March.

On the two nights following the attack on Merseyside, the Luftwaffe's effort was mostly directed at Manchester, where the situation was soon a good deal worse than it had been on the Mersey. Reinforcements sent there included forty pumps from London. A week after these raids, London suffered an attack in which much of 'The City' was destroyed by fire. The Manchester and London raids impressed people as marking a change in German tactics – a switch to specifically fire-raising attacks.

In fact, German records of bomb-loads lend little support to this idea. It was the shortage of fire-watchers in commercial premises on the weekend before Christmas that allowed the fires to get so badly out of hand in Manchester, and the same thing happened in the City of London – with rather less excuse – the weekend after Christmas. In both cases the attacks were successfully concentrated on central districts where the fire-risk was great and the results most noticeable. There can be no doubt that Liverpool would have suffered the same fate, and for the same reasons, if the raid there had not been more scattered.

A radical shake-up of the fire-watching system followed, involving an element of compulsion.

Although not yet the main focus of attention, Liverpool was the subject of several more or less official reports in the wake of the December raids and much local thought was put into the lessons that might be drawn from them.

An investigation by Mass-Observation[35] found that morale in Liverpool was, by a substantial margin, the highest of any blitzed town that the observer had visited. Some of the reasons given are interesting. It was thought, for instance, that the large numbers of sailors living it up on shore leave raised spirits all round. On the other hand, it was suggested that life in Liverpool between the wars had been so hard that it would take more than a few air raids to make things significantly worse. It was also thought that public confidence in the Council, and especially in the Emergency Committee, was lacking: "The surest way to get a big laugh from intelligent Liverpool people is to ask them what they think about their local government and political leaders...at a later stage in the war this lack of confidence might become significant." There were also reservations about emergency feeding arrangements, which it was thought might break down in the face of a more concentrated attack.

One problem that became apparent towards the end of 1940 was that the shipping shortage caused by the convoy system and war losses was being aggravated by slow turn-round times in port. This was not caused by the weight of traffic so much as changes in shipping patterns, with vessels using strange ports and carrying loads for which they had not been designed – and once ashore, cargoes might have to wait for specialised railway wagons to be found before they could be moved inland. Around December there was apparently a press campaign (not traced) suggesting that the blame lay in the organisation of the ports – especially Liverpool.

The upshot was the appointment of Mr. J. Gibson Jarvie, Chairman of the United Dominions Trust, as Regional Port Director for the North West, covering ports from Holyhead to Silloth. (Others were appointed for the Clyde and Bristol.)

Jarvie's remit was to improve the turn-round time of ships, to see that the best use was made of existing transport facilities, and generally to speed the passage of goods. He took up his post in January, primed to expect the worst, only to find that he had been misinformed and that the local authorities were coping well with the effects of the December raids. There was no sign of the chaos Jarvie had been led to expect and many of the problems that did exist were not the fault of the MDHB or Liverpool generally. "The present inspired campaign (it is obviously inspired) can do nothing but harm."[36]

Wing-Commander John Hodsoll, the Inspector-General of ARP, was another visitor to Liverpool whose impressions were decidedly favourable.[37] The salvage arrangements were better than many he'd seen, especially in the docks; care of the homeless was good, and so was morale among the civil defence personnel. He noted that demolition with explosives had been required at short notice in both Liverpool and Manchester to prevent the spread of fire – this was all that had saved the Central Telephone Exchange in Manchester. Explosives experts, military or otherwise, had needed to be found quickly and he thought that better arrangements ought to be made for the future.

"Liverpool struck me as being generally right on top of their job...They were taking the greatest pride in meeting whatever situation might arise and although pleased to see the Regional Commissioner after their most severe 'blitz' told him quite plainly, I gather, that they did not want any help or interference and were perfectly capable of meeting every situation themselves. From what I saw, I should think this is probably quite true and of course a city of this size has very large resources."

One thing to catch his eye was the warehouse problem. "They are very big, they are old and they are, most of them, stuffed with inflammable goods from top to bottom. In ordinary times they are left completely unattended." They simply did not have the staff that shops and office buildings could call on to do one night a week. For the moment, volunteers were called in along with a few hundred men from the Army and Home Guard.

Another problem that seems to have aroused general agreement was the danger of the surviving timber stocks. The Regional Commissioner and the authorities in Liverpool and Birkenhead were all anxious that Hodsoll should use his influence to get it removed – the General Manager of the Dock Board, Sir L. A. P. Warner, thought that "all the Fire Watchers in the world" would not protect timber from incendiary bombs. Hodsoll needed little convincing: "Apart from the very serious losses of timber of which there is already a shortage, it seems criminal to leave these enormous stocks in the Docks where they will inevitably be destroyed and may cause the destruction of equally valuable properties and goods in their vicinity." He suggested that "the Fire Co-ordination Committee" should do what it could to move timber stocks out as a matter of urgency and, if possible, "get the warehouses in the really vulnerable areas cleared altogether" – admittedly not an easy task.

Jarvie also commented on this. After labour problems,[38] the worst cause of congestion was the failure of certain Government departments notably the Ministry of Supply – to take delivery of goods waiting for them at the docks. Much of the timber stored in the danger area turned out to be pit-props left in the yards through mismanagement in Whitehall. Some think the timber merchants were at fault in refusing to move their stocks out of town at their own expense. Apart from the obvious unfairness of expecting them to bear the cost of a measure intended to benefit the city as a whole, I am sure that if the timber merchants' attitude had been the only problem it could soon have been overcome by an order under the Defence Regulations.

The timber was not moved.

In view of the fire at Gladstone, the Port Emergency Committee issued new instructions: no inflammable goods were to be stored on the top floor of three-storey sheds and all shed doors were to be left partly open at all times to allow rapid access for fire-fighters as well as reducing the effects of blast. As this last rule was to be applied to bonded premises as well, it may be imagined what sort of problems it created in a dock area.

The Royal Navy was most unhappy with the arrangements for fire-fighting in the docks, though their criticisms of the Merchant Marine seem to have been unfair and this casts doubt on their other opinions. It is odd that while lashing out in all directions they made no comment on the fact that life in Gladstone Dock would have been a lot simpler if only the ***Glenorchy*** and ***Eurybates*** had arranged to have lines strung across the dock at nightfall in case they needed to move in a hurry. There was no difficulty in arranging this and some masters had done so – only to be reminded that the practice was strictly forbidden by the Dock Board.[39] It is true that no vessel of any size was lost in the port as a result of shed-fires prior to the 3rd May 1941, but one or both of the ships moved from South Gladstone 1 would almost certainly have been lost if the sheds there had not been set further back from the quayside than was usual. The Board's objections have not come to light.

On occasion, Hodsoll could be scathing in his comments. He was particularly brutal when it came to the performance of the fire service in Bootle, suggesting that a startling number of auxiliary firemen failed to report for duty on the second night of the December raids and querying the competence of the Chief Fire Officer, Mr. J. F. Collins. The Regional Commissioner was sufficiently concerned to suggest transferring Bootle's brigade (which had no connection with the police) to Liverpool. Liverpool would have been only too glad to accept, and Bootle's objections would probably have been overridden if nationalisation had not become a hot issue soon after.

That Hodsoll's judgement of Collins was not the universal one is shown by the award of the MBE to the latter – for his courage, endurance and outstanding leadership during raids. As this was gazetted on the 13th June 1941 it is *just* possible that it relates to his performance in May. (Liverpool's Chief Fire Officer, Mr. Owen, received the MBE in the 1941 New Year Honours, said to be partly in recognition of the Liverpool fire service's good work generally.)

However, the experience of December did lead to changes in the Liverpool fire service. In the LFB, men were given temporary promotion – two to inspector and twenty to sergeant – so that there would be officers available to supervise "at each important fire." Also it was agreed that henceforth the LFB and AFS would act as a single unit and, apparently for the first time, equivalent ranks were specified (LFB inspector = AFS divisional officer, LFB sergeant = AFS section officer, etc.). The senior man present, whether regular or auxiliary, would take charge.[40] These measures, which seem rather belated, hint at problems that had arisen.

Efforts to obtain a large fire-boat were redoubled – the attack on the ***John A. Brown*** in the river had been alarming – but the difficulties still proved insuperable. The Dock Board had also been seeking a new salvage-boat since the previous April as the ***Salvor*** (213) was over thirty years old and no longer fit to leave the river in any but the best weather. It was resolved in January 1941 that the Board's ***No. 20 Hopper*** should be converted for salvage and fire-fighting duty as the ***Watchful*** (though for some reason her name could not be changed officially during the war).

Before the raids started, Allerton Fire Station had been prepared as a reserve HQ in case of damage at Hatton Garden, with a duplicate network of direct telephone lines to all the regular and auxiliary fire stations. (It was close to the main ARP Control Centre, where the Emergency Committee sat and from which the other civil defence services were directed.) In February, the Chief Constable proposed that the same principle should be applied in each of the eight divisions of the city, with the local AFS Divisional HQ being equipped to take over from the LFB District Fire Station.[41] This was agreed, but it is not clear when the work was completed.

Commander Aylmer Firebrace, formerly Chief Officer of the London Fire Brigade, had been seconded to the Home Office to study the problems of fire defence. His job involved visits to provincial towns during and after raids to offer help and advice and to report on how the different brigades were coping. On the 6th March Liverpool was sent such a report. The main points made by Firebrace were as follows, interleaved with the responses of Mr Winstanley as reported to the Watch Committee on the 27th. (All are in my words. It may reasonably be supposed that the Chief Constable's pronouncements on the fire service noted here and elsewhere were made after consultation with the Chief Fire Officer if not entirely at the latter's instigation.)

FIREBRACE: There is still a shortage of towing vehicles for trailer pumps. Every such pump that can be manned ought to have one. The dock trailer pumps ought to be the first to be provided with towing vehicles rather than the last as now. Too many towing vehicles are out of action awaiting repair.

WINSTANLEY: Liverpool has been authorised to acquire 294 towing vehicles, of which 247 have been obtained. They are not easy to find within Hom Office price limits and it may be necessary to start requisitioning. On the 15th March (just after a heavy raid) there were 98 in for repair owing to a shortage of labour, which applies to outside garages as well. The ones available have to be put where they are the most use; in contrast to most districts of Liverpool, there are no hills in the docks, and it is not safe to drive round them in the black-out anyway. (There were in fact half-a-dozen self-propelled pumps on the docks. One snag with the manhandling of trailers was that ancillary equipment had to be piled on top and tended to fall off.)

FIREBRACE: When enough towing vehicles have been obtained, reconsider the arrangements for mobilising pumps. At present, additional pumps for dock fires are sent from the town rather than from points nearer to hand in the docks – presumably because they lack towing vehicles. This leads to delay.

WINSTANLEY: Reinforcements are now allocated by the eight district control centres. It is generally quicker to send them through the streets rather than through the docks. Anyway, sending a pump from one dock to assist at another would leave the first unprotected.

FIREBRACE: The accommodation for firemen in the docks is not good and might discourage part-time volunteers (mostly dockers). All dock pumps ought to be fully manned at dusk each evening.

WINSTANLEY: Agreed, dock accommodation could be improved if the money can be found. I am not optimistic about this bringing in more volunteers. (Among the full-time firemen a posting to a dock station was seen in much the same light as that in which the German soldier viewed a posting to the Russian front. It was actually used as an unofficial punishment for the insubordinate.) We are trying to improve the manning of dock pumps at dusk.

FIREBRACE: Get two more fire-floats.

WINSTANLEY: Agreed, but how? We are still trying to get one for the river.

FIREBRACE: What are your plans for introducing a Fire Brigade wireless service as suggested last December?

WINSTANLEY: The value of this would be limited as only one frequency can be allotted to the Fire Brigade and the Police. When we have enough equipment for the Police we will experiment with its use in the Fire Brigade.

FIREBRACE: The Fire Brigade ought to be separated from the Police.

WINSTANLEY: We see no advantage in the change. Anyway, the organisations are so closely connected that this would involve confusion at a bad time – changing horses in mid-stream.

An experienced fireman in possession of all the facts might say differently, but it seems to a layman that Liverpool's responses are reasonable enough for the most part. No doubt the people in charge of Liverpool's defence might have arranged things better than they did, but they were not fools and criticism from outside ought not to be accepted without reservation.

On the 6th February Hitler ordered the Luftwaffe to concentrate on the ports. From his point of view this reinforcement of the U-boat blockade was sound policy. With the East Coast and Channel ports harassed by the enemy, and the Port of London's trade cut to a quarter, the bulk of the country's seaborne trade was concentrated on the Clyde, the Bristol Channel, and the Mersey – especially the last. Consequently, these areas, with other ports such as Belfast, Hull and Plymouth, were now the prime targets. Liverpool also acquired additional importance from the 7th February when the Headquarters of Western Approaches Command (responsible for all Atlantic convoys) was moved from Plymouth to Derby House, behind Liverpool Town Hall. Admiral Sir Percy Noble took command ten days later. (This was quite separate from the local command under the Flag Officer in Charge (FOIC Liverpool) based in the Liver Building at the Pier Head. This was responsible for Liverpool as a Naval port, catering mostly for convoy escorts – to be found in Gladstone Dock with the overflow in Brocklebank and Albert – as well as a number of minesweepers and other small craft mostly berthed in Birkenhead Docks. The Mersey did not usually see anything larger than a destroyer except for vessels under construction at Cammell Laird or in for repair – Gladstone Graving Dock contained the occasional battleship.)

The winter weather precluded anything more than relatively light raids in January and February. One of the Chief Constable's most serious worries at the beginning of March was that the troops brought in to protect warehouses had been withdrawn, leaving them as vulnerable as they had been in December except for the addition of a few wardens from other districts. "The Committee will realise that many of the fire parties employed by the occupiers and indeed not a few of the wardens are well past their physical prime and they would certainly be unable to mount the staircase of a high building quickly enough to deal with a fallen incendiary bomb before it started a fire."[42] The Emergency Committee put the problem to the Regional Commissioner and (whether or not as a result of this approach) several thousand soldiers were allocated to this duty nationally from the night of 10/11th March. Merseyside got two thousand of them.[43] For once, precautions had been taken just in time to be of use as the next heavy attack followed two nights later.

On the night of 12/13th March 316 aircraft were sent with 303 tons of HE and 64,152 incendiaries – on the face of it by far the heaviest fire raid on Merseyside. As in December, there was a high proportion of mines and heavy bombs. It was a clear night with a full moon and over 500 fires were started. 65 aircraft carried 58 tons of HE and 4,392 incendiaries on the following night and there was a light raid on the night of 14/15th, but all the events mentioned below occurred on the first night unless otherwise specified.

The main weight of the attack fell on the Cheshire side, mostly on residential property, and casualties in Birkenhead, Wallasey and Bebington were heavy. In some ways Wallasey had the worst of it; within two hours of the first raid starting, the trunk main was broken, leading to a complete failure of the water supply. Hits on the power station and gas works deprived the borough of all power supply as well.

In Liverpool the raid was worst around the centre, where the most serious fire seems to have been at the Head Post Office in Victoria Street. This was attended by four turntable escapes, six pumps (all but one of them regular LFB appliances), a hose-laying unit and a mobile dam. These were all able to leave within six hours of the call, by which time much of the top floor had been burnt out. The most important facilities on that floor had been the trunk telephone exchange for Merseyside and North Wales and the telegraph office – both damaged by water mainly. The hundred teleprinters were all saved and carried down to the basement where facilities for setting them up had been arranged in case of such an event. The GPO was also prepared for the loss of the trunk exchange and this service was transferred at once to the exchange building in South John Street. There was no actual break in the service, but only a limited number of lines were now available.

Work had already been started on the provision of a trunk exchange and telegraph office in Lancaster House, Old Hall Street. This building had been completed only recently in connection with pre-war plans for the introduction of automatic telephone working. The war had delayed the programme, but some equipment had been installed (though here too damage was caused by a bomb in March); accordingly, steps were taken to get trunk and telegraph facilities working in Old Hall Street while repairs were also started to the Victoria Street trunk exchange. In the meantime, Liverpool had been put in the dangerous situation of having no reserve for either service.[44]

Incidents at the docks in Liverpool were few; they included a parachute mine in the avenue north of Huskisson 2 that caused more damage to the sunken ***Europa.*** (She was raised a few days later and dry-docked for repairs.) On the night of 14/15th nine HE bombs fell around Kirkdale carriage sidings, one of them blowing in the side wall of Spellow tunnel. Single-line working was restored soon after.

Birkenhead Docks were more seriously affected, the flour mills getting the worst of it. (Merseyside was then the greatest flour-milling centre in Europe, the industry being concentrated mainly at Birkenhead and Ellesmere Port.) Vernon's mill (East Float, north side) was only slightly damaged, and Rank's (West Float, south side) was able to restore production from late April. Paul's mill, to the east of Vernon's, was all but destroyed on the first night; and the dockside buildings of Buchanan's, (west of Vernon's) including warehouses and silos, went the same way twenty-four hours later. Buchanan's were able to restore production gradually in May. The surprising thing was that only a small quantity of flour and grain had been lost in these mills and, taking those not seriously damaged and their spare production into account, overall flour production hardly faltered at all.[45]

It was a bad time for ships awaiting repair after previous incidents most, if not all, in Birkenhead. The ***John A. Brown***, already mentioned, was shaken by an HE bomb under her stern while in dry dock; and the ***Elax***, another December victim, was hit by a bomb in Bidston Dock. She was later anchored in the river as a storage ship until new engines were fitted a year later. The ***Catrine*** (5,218), also in Bidston, had been mined in Liverpool Bay on the 29th December and brought in by the Marine Department – she too was hit by a bomb. The Swedish steamer ***Buenos Aires*** (5,646) had been mined on the 31st December and was now further damaged by fire. She was declared a constructive total loss and left the Mersey under tow in February 1942 for use as a supply ship at Scapa Flow. The ***Lady Connaught*** (2,284), yet another ship mined in the Bay – 27th December, was also damaged along with several vessels that had not previously been in trouble locally.

The worst problem for ships in March was mines. The ***Tacoma City*** (4,738) had just arrived from New York with "7217 tons steel trucks" and 405 tons of general cargo. She was at anchor in the river, moved on Admiralty orders to take her clear of suspected mines, and moored again just off Rock Ferry light – near to the training ship ***Conway*** (the last of the wooden warships that had long been a feature of this stretch of the river). When the ***Tacoma City*** swung to the tide an unsuspected mine exploded beneath her at 1400 on the 13th. She broke in two and with her steel cargo there was no hope for her; the stern section sank like a stone and the rest followed in three minutes. All but four of the forty-five men aboard managed to get onto rafts and were saved by boats from other craft including the ***Conway.***[46]

The minesweeper HMS ***Restrivo*** went round the river in the afternoon, setting off two mines near the wreck of the ***Innisfallen*** and a third not far from the ***Conway.*** (It was not possible to sweep where mines might damage ships at anchor.) At around 2000 that evening the ***Ullapool*** (4,891), carrying 7,605 tons of wheat, was virtually cut in two by another mine 1,500 feet off Prince's Landing Stage. A ferry, the No. 4 pilot boat, and ***Restrivo***[47] did what they could to rescue the thirty-eight crew and a pilot who were either in the water or clinging to the rigging, but even as they did so the alert sounded for the next raid and the restricted lighting allowed for ships was killed at once. Fifteen of the crew were lost.

During the raid that followed, a bomb landed on the quay near the east end of the West Float, north side, without exploding. The ***Myrmidon*** (6,278) was moored here, with her stern to Duke Street Bridge, having nearly completed loading a cargo of government stores. It was decided that she ought to be moved away from the UXB and, at about 0400 on the 14th, two of Rea's tugs arrived to take her across the Float to moor alongside the ***Empire Simba*** opposite. The ***Empire Simba*** (5,691) had been bombed off Anglesey on the 1st March and abandoned in a sinking condition only to be brought in by the MDHB's Marine Department three days later – she was still being kept afloat by pumps. The ***Myrmidon*** was taken across the Float broadside on and was about a hundred feet from the other ship when a great explosion blew her stern out of the water and the hatch covers over No. 6 hold were thrown into the air. She was tied up alongside the ***Empire Simba***, which had also taken further damage, and sank by the stern. The stern tug, the ***Minegarth***, was damaged as well, but was kept afloat.[48]

After the previous night's raid the parachute from a mine had been found on the ***Empire Simba's***

The warehouse of Rank's Ocean Mill, Birkenhead, with a fire-float in action.

Buchanan's flour mills.

deck, which suggests a failure of communications somewhere though other explanations are possible – there might, for instance, have been a second mine in the area. The *Myrmidon* was repaired in time to set off another mine in the river on the 5th June. It was not till the first week of April that all the mines in the East and West Floats were cleared. A week after the March raids two searchlights were set up at Liverpool Pier Head and Egremont Pier specifically to mark the fall of mines in the river.

One of the most damaging blows in March was the sinking, on the first night, of the *Mammoth* (1,542), then the second largest floating crane in the world and one of the Dock Board's most valuable and hard-worked assets. She was moored at the Esparto Quay, just west of the *Myrmidon's* berth, and was hit by two HE bombs, one hitting the starboard engine room and the other falling through the port aft tailshaft compartment to explode underneath the vessel. As she began to take on water an appalling prospect opened up. At best, she would be a difficult salvage job; but if she turned over, her towering jib would be wrecked beyond repair as well as causing damage to anything in its path – or obstructing the Float if she turned that way.

Both the watchmen on board were injured, but one of them – Bob Wright, who had had his heels sliced off by shrapnel – managed to hobble round casting off the moorings so that they would not hold her up on one side. For an hour the *Mammoth* wallowed in the water, listing to starboard and then going down by the stern, but at the last she settled on an even keel. She was indeed an awkward salvage job, but she was at length restored to grace the Mersey for another forty years and more.[49]

In spite of the enormous numbers of incendiaries dropped in these raids most of them had been caught early, the soldiers brought in for this purpose being particularly effective. To cope with the many fires that did take hold, large-scale reinforcements were sent to Wallasey and Birkenhead, Liverpool sending foam compound to Wallasey on the afternoon of the 13th and a turntable ladder later that night. Liverpool's situation was not so bad, but twenty-four pumps were brought in, including thirteen from Manchester, as well as three turntable escapes from Wigan, Southport and Birkenhead! It was reported to the Liverpool Watch Committee that Bootle called for help early on the night of 12/13th and was sent twelve pumps including three from Liverpool.[50] This is curious as Major Salt reports only three HE bombs and a few incendiaries landing on Bootle on this night and the borough was only slightly affected by the raids that followed. It may be that for 'Bootle' we should read 'Birkenhead'.

The Liverpool Watch Committee was delighted to record that: "the entire organisation worked faultlessly"[51] and in Wallasey the provision of mobile dams around the town had countered the failure of the mains to good effect. A park lake had been drained and was refilled as soon as possible from the docks using over a mile of six-inch steel piping laid by the AFS and Royal Engineers.[52] The general impression, among outside observers as well as locally, was that the work put in on the fire defences since December had proved its value and that the future could be faced with confidence.

Attempts at improving Liverpool's ability to cope with fire continued. A review of cars laid up on account of wartime conditions produced only a miserable handful that could be requisitioned as towing vehicles. Conversely, the wooden ladder of one of the two ancient turntable escapes actually snapped while in use; it was lucky that this happened while it was engaged in demolition work after the March raids and not at a fire. Both were condemned at last and converted into mobile water carriers.

It was agreed that fifty auxiliary firemen with some mechanical skill should be transferred to the Divisional HQs where they could help to look after the existing towing vehicles. Moves were also made to acquire two more fire-floats for the docks and the necessary pumps were ordered. The remaining light trailers in the first-line strength had been replaced by large trailers and six "escape carrying units", with twenty-one pumps added to the second line. On the other hand, the number of part-time volunteers had fallen to 2,061; no reason is given, but some will have found the work too arduous. Winstanley recommended an increase in the full-time establishment to 2,682 officers and men, and this was put to Home Security. At the same time the Ministry was advising Liverpool to prepare accommodation for reinforcements up to the number of 2,600 men as against the thousand already allowed for.[53] (In April it was reported in the Royal Navy that the whole system of fire-fighting at Liverpool had been reorganised since the 1st February,[54] but this appears to have been a wild exaggeration – perhaps based on Firebrace's suggestions.)

In March and April Winstanley was frequently before the Emergency Committee with plans for additional water supplies, all of which were approved. The Liverpool Gas Company agreed to make a gas-holder available at their Caryl Street depot at the south end – 1,500,000 gallons. When the Home Office offered 20,000-gallon dams three were requested for use in the city centre. A former oil tank on LMS property at Townsend Lane was acquired – 34,500 gallons. Another 20,000-gallon 'sump' was requested on the 29th April – to go to Maiden Lane where it would be useful in the event of fire at the LMS sidings at Townsend Lane. There were also to be three 100,000-gallon pits to cover the factories in the Edge Lane area. Little, if any, of this would be ready in time for the next heavy raids, but it would plainly be unfair to suggest that the need for emergency water supplies was not recognised.

April started with two raids on the Bristol area. On the night of 7/8th there was a heavy raid on Glasgow as well as quite a bad one on Merseyside (65 tons HE and 13,556 incendiaries) – but this was scattered and ineffective. Attacks on Coventry, Birmingham (twice), Tyneside and Bristol followed. Belfast was the main target on the night of 15/16th; visibility was bad and fifty-one aircraft turned to Liverpool as an alternative, but they did not have much success there. Then it was London (very heavy), Portsmouth, London (heavy again), Plymouth three nights running and Sunderland.

Liverpool had a number of alerts during which nothing happened, sometimes caused by aircraft mining the approaches. At this time the port was as busy as it had ever been; in the week ended 26th April it handled 136,400 tons of food and animal feed – nearly twice the previous best and half the total for all ports.[55] The total for all types of cargo was 181,562 tons – quite exceptional – and the week to 3rd May was only a little quieter at 145,596 tons.

After alerts on the two preceding nights, there was a raid on the 26/27th that was intended as a major attack, with 113 tons of HE and 15,336 incendiaries. Visibility was poor, however, and the Luftwaffe scattered bombs and mines along the Lancashire coast from Liverpool to Southport by way of Bootle, Formby and Ainsdale. Casualties in the leafy suburbs were much lower than they might have been in the crowded terraces of the city and military damage was negligible. The geography of the Mersey estuary is so conspicuous that decoy fires and interference with navigation beams had only limited effect in deceiving the enemy, but on this occasion incendiaries set light to a pine wood near Southport and following aircraft unloaded tons of high explosives on the fires. This sort of luck could not be expected to hold.

By the end of April, Merseyside had suffered about seventy raids in all. Of these, most had affected the docks in some way but only half a dozen really seriously. In fact the worst casualties in relation to population had occurred in the largely residential borough of Wallasey, which had been designated before the war as a 'neutral' area for evacuation purposes – meaning that no-one was to be moved in or out except for the parts nearest to the docks. There were 329 dead there, followed by Birkenhead – 403, Bootle – 152, and Liverpool – 1,263. Another 120 had died in the neighbouring boroughs, mainly Bebington and Crosby.

Damage to the docks had been extensive - warehouses and timber yards had been destroyed, and dock sheds were open to the sky – but the long term effect of the damage to date on the working of the port was minimal. Sunken ships were perhaps a bigger nuisance; the ***Lyster***, ***Silvio*** and ***Mammoth*** still lay in the docks where they had been hit, while the river contained the ***Innisfallen***, ***Ullapool*** and ***Tacoma City***. All these, for various reasons were particularly awkward wrecks to clear. The Marine Department had not been idle; many other vessels had been raised and repaired, and frequently they had to drop everything to go to the aid of crippled vessels beyond the bar. The number of vessels needing repair was itself a burden as they were queueing up for access to the graving docks or occupying quays while the local ship-repair firms worked on them.

On the night of 27/28th April Portsmouth was attacked, and two more heavy raids on Plymouth and Devonport followed. (Plymouth was one of the very few places that might claim to have had a worse time than Merseyside.)

In Liverpool, a "Queen's Messenger Food Convoy" came from Manchester on Monday the 28th and parked for a while in front of St George's Hall. It consisted of two sets of five vehicles intended to provide food in bombed areas. The Lord Mayor inspected them and "expressed his appreciation of the fact that Liverpool was to have one of these canteens, probably before the end of the week."[56] The circumstances in which one set did in fact return within the week were hardly what the Lord Mayor had in mind.

The Port of Liverpool was closed on Naval orders from 2110 on the 30th to 0730 next morning for fear of mines – justified: one was detonated by a minesweeper in Liverpool Bay on the 1st May. With the way cleared, the normal work of the port continued.

At 1312 the sirens wailed, followed by the 'all-clear' at 1341 – just a reconnaissance flight.

SHIPPING MOVEMENTS – 1st MAY

Inward	*G.T.*	*From*	*Outward*	*G.T.*	*To*
BARON INCHCAPE	7005	Bombay	**CITY OF RANGOON**	6635	Rangoon
CLAN MACDOUGALL	6843	Glasgow	**EASTERN COAST**	1223	Leith
EUTHALIA	3553	St. John (New Brunswick)	**EIKHAUG**	1436	Cardiff
GRONINGEN	1206	Belfast	**HYDROUSSA**	2038	Father Point (Quebec)
			RINGEN	1499	Cardiff
			SANGARA	5445	Lagos (via Glasgow)
			ZEUS	5961	Father Point (Quebec)

This information is taken principally from Lloyd's Shipping Index and MDHB pilot logs, but neither source is exhaustive. The date of entering or leaving the Mersey is given, but accuracy on this point is not guaranteed as some of the dates in Lloyd's Index may refer to docking or arrival at the bar. Vessels under 1000 tons gross are omitted, eliminating a large amount of coastal traffic. The Royal Navy, local ferry services and transfers within the river are also excluded.

The following is a sample of the day-to-day activity of the port not mentioned in later lists, with a bias to vessels mentioned elsewhere.

The ***Marton*** was moved from Canada to Langton No. 2 Graving Dock (lower) so that she could be checked for possible underwater damage from a near miss. In the West Float, the Upper Mersey Navigation Commission's tender ***Jessie Wallwork*** was working on the recovery of the ***Mammoth***. The ***Euthalia*** docked by the Brunswick silos and began to unload her cargo of wheat – the ***Baron Inchcape*** docked at Canada. A smaller coaster, the ***Busiris***, started discharging coal from South Wales at East Bramley-Moore – doubtless of better quality than the Lancashire coal that was exported from the same dock. The ***Mobeka*** was moved from Toxteth Dock to Queen's and the ***Brittany*** from Carriers' to Alexandra to take on their next cargoes. The ***Jean Jadot***, which had just finished unloading at Canada 3 crossed over to the coal hoists to take on fuel, while the ***Baronesa***, having filled her bunkers there, was found another berth in Canada pending her departure – due on the 2nd.

Oil-fired ships were supplied at their berths by small oilers such as the ***Chilol***. Having exhausted her previous supply (taken from the ***Elax***), she now took on more from the tanker ***War Pathan*** in the river and returned to Gladstone Dock to refuel convoy escorts. There were many of these small craft busy about the river; the Lever Brothers' barge ***Erasmic*** was alongside the ***Malakand*** in Huskisson, transferring ninety-two tons of soap from Port Sunlight for export to the east. Two more small tankers, with the appalling names ***Canemola*** and ***Brimolco***, left for Bromborough after taking over a thousand tons of molasses from a pipeline at Huskisson.

In Canada, the minelayer HMS ***Adventure*** landed a detachment of Royal Marines for drill and then gave the ship's fire party their daily exercise. Most of the vessels reported as sailing on the 2nd left the docks to anchor in the river overnight.

NIGHT – 1st/2nd MAY

SUNSET 2040
BLACKOUT 2110
ALERT 2234-0028
BLACKOUT ENDS 0507
SUNRISE 0537
MOONLIGHT TO MIDNIGHT

On the first night of May fifty-nine aircraft were ordered to Liverpool, of which forty-three claimed to have found the target. These carried 48 tons of HE bombs (up to 500 kgs) and 4,032 incendiaries. As the first raiders were heard, the action opened at 2246[57] with the switching on of searchlights and the roar of AA guns putting up what the press liked to describe as a barrage. It was in fact more a matter of random shooting, which encouraged those on the ground and probably deterred some of the more inexperienced pilots above. Over 1,600 rounds were fired before the guns stood down at 0025. Though Liverpool was plainly the Luftwaffe's main target for the night, it was the Cheshire side of the river that suffered first, with a bomb on Wallasey at 2250. Other incidents to the west were concentrated in the next forty minutes, but the only one of consequence occurred at 2356 when a train ran into a crater on the main line between Rock Ferry and Bebington, blocking all lines for a time.[58]

The first HE bombs on the Liverpool side fell at the south end at 2310, blocking the railway lines leading to Garston docks. These also caused slight damage to the British Thermit Company's works (carbon-free metal alloys) on the north side of the line and the gas works on the south side. Ten minutes later HE bombs fell around Low Hill, east of the centre, mostly on houses. These were followed by fire-bombs further east, the only ones recorded as doing any damage on this night. To the north of the railway complex at Edge Hill – Liverpool's Clapham Junction – there was a concentration of industry that included the Automatic Telephone Company and Meccano – both now engaged in war work. The Luftwaffe got Crawford's biscuit works, which may well have been similarly engaged. The fire here was tackled at first by the AFS, with pumps based at the works itself as well as nearby Edge Lane. Before long the fire was reported to be out of control and a call for help went out at 0035, quickly answered by an LFB pump from Derby Lane. Order was then restored in half an hour, and the loss of a single-storey block of offices was thought to be of little consequence.[59]

From 2330 several districts were hit at once, most seriously to the south among the residential property on both sides of Smithdown Road, north of Sefton Park. One of the first incidents here occurred when an HE bomb hit a dairy in Arundel Avenue. "The proprietor of the dairy was fire-watching with his two sons when a bomb hit the shippon and shop, burying 19 cows. The father and one son were taken to hospital with severe injuries and the other son escaped with a shaking. Two cows were flung by the force of the explosion into the street where a policeman riding a bicycle ran into them in the darkness. Next door a great dane was buried under debris but extricated himself."[60] Eight of the cows were killed.

At midnight more HE fell around the centre. One hit the roof of Lime Street Station over platforms 8 and 9, damaging two trains and injuring a passenger. More seriously, all lines out of the station were blocked for a time by UXBs (unexploded bombs) – notably one in the cutting between Overbury and Kinglake Streets that removed itself by exploding at midnight during the next night's raid.[61]

The docks were affected only at West Brunswick where an HE bomb started a fire in bags of nitrate, dunnage and wooden partitions. This was tackled by two AFS pumps from Coburg Dock and two Fire Brigade pumps called from Hatton Garden at 0001. The fire flared up quickly and destroyed one section of the shed, but was brought under control within twenty minutes of the larger pumps arriving.[62]

A few aircraft dropped mines in Liverpool Bay, causing the port to be closed till 0730 again – this applied all week. There was also scattered activity in other parts of Lancashire, especially at Blackpool where the RAF airfield at Squire's Gate was attacked. East and north Liverpool and Bootle were untouched, however, in spite of an untoward incident in the latter town. During the raid, a senior policeman was strolling down Oriel Road when he saw a stream of light shining from Trinity Road. Shocked at this flagrant breach of the blackout regulations, he rushed to identify the culprit and found that the pedestal lamps outside the Town Hall were the source of the unlawful light. Before he could reach the Police Station to do something about it, the lights had been extinguished. It turned out that they had been put on by accident and the person responsible was later fined – although the bulbs ought really to have been removed from the lamps.[63]

The attack was broken off early, apparently because of deteriorating weather on the continent, and put little strain on the defences – all rescue work was completed during the night.[64] First reports put the number killed at thirteen. Six months earlier this might have been classed as a serious raid, but not any longer.

Fish Street, off Grafton Street, Liverpool – 1/2nd May. Five street fire-watchers were killed here, but the ugly little shelters did their job.

Friday 2nd May

The local press reported the usual crop of 'human interest' stories, with no reference to anything of any conceivable military importance being hit. The greatest inconvenience would have been caused by the closure of the main passenger station, but at least Lime Street did not handle the weight of commuter traffic that some of the other stations did. Several hundred people were temporarily displaced by UXBs, of which one at least went off just before noon – at Dunstan Street,[65] near the Edge Hill railway yards.

Continuing the programme of improvements in water supply, Liverpool's Chief Constable noted that some six-inch steel piping was on offer and proposed the acquisition of five and a half miles of it.[66] It would be laid down to enable water to be pumped from the docks, park lakes and the canal to industrial areas in the event of further damage to mains.

In London, the sequence of lighter and not very effective raids on Merseyside had been noticed and Home Security wondered what the German strategy might be – they were hampered in not knowing that some of the raiders on the 7/8th April and all of those on the 15/16th had diverted to Liverpool because of unfavourable weather over their primary targets. In view of the way the enemy had been touring the ports it was concluded that a heavier attack on Liverpool was likely in the next few weeks and that: "all possible steps should be taken to minimise the dislocation that will be caused by a 'blitz' on the Liverpool area."[67]

In Liverpool too it was known that one raid was often followed by others on successive nights, and concern was expressed at the number of ships loading dangerous cargoes. In particular, there were four taking on about 1,500 tons of HE bombs each: the ***Glen Beg*** and ***Martand*** on the Birkenhead side; the ***Mahout*** and ***Malakand*** in Huskisson Dock. The two in Birkenhead would have been loading direct from railway wagons on the quayside. Ammunition trains arriving at Huskisson Dock with around 300 tons of 250-lb and 500-lb bombs (for the RAF in the Middle East) were split, half going to each ship. The bombs had then to be transported through the sheds before loading onto the ships. Wagons that could not be dealt with before nightfall were withdrawn from the dock area for safety.

The suggestion that the ships might be removed as well – taken out of the river overnight – was rejected in view of the risk from mines and the delays in loading that would be caused by inconvenient tides. Alternatively, the Dock Board's ban on the stringing of lines across the docks at night could be rescinded – at least for these ships. For reasons that doubtless seemed compelling at the time, the Dock Board refused to make any exceptions to its rules and nothing was done.[68]

There must have been a good few people keeping their fingers crossed for a quiet night.

* Convoy sailed Halifax 16th April. (The amount of traffic on this day exemplifies the problems created for the ports by the concentration of ships into convoys. Finding berths for everyone before the tide fell too low was often impossible.)

SHIPPING MOVEMENTS – 2nd MAY

Inward	*G.T.*	*From*	*Outward*	*G.T.*	*To*
BANFFSHIRE	6479	London	**AGIOI VICTORES**	4344	Lagos
GRENA	8117	Port Arthur to Stanlow	**BARON CAWDOR**	3638	Kingston (Jamaica)
HEDERA	2327	Barrow	**BRITISH PRINCE**	4979	Norfolk ex Manchester
INDOCHINOIS	6966	Duala	**BURMA**	7821	Durban
KING ARTHUR	5224	St. John* to Manchester	**COLONIAL**	8309	Beira
MANCHESTER DIVISION	6048	St. John* to Manchester	**EASTERN STAR**	5959	Halifax
MANCHESTER SPINNER	4767	Norfolk(Virginia)* to Manchester	**EDAM**	8871	New York
MARY KINGSLEY	5021	Barbados*	**EL MIRLO**	8092	Kingston (Jamaica)
MOENA	9286	Sourabaya*	**FALCON**	1025	Belfast
NAROCZ	1795	Glasgow to Runcorn	**GAND**	5086	Sydney (Nova Scotia)
OLAF FOSTENES	2994	Halifax (Nova Scotia)	**GYDA**	1695	Montreal ex Manchester
PELAYO	1346	Valencia	**HÖYANGER**	4624	Vancouver
REMBRANDT	5559	Vancouver* to Manchester	**LUCERNA**	6556	Curacao (Dutch W. Indies) ex Manchester
ROOKLEY	4998	* to Manchester	**MALANCHA**	8124	Curacao
SOURABAYA	10107	Aruba (Dutch W. Indies)*	**SAKARA**	2743	Ridham Dock ex Manchester
STANFORD	5969	St. John* to Manchester	**SOMMERSTAD**	5923	Point Breeze
TREGARTHEN	5201	New York	**TUREBY**	4372	Montreal ex Manchester
TUDOR QUEEN	1029	London			

NIGHT – 2nd/3rd MAY

SUNSET 2042
BLACKOUT 2112
ALERT 2220-0237
BLACKOUT ENDS 0505
SUNRISE 0535
MOONLIGHT TO 0045

The second night's raid was a much more serious affair, affecting every division of Liverpool as well as much of the surrounding country. Sixty-five aircraft were said to have arrived, bearing 105 tons HE and 6,042 incendiaries, and this time the HE included fifteen 1000-kg bombs and sixty-six mines – 75 tons between them. It seems that half the mines claimed actually did land in the target area – a very high proportion – making this a much heavier raid in relation to others than the reported bomb-load suggests. (see Appendix I) Liverpool city centre was the focus of the attack, which was pressed continuously from about 2230 to 0200. HE and fire-bombs were mixed throughout, with the mines added after the first hour. The night before there had been reports of a new kind of incendiary device in the form of red and white rockets seen at Upton on the Cheshire side; now there were more of them, shooting along the ground.[69]

The guns fired 4,732 rounds, apparently with some success – at any rate, the Royal Artillery claimed an aircraft seen to crash off the mouth of the Dee at 2315. It was hoped that an orange flash and explosion over the North Docks at 0212 might signify another – the colour suggests the premature explosion of a mine.[70] Again, the raid ended early, though only light, harassing attacks were to be expected for the last couple of hours.

The mines were scattered widely. In Wirral, the railway line from Hooton to West Kirby was closed on account of them; so was the main Chester-Birkenhead line. One in Higher Bebington only broke windows, and one in the Manchester Ship Canal at Stanlow caused slight damage to a ship. (In the canal they would act as sea-mines.) HE and fire-bombs caused a 'medium' fire at Cammell Laird and a large one at the Admiralty store, Abbey Street Gate – both in Birkenhead.

South Lancashire – Formby, Rainford and Haydock – was treated to a similar mixture, and even Ramsbottom, nestling in the Irwell Valley north of Manchester, received a pair of mines – which were probably claimed as falling on Liverpool. One landed in Huyton, damaging 200 houses around Sheppard Avenue. Another fell at Bibby's Farm, just in Liverpool, causing more blast damage in Huyton; but these and several HE bombs caused no worse casualties than six slightly injured.

At 0011 two came down in the Crosby area. One landed in Crosby Road South (by Parker and Pritchard Avenues) killing fourteen – this is apparently the one that put the main transmitter of Seaforth Radio Station out of action for several hours. The other landed on the railway embankment (North Mersey branch) that formed the boundary between Crosby and Bootle, causing great damage in Bulwer Street to the south.[71] The same railway line was hit by a second mine near the Railway Signal Company's works in Fazakerley and was thoroughly blocked as a result.

Another landed squarely in Bootle, in Cyprus Road by Marsh Lane Station. This caused much damage in Marsh Lane and Malta Road; Chadburn's (Ship) Telegraph Company's works (manufacturing control gear for torpedoes among other things) was damaged by blast, and fires started in neighbouring timber yards. Other damage in Bootle was slight, with only one HE and a shower of fire-bombs that started a serious fire at Bedford Road School.

Liverpool was hit hard. Quite a number of mines fell on the city: two on Croxteth Hall Estate, one at Pemberton Road, Old Swan, two near Smithdown Road, two near the Palm House in Prince's Park that failed to go off – there were others at Bowland Avenue, Linnet Lane, Coltart Road and Hunslet Road.

The Pemberton Road mine exploded outside No. 66 at 0110. Rescue parties and ambulances were sent for at 0115 – the AFS were already present. The first rescue party arrived at 0130 and the incident post was set up in Old Swan Bridewell ten minutes later. A second rescue party came at 0205, with two ambulances and a 'Water turncock' to cut off the damaged mains. Work continued till after the 'all-clear', but casualties in the shattered terraces

Bulwer Street, with the railway embankment on the right - the Rimrose Brook runs between. An Anderson shelter has been thrown up out of the ground, but it seems that no-one was killed here.

Chadburn's (Ship) Telegraph Company, Cyprus Road - looking towards Marsh Lane Station.

Grayson Rollo's Bridgewater Street establishment.

were surprisingly low and only one body had been recovered by that time.[72]

The Smithdown Road pair went off at the same time. One blasted a huge crater in Toxteth Park Cemetery and blew out windows in Smithdown Road Hospital. The other hit a garage and damaged houses, killing one woman. There was a surface shelter eighty-five feet away, containing about twenty more people than the fifty it was supposed to hold. All the walls were sucked outwards, but without precipitating a collapse, and only a man standing at the entrance was killed here.

While some of the mines on this night did worse things, they were proving an expensive way of killing people.

HE and fire-bombs were also widely spread. Brunswick Goods Station was hit by HE at midnight, there were heavy casualties in Fern Grove also near Toxteth Park Cemetery, and the Automatic Telephone Company's works at Binns Road was damaged by fire.

In Kirkdale, the Fountains Road/Chancel Street area was hit early in the night when five HE bombs fell at 2225, demolishing fourteen houses. Among the people who moved in to help at Chancel Street was Sergeant Thomas Smith of the Liverpool City Police. "With other officers, he began rescue operations in one stricken street where people were trapped. Hearing voices beneath the debris of two houses, Sergeant Smith began tunnelling with a broken slate by the faint light of a bicycle lamp. Gas from a broken main fouled the air, and the officer had to scoop away earth for twenty yards before reaching the trapped people. After dragging out a man and woman who were removed to hospital, Sergeant Smith again entered the tunnel and, when within a few feet of two other people, he was suddenly trapped by a fall of debris.

"Gunner Thomas Scully, R.A., of 9 Meybrick Road, Liverpool, who had been passing debris out of the tunnel, quickly made a new exit at the rear of the tunnel, and eventually managed to release a man and a woman and Sergeant Smith, who was exhausted and removed to hospital. Gunner Scully stuck tenaciously to his task, and it was largely through his efforts that the three people were rescued alive."[73] Sergeant Smith was awarded the George Medal.

In Everton, a 250-kg bomb fell by St. Brigid's Church, Bevington Hill, at 2315. It landed in the area between the street and the side wall of the crypt, which had been converted into a shelter. Thirty feet of the wall collapsed, bringing down part of the church roof as well as a large section of the reinforced concrete roof of the shelter. There were some three hundred people sheltering there at the time. The situation was alarming, but seven Rescue Parties were on the scene within six minutes and most of the occupants were released quickly – the last in a little over two hours. This was thought at first to be the worst incident of the night, but it turned out that only seven people had been killed.[74]

Things were at their hottest around the city centre. During the raid, Cecil Moores of Littlewood's visited the Company's Hanover Street parachute factory where his party went up to the roof to see how things were going. There were fires in the north – apparently around Leeds Street, behind Exchange Station, where the Company's old pools building might be at risk – so they decided to have a closer look. "When we reached Leeds Street a fire had just started in our building, and the fire-watchers were playing on the flames. They soon went away to get assistance, and it was fortunate they did for a high explosive bomb fell plumb on the building next door, hit a gas main, and within seconds that building and ours was just a raging furnace. All we could do was stand by and watch them burn."

Learning that another bomb had damaged the rear of Littlewood's Old Hall Street head office, Mr. Moores directed that the night shift at Hanover Street – where there were 450 working – should be abandoned for the time being.[75] Not far from Old Hall Street, a bomb in Lumber Street caused serious damage to shops and offices as well as bringing down a substantial section of the roof of Exchange Station over the platforms used by local electric services. (Not the part that was missing during the station's later years – that was removed for use in replacing the damaged section.)

One of the Wrens handling signals at Western Approaches Command was Edith Pargeter, then just beginning to establish her reputation as a novelist. The characters and incidents of her early (and recently reprinted) novel, ***She Goes to War***, are fictional, but the Liverpool background is authentic first-hand reporting. In the concrete bunker under Derby House, the sounds of raids were muted, but on this night an HE bomb landed close by – evidently across Rumford Street.

"That was a bang, if you like. Busy about our lawful occasions, we were suddenly struck by what felt like a hammer-blow against both ear-drums. I suppose we all jumped wildly; I know we all stood fixed for a moment afterwards, frozen to the ground, while the first reverberations quitted our ears. Then Seldon, who has nothing even remotely resembling a nerve in her body, remarked complacently; "That was a bomb." Curiously enough there was a distinct pause before the block collapsed; we heard that too, a slow, slithering, grinding roar that went on for several minutes in a series of diminuendos. We couldn't tell from which direction it came. From our fastness sounds have no direction at all. But next morning we found a ruin on our back doorstep, and the sunlight flooding in at windows which ordinarily it never sees."[76]

South of the city centre there was a good deal of activity on all sides of the LMS Park Lane (Wapping) Goods Station. To the north a cable store, rice mill and sack warehouses were demolished and burnt. To the south there were bad fires among warehouses and bottling works, and at the GWR depot in Chaloner Street – hit by HE at 2320. Grayson Rollo's ship repair works between Bridgewater and Watkinson Streets was hit by HE and incendiary bombs at the same time and burnt out. Water for this fire was taken from Queen's Dock.

Further south there were fires at West Coburg Dock and the Royal Southern Hospital, Hill Street. The latter was now HMS *Wellesley*, a Royal Navy depot and shore training establishment for gunners on merchant ships. Half the south-east wing was demolished by HE and the fires here were extensive.[77]

To the east, a parachute mine on Cornwallis Street at 0035 wrecked St. Michael's Church, Pitt Street, with the houses opposite, and caused serious damage to the Corporation Baths (a useful source of water). A workshop in Cornwallis Street was demolished and left with one of the outside walls leaning inwards dangerously. When groans were heard inside, four men went to investigate; three were police, Sergeant C. J. Gartland, PC Collier Baker and PC J. E. W. Uren – the other was Thomas Tolen from an ARP Rescue Party. In the darkness they found a fire-watcher, Anthony McQueen, almost completely buried in rubble.

The four had not been working to free the man long before it became apparent that a wooden beam carrying the floor above was sagging under the weight of debris. Uren put his shoulder under the beam while the other three worked desperately to get McQueen out as quickly as possible. Before long, Baker was forced to join Uren in holding up the beam, so that only Tolen and Gartland were left attacking the rubble. After an hour, the building showed unmistakable signs of imminent collapse. Seeing that the time for careful extrication of the injured had passed, the Sergeant, who was something of a strongman, told McQueen that it looked as though he was just going to have to pull him out. McQueen agreed and Gartland threw his arms round him and – at the second attempt – hauled him clear. Tolen and Baker were able to get out, but Uren was now flagging under the weight of the beam and could not let go with any prospect of reaching safety before the whole lot caved in. Sergeant Gartland returned to take hold of him and pull him clear, whereupon the beam gave way and the accumulated debris crashed down onto the place where they had been working. All four rescuers received the George Medal.[78]

It may have been the mate of the Cornwallis Street mine that caused much trouble to the west. Sheds at the north-east corner of Queen's Dock were partly demolished along with some smaller buildings at the south end of the great Wapping Dock warehouse and 150 feet of the Dock Board's boundary wall. Park Lane Station across the road was badly blasted, and three spans of the Overhead Railway were brought down just to the north of Wapping Dock Station.[79] The mine that did this was one of the best-placed of the night, as it not only cut the Overhead line and the dock line below – it also blocked the connection between the dock line and Park Lane Station.

The main line of the dock railway was a vital artery for goods traffic, most wagons transferred between docks and railway goods stations passing over it to a greater or lesser extent – often greater when the usual routes were blocked by enemy action. Craters were soon filled and damaged track easily replaced, but the Overhead Railway ran over the dock lines for most of its length and when that was brought down the job of removing the massive girders was very much bigger. And on this night it happened again – to the north of James Street Station, which was completely wrecked when another two spans were demolished.

This brings us to the Pier Head area, where some of the worst damage of the night occurred as the raid was drawing to its close. At 0010 a mine caused extensive damage at the north end of South Castle Street, and was followed by HE. Three fire-watchers, including the managing director, were standing at the doorway of Burnyeat, Dalzell & Nicholson's premises at the corner of Litherland Alley, towards the Canning Place end. All were blown down the passageway inside. The managing director and one of the others survived, but the man in the centre had the misfortune to be exceptionally tall and was killed instantly when his head hit the lintel.

There was a bad fire at the former White Star Building in the Strand, whose tenants now included the Dutch consulate, J. H. Lamey Ltd. (Tugs), and the Larrinaga Steamship Company. Men from the Dock Board's fire party were helping here when a mine exploded at 0145, causing serious damage to George's Dock Building and the MDHB Office. George's Dock Building was built round one of the main ventilation shafts of the Mersey Road Tunnel; the plant for this was only slightly affected, though most of the offices were rendered uninhabitable by blast, fire and water.[80]

The Dock Board Building formed a quadrangle round the central dome. As a result of the blast from the mine fires started, and soon the whole of the east side was in flames causing the Board's men to hurry back from the Strand. The Fire Brigade and AFS were soon here in force, helped by escapes from Birkenhead and Southport (there were eventually seventeen pumps on this job). Water was taken from Canning Dock and the Landing Stage. While

St. Michael's, Pitt Street.

Three spans of the Overhead Railway on the floor. The clock stands at 1220 - probably the time the mine went off. The missing section of the battered Wapping warehouse has already been tidied up after damage sustained in September. Thoughts of turning the warehouse into up-market flats would then have been considered eccentric.

the whole of the east side was gutted, they managed to restrict the fires elsewhere to the roof and top floor – though here the flames raced through all four sides of the building. Although the building was saved, most of it was rendered unfit for use for the time being – both this and the White Star (later PSNC) Building now have somewhat simplified architecture about their upper storeys.

Next door to the Dock Board Offices was the Cunard Building, which was also badly damaged, particularly the section occupied by PSNC, but was saved by its own fire party. Likewise, the Goree Piazzas were knocked about – these being blocks of ancient warehouses that had somehow survived amid the Edwardian splendours of the Pier Head.

It was in the area of George's Dock Building that an ambulance had just arrived with a woman driver to pick up casualties, "when a heavy explosive bomb dropped, killing her and her patient and a constable. Another constable was injured and the ambulance reduced to a mass of twisted metal. Firemen engaged at another fire just across the road were lifted into the air and flung on to their backs. It was only the corner of another building which saved them from serious injury."[81]

At the same time as the mine went off, the Corn Exchange in Brunswick Street was more or less demolished by HE. Fire broke out in the debris, fuelled by broken gas mains, and the place was soon an inferno while Weaver Buildings burned on the other side of Drury Lane. Each building had people trapped in the basement and four Rescue Parties moved in while the fire service tried to hold off the flames. Three were brought out of Weaver Buildings after a few hours, but the parties working in the Corn Exchange had to break through dividing walls and it was mid-day before they were able to bring another three out from under stone steps behind the boiler house.

Just south of the Pier Head, three mines had fallen into the docks – one each in Salthouse, Canning Half-Tide, and Albert. The last was seen by another young novelist, Lieutenant Nicholas Monsarrat, on HMS *Campanula.*

"*Campanula* herself came nearest to dissolution from a huge land-mine which, floating down by parachute and silhouetted impressively against this bombers' moon, fell into the dock-basin with a gentle splash about twenty yards astern of us. Not knowing what sort of activity could touch this sneaky weapon off – it might be noise, electrical interference, temperature change, a certain pattern of vibration, or the simple lapse of time – we closed down everything we had, from the bilge pumps to the radio set, and, moving on tiptoe and talking in whispers, pulled ourselves out of the neighbourhood with our own strong arms."[82]

There were believed to be four more mines in the river, but these could be dealt with by minesweepers. The three in the docks would need careful handling.

The effects of night bombing were largely a matter of luck, and, for all that this was a bad night, luck was with the defenders this time. The mines caused a great deal of damage, but none of them – in or out of Liverpool – caused the ghastly carnage of which they were capable. Some of those that exploded killed no-one, and even at Coltart Road and Linnet Lane, which (along with Fern Grove) seem to have been the worst incidents, the death-roll did not exceed about twenty. What they did do was store up trouble for the future; even the ones that had not gone off blocked roads and closed docks, and a phenomenal number of windows had been shattered in the city's business quarter. This was a significant breach in the defences if more fires should be started before they could be boarded up.

SATURDAY 3rd MAY

Edith Pargeter: "It was eerie coming out into daylight next morning, after our reliefs took over. It was a glorious morning, drenched in pale but dazzling sunlight, except that a curious fawn-coloured haze seemed to hang in mid-air over the streets. But if it was sultry overhead it was glitteringly bright underfoot. We walked to our transport over ground white as hoar frost with glass literally blown to powder. Every window was out; we'd expected that, but I for one hadn't dreamed how it would be. There were great glittering slivers lying on top of the frost, but most of the glass was so fine it might never have been glass at all. The street glistened like the whitest mica you ever saw, and rang underfoot."[83]

The local press followed the official communiqué in reporting a heavy raid on Merseyside: "Early reports suggest that the number of casualties may be large and that a substantial amount of damage was done."[84] Still, there was nothing the local forces could not cope with, though transport difficulties were multiplied through damage and unexploded bombs and mines. The main roads closed in the centre of Liverpool included Strand Street, South Castle Street, James Street and London Road (an unexploded mine). Whatever their virtues otherwise, tramways are inflexible in these circumstances and Liverpool's bus fleet was so small that vans had to be used to transport Saturday morning workers. Several of the main railway lines into the area were blocked, and no trains ran on the Overhead. Following damage to that company's head office in James Street, temporary offices were set up in a train at Pier Head Station.

Life went on. Theatrical entertainments on offer for that evening were all on the light side; Evelyn Laye and Fred Emney were at the Empire with a supporting company that included Beryl Reid, Comedienne, and the D'Oyly Carte Opera Company were ending the second of their three weeks at the Royal Court with ***The Gondoliers***.

It was also the first day of Litherland's War Weapons Week, in which it was hoped that the town would raise £100,000 in War Bonds. The festivities started with speeches at the Town Hall, followed by a Home Guard parade past the war memorial. Almost at once, the indicator – a bullet – was raised to £45,000. This was erected in Linacre Road, and had a miniature barrage balloon floating above it. Two centres were opened for the sale of bonds, and people looked forward to a week of varied entertainments and official functions.

Rescue work continued throughout the day at several of the more serious incidents. That at Pemberton Road was closed at 1145 with only one person reported killed. Less than half an hour after, a body was found on the rafters of a house in Woodhall Road and two more people were reported missing. Work resumed until the victims were found late that evening.[85] At 1930 hours Blackpool was advised to have a rescue party standing by for Liverpool, which was ordered out at 0120 on the 4th.[86] This suggests that Liverpool had been identified as the night's target – possibly by the switching on of the German navigation beams in advance. Home Security certainly thought that Friday night's raid was: "a prelude to further and more systematic attacks."[87]

It was on the Saturday that shipping was first affected. At an unspecified time, the mine in Albert Dock detonated spontaneously. Fortunately, this and the other docks containing mines were among the oldest, smallest, and least important on the Mersey (they are now preserved as relics of dock-working in the days of sail). Albert Dock, surrounded by immense and majestic warehouses, was used to store sundry Dock Board vessels – including two spare lightships at the south end – and the west side had been taken over by the Navy as a berth for corvettes. Six of these had sailed on the Friday, leaving only ***Tulip***, ***Periwinkle*** and ***Campanula*** to be threatened by the mines. Most mines dropped at this time were magnetic, designed to take account of the surroundings on arrival and then explode only when a change in the local magnetic field was detected. This meant that, in theory, any ships near the mine when it fell were safe so long as they were not moved. Apparently nothing was in Albert –

apart from *Campanula* the night before – but the mine went off anyway, blasting the bow off the lightship *Sirius* (174) and sinking both her and *No. 2 Surveyor* – a seven-ton launch. *Camel No. 4* (310) was left badly damaged and down by the stern.[88]

At around 2000 the coaster *Corbet* (468) was passing the entrance to Herculaneum Dock at the south end with a cargo of coal from Garston Docks for Belfast when she set off another mine. She heeled over at once and sank quickly, only one man being saved of the nine on board.[89]

These events added to the work of the salvage men, one of whom was in the news that day – Charles Brock, Superintendent of Salvage Plant for the MDHB. He had been awarded the MBE, the citation reading: "Mr. Brock has displayed outstanding ability and devotion to duty during enemy air raids and set a magnificent example when assisting to fight fires and attending to damage by high explosives. He has carried out his work under intense aerial bombardment without any consideration of personal safety."[90]

He was going to have to do it again before another day dawned.

SHIPPING MOVEMENTS – 3rd MAY

Inward	*G.T.*	*From*	*Outward*	*G.T.*	*To*
ABOSSO	11330	Lagos*	**INGER**	1418	Cardiff ex Manchester
ADDA	7816	Lagos*	**MEROPE**	1162	London
AFRIKA	8597	Mauritius*	**NARKUNDA**	16632	Troopship
ALPHACCA	5759	Bombay	**ORDUÑA**	15507	Troopship
BRITISH ENDURANCE	8406	New York to Stanlow	**SLIEVE DONARD**	1116	Holyhead
CITY OF AUKLAND	8336	Rangoon*			
DORDRECHT	4402	Calabar (Nigeria)			
MACGREGOR LAIRD	4992	Forcados (Nigeria)* to Manchester			
MOSDALE	3022	St. John			
NEW BROOKLYN	6546	Duala*			
PRINCESSA	8731	Buenos Aires* to Manchester			
RHESUS	6530	Rangoon*			
SELLINGE	2327	London			
SILVERSANDAL	6770	Vancouver			
TRENTINO	3079	Lisbon			

*Convoy sailed from Freetown (Sierra Leone), 8th April.

NIGHT – 3rd/4th MAY

SUNSET .... 2044(BST)
BLACKOUT .... 2114(BST)
ALERT .... 2230(BST) – c.0450 (DST)
BLACKOUT ENDS .... 0548 (DST)
SUNRISE .... 0633(DST)
MOONLIGHT TO 0130 (BST)
(From this date the blackout ran from three quarters of an hour after sunset to three quarters of an hour before sunrise - it had been half an hour previously.)

This was by far the worst night of the war for the towns on the east bank of the Mersey. 298 aircraft claimed to have dropped 363 tons of HE and 49,706 incendiaries Details of the types of bombs dropped are not available, but there were at least two 1,000-kg bomb-mines – a new type that as their name implies, acted as mines in water but were dropped without parachutes. Light attacks were made on other towns as widely scattered as Hartlepool, Barrow-in-Furness, Bristol and Great Yarmouth. A few bombs of the Mersey's quota fell on the Cheshire side, at Birkenhead, Wallasey, Bebington and Runcorn – one near Mold, Flintshire killed four shepherds. Some others were scattered across Lancashire , most of them on the fringes of Merseyside such as the two mines at Huyton. Mines were also laid in Liverpool Bay. Otherwise the weight of the attack was heavily concentrated on a strip of land within two miles of the Liverpool dock wall, from Liverpool city centre to the southern parts of Crosby and Litherland. Conditions were near perfect for the bombers with light cloud and the moon in the first quarter. Liverpool's luck was out.

The guns fired about 5,000 rounds and were restricted to a maximum height of 12,000 feet from 2315 to 0015 to allow the night-fighters to have a go over the city.[91] Neither arm seems to have had much success, but just after midnight a Heinkel 111 bomber flying at around 500 feet hit the cable of one of the balloons moored on ships off the river mouth and was seen to crash into the sea. The cable was one of those fitted with an explosive device, which may have helped.[92]

Reference to the duration of the alert suggests a steady attack over a period of some five hours (not six – see below). In fact there was a devastating attack concentrated in the first hour or so and then tailing off rapidly to a few planes, evidently to harass the defenders and discourage people from coming out to tackle the fires. It started with flares in the West Derby area, the first bombs following soon after 2300 (some say 2230). The Liverpool Engineer's Department record shows 55 timed incidents in the next half hour, then 50 – 37 – 22. There were another fourteen in the half hour from 0100 and only fifteen from 0130 to 0500.[93] (The Engineer's Department was concerned with a limited range of incidents, such as those involving rescue parties, blocked streets or damaged sewers, and there may be omissions in the later period on account of poor communications.) Decoy fires lit on the Dee estuary to divert some of the attack had only limited success.

HE bombs, mines and incendiaries were mixed throughout the raid, and there were more reports of "bombs which appeared to discharge rockets on hitting the ground."[94] Later in the war the Germans certainly did use bombs containing a relatively small charge of high explosive together with a number of incendiary devices that were scattered by the blast. The ones now landing on Merseyside seem to have been of this type and may well have assisted in creating the serious fire situation that developed during the raid.

It is most regrettable that on this fearful night Liverpool's ordeal was compounded by a second disaster – the catastrophic failure of the fire services to cope with the situation. This was not just the result of an exceptionally heavy raid and failure of the water supply; the organisation that had worked faultlessly in March failed utterly in May.

The main reason is plainly stated in a report made by Wing-Commander Hodsoll a few days later: "There was a muddle over bringing in reinforcements which either did not arrive or were extremely late."[95] No further information has come to light as yet. The nature of the "muddle" is obscure, nor can I say when the reinforcements ought to have arrived or when they actually did. The consequences will become all too apparent in what follows. The fact of the fire services' failure is hardly news as it was openly referred to in the local press before the month was out. George Eglin, writing about Liverpool's war in the ***Echo*** in 1957 and 1966, touched on this matter, but where one might have expected later accounts to reveal more one finds instead that the subject is dropped altogether.

In view of the concentrated attack in the first part of the raid, it will be understood that the need for large-scale reinforcements was – or ought to have been – apparent early on in the night. It could take as much as two hours to drive from Stockport to Liverpool in the blackout. (The drivers of two precious, full-size appliances coming from Manchester along the East Lancashire Road may have been trying to improve on this sort of timing when they ran full tilt onto the islands at roundabouts – they had to observe the blackout like everyone else. They became hopelessly bogged down and the crews had to hitch lifts from those following.) When reinforcements were needed from further afield speed in calling them in was of the most vital importance. This was one way in which a heavy raid was much worse for a smaller city than one of the same weight on – say – London. The whole subject is shrouded in such obscurity, however, that little detail can be given and it is impossible to attribute blame; there may indeed have been nothing worse than pardonable errors under extreme stress. If human error *was* involved, the mistakes did not necessarily arise in the Liverpool fire service.

It is interesting to compare what happened when London suffered its last heavy raid a week later. The target was identified from the placing of the German navigation beams nearly six hours before the first bomb fell. Steps were immediately taken to call in reinforcements for the 2,500 pumps already in Greater London and some London pumps in Birmingham were on the road within an hour of the raid starting.[96] In spite of this, very serious fires developed; largely because of difficulties with water-supply – the Thames at low tide was a much more difficult source to extract water from than the Liverpool docks. It is true that parts of Liverpool suffered from the failure of water mains, but most of the fires there were within easy reach of the docks if only there had been the pumps to take advantage of the fact.

It is certain, as will become clear, that many firemen upheld the finest traditions of their service, some of them giving their lives. It must also be remembered that there is inevitably a bias in favour of disaster; buildings destroyed or gutted loom larger in the records than buildings saved from serious damage by the efforts of fire-watchers, AFS, and regular firemen.

The events of the raid were confused at the time, and it appears that some aspects of what happened have been suppressed to this day so that nothing like the full story can be told. An additional source of confusion arises with the change from British Summer Time – then continued throughout the winter months – to Double Summer Time.

Officially, the hour went on at 0200 BST (0100 GMT) but few of those actively engaged will have paused to adjust their watches at the appointed hour. Unfortunately, it is apparent from those records that *do* refer to the change (mostly ships' logs) that 0100 BST was a popular time for making the adjustment, one of His Majesty's Ships even doing it at 2300 *the previous day*. To make confusion worse confounded, references to Summer Time may mean Double Summer Time – and some call it Mid-Summer Time (MST). It follows that times quoted in this section are more than usually unreliable. I have simply passed them on as given, adding BST or DST in brackets where the records make it clear which is meant.

THE HOME FRONT

Of the few Incident Officer's Record Sheets to survive, that for the area between Edge Lane Drive and Queen's Drive was almost certainly selected as a result of its being the first of this night (by Liverpool Engineer's Department reckoning). What happened there is in no way remarkable and is thus a fair representative of the many other domestic tragedies scattered across the city.

The Incident Officer was Constable Harris of 'G' Division, who reported that HE had fallen at 2240, damaging houses in Heliers Road and Withnell Close. There were people injured and trapped, but no roads blocked. The Incident Post was set up at the ARP post in Saville Road and ambulances sent for. A Rescue Party had arrived by 2300 and was sent to Withnell Close. Three seriously injured children were brought out of one house at 2320.

At 2315 more HE dropped behind a house in Whitehouse Road. There were no casualties here, but gas and water mains were affected. Ten minutes later bombs hit houses in Ringcroft Road and Anstey Road. A call went out for ambulances and Rescue Parties, which were needed in both roads. At 2330 fires were seen in the damaged houses in Withnell Close. Men were sent to deal with them and they were reported out by 2355. Another Rescue Party arrived and four people were sent to hospital from Ringcroft and Anstey at 2340. Another two only slightly injured – followed from Ringcroft five minutes later. There was believed to be a child still trapped at that house.

An ambulance was called at 2350 to take an injured woman from Anstey Road, and another at 0140 for a woman from Whitehouse Road. At 0145 a waterman was sent for to tackle a bad escape at Anstey Road. The last ambulance was called at 0243 when the child at Ringcroft Road – a four-year-old boy – was brought out dead.

At 0415 the Rescue Parties left the scene. The warden had ensured that everyone was accounted for and the homeless accommodated. The Incident Officer reported 'the incident' closed at 0430. There were two dead and twelve injured – six seriously. No

Banks in the front line - the corner of Smithdown Road and Langdale Roads. HE, reported 0045, 4th May. There were four killed here.

roads were blocked and water and gas mains had been attended to. One is left with the impression that everything had been handled with speed and efficiency, and by all accounts this was generally the case with the rescue services.[97]

To the east, HE fell on the large underground shelter by the Rocket Hotel, Queen's Drive, just after midnight. Some people had been moved there after being bombed out earlier in the night and about thirty were killed. The Huyton mines were a little further out – at Reva Road and Swanside Road close to the Liverpool boundary, but casualties there were not heavy.

In the south and east of Liverpool there was relatively little activity, though it may not have seemed so to those involved in such incidents as there were. The demolition of seventeen houses in Alt Street, north of Prince's Park, was the worst domestic incident in these parts. A mine caused serious damage at the Corporation yard in Smithdown Road, killing most of the heavy rescue squad whose lorry had just returned from Lewis's store. Sudley Road and Rose Lane Council Schools were also badly knocked about.

From central Liverpool north to Walton and Bootle, however, there was a broad swathe of destruction. While the Northern and Southern hospitals had been evacuated as being too near the docks, Mill Road Infirmary and other establishments continued their normal civilian work. They also acted as casualty receiving stations during raids, Mill Road being the biggest of these. As soon as was practical, air raid victims were loaded onto special ambulances converted from old single-decker buses so as to hold ten stretcher cases and taken to emergency hospitals in safe areas on the outskirts. Ordinary coaches were called in as necessary for the walking wounded. Soon after 2330 a mine exploded in the courtyard between C and E blocks at Mill Road, bringing them both down in a cascading avalanche of bricks.

The emergency operating theatre was in a basement under one of the demolished blocks. A young Greek seaman had been brought in with a perforated ulcer and had already been anaesthetised when the sirens went. The surgeon, Mr. Digby Roberts, opted to continue with the operation, and the first incisions had been made when the roof fell in.

One of those present was Glenys Pierce, a junior theatre sister. "The first thing I remember was hearing Mr. Roberts saying that he had lost his glasses. There was a slab of stone across my body and, from above, everything was falling in. The patient was still anaesthetised, but the table was tilted like a seesaw. There was a nurse who had fallen through the hole into the basement. She was hysterical, clutching her head and crying that she could not see. I could see a way out through the blown out window and I got her out through there. I told the rescue party how to get into the basement and took the nurse to the out patients."[98]

Among the rescuers was Mr. D. Guyers, leader of the local street fire parties; he and John Wilkinson answered the Chief Warden's call for volunteers and went down into the operating theatre. They got the staff out first, then found the seaman. "We were getting a bit nervous for our own safety when we spotted a bare leg moving. We tried to get the body but only succeeded in clearing the debris. There was a block of concrete on top of his table, which had turned over with him underneath."

"We could not get him out, although I could take the weight of the stone, so we called for more help and were joined by a soldier. Together, John and this soldier pulled him out while I took the weight of the stone. We had no torch and could not see very clearly, but everything was burning. Three-handed we couldn't manage, then we spotted a torch coming along a passageway. It was a policeman. He said the building was in a bad state but he knew the way out if we hurried, so the four of us carried the seaman out. When we got him out I found Dr. Bradley, himself injured about the face, and brought him to the man; his stomach had been opened and his intestines were protruding. Dr. Bradley said he was as good as dead but tore his coat and bound it round the man's stomach."[99]

In fact, the operation was successfully completed at Walton Hospital.

When the blast came, Gertrude Riding – Matron, Dr. Leonard Findlay – Medical Superintendent, and William Gray – his deputy, were leaving the casualty receiving ward where the victims of the night were already beginning to come in. All three were caught in the blast and thrown under falling debris, Mr. Gray being killed instantly while the other two were knocked out.

Miss Riding came round to find things still falling about her and Dr. Findlay calling: "Where are you, matron?" She tried to move, but found that her arm was caught under Mr. Gray's body. "Dr. Findlay got me out. Fire was blazing and it was very difficult to realise what was happening. One of my eyes had gone completely, and the other was so affected that I had to keep it open with two fingers in order to see at all. I heard a nurse calling for help, and I removed some bricks and stretchers that had fallen on her and pulled her free. She was an auxiliary nurse, and the patient she was bringing in was dead. Further along I heard someone else calling for help. It was Father Maloney, a hospital chaplain. He was pinned down, and I could not lift him bodily, but a few minutes later a porter came along and with other help he was rescued."[100] Soon after, Miss Riding collapsed from the strain of her exertions and her injuries and was taken to Alder Hey Hospital.

The state of the Infirmary after the blast was that C and E blocks had been demolished (including half the maternity unit and the X-ray department) and A, B, D, F and G blocks were badly damaged along with the Admin block and boiler house. Fires broke out in the ruins and among cars and ambulances wrecked in the yard. Only the Out-Patients' Department was intact, and that was without electricity.

As the extent of the disaster became apparent the civil defence services swung into action to good effect. The incident post was set up by Police Sergeant Carson at 2355, the first message out being a request for Fire Brigade assistance. There was an AFS squad attached to the hospital and a Fire Brigade pump arrived from Durning Road within minutes; between them they had all the fires out or under control by about 0100.

Also at midnight the call went out for "All available rescue, first aid and ambulance help." Two rescue parties and two first aid parties arrived. At 0045 Control was told: "Many trapped under debris, extra rescue and first aid required." Within five minutes thirty men of the Pioneer Corps arrived, but a further message had to be sent at 0125: "More rescue parties required, Mill Road Hospital now closed for reception of casualties." A few minutes after this another forty soldiers came.[101]

After the initial chaos of shocked and injured people blundering about in the darkness and mothers with babies escaping from the wreck as best they could, order was established – largely through the efforts of Dr. Findlay. In spite of being shaken and badly burned, he organised rescue work well into the following day before accepting treatment himself.

While the raid continued and more bombs fell in the area, four hundred patients were assembled in the Out-Patients Department to await the buses and ambulances that came to take them to other hospitals, and people came to help from nearby houses bringing tea and comfort. An emergency dressing and reception station was set up in the main hall with stretcher cases scattered round the floor. Casualties from outside were still coming in, including one old lady "with a shattered hand hanging at a grotesque angle from her wrist",[102] and nurses did the best they could with dressings and drugs recovered from damaged cupboards.

Birkenhead responded to a request for help by sending eight ambulances and eight first-aid parties to Mill Road where their contribution must have been welcome, though there was in fact no shortage of ambulances in Liverpool. The Liverpool ambulance service was not pleased at having its record of never calling in reinforcements spoiled in this way, and subsequently had to content itself with the claim that it had never *needed* help.[103]

After four hours the work of evacuation was complete, and with hopes of finding more survivors dwindling, the dead became a consideration. The number killed could only be guessed at as yet – they would include fourteen ambulance drivers and seventeen members of the hospital staff. About seventy people had been seriously injured. Dr. Findlay received the George Medal, and Miss Riding the OBE.[104]

Six hundred yards to the west, where two and three-storey terraces climbed the hill above Shaw Street, the first HE-bomb was reported as blocking Eastbourne Street at 2323. A few minutes later three houses were demolished where Plumpton Street meets Exmouth Street, and a mine demolished much of Plumpton Street and Fitzclarence Street at 2350. Given the uncertain accuracy of these timings this may well have been the companion of the Mill Road mine. Another mine blasted Westbourne Street and College Street North – behind the Collegiate School – at 0110.

This is the background to the story of Corporal (Acting-Sergeant) James Garrigan of 136th Company, Pioneer Corps. Everyone who was not needed to mind the Company's base – the Drill Hall in Everton Road – was sent out to help locally, and it may be that the men sent to Mill Road came from here. Sergeant Garrigan, an Irishman and First World War veteran, took a party of ten volunteers to Plumpton Street and was given the job of rescuing a woman and her little girl from the ruins of a public house. Both could be heard calling out, but it was two hours before the men were able to bring out the girl, who was found lying on her mother's lap. She was put in the relative safety of a nearby house while an ambulance was called for. This was a three-ton lorry fitted up by the Pioneer Corps. It arrived, the driver walked twenty yards or so to the pub where the men were still working – and then a mine exploded.

When Sergeant Garrigan climbed out of the crater into which he had been thrown – the one by the pub – he found that the ambulance had been completely destroyed and six of his men were dead or missing. Also, the house in which they had placed the girl for safety had been demolished and there was plainly no hope of rescuing her a second time. Although badly shaken, Garrigan got his remaining men back to work and the mother was brought out only to die soon after. It was only one of many incidents where gallant struggles were miserably rewarded. Sergeant Garrigan received the George Medal. Over thirty were killed in this area, including a warden, a first-aid worker and fire-watchers as well as the six men from Garrigan's party.[105]

West again, towards Exchange Station, an HE-bomb landed on Holy Cross School in Addison Street. "About 120 people were in the shelter underneath and not a living soul escaped. Mangled bodies lay everywhere amongst the debris, most of them mutilated beyond recognition. Air Raid Precautions Officers and military personnel worked hard to shift the wreckage hoping to find someone alive, but after hours of labour their only reward was to see a dog and a cat crawl to safety."[106] The list of Civilian War Dead records 73 killed in and around Addison Street, which may be an understatement.

At St. Mary's Church in Highfield Street – over the road from Exchange Station – there were hundreds sheltering in the crypt. When the church caught fire Warden Joseph Owens led the people out through the burning streets in small parties to find places in other shelters.[107] The church was gutted.

Further north another basement shelter was hit at Gildart Gardens at 2310. 134 people were rescued from this one before the roof collapsed and the wreckage caught fire with some still inside.[108] There were about thirty killed here and in Ford Street. At St. Martin's Market in Scotland Road (better known as Paddy's Market) St. Martin's Hall was gutted, while the Wholesale Fruit and Vegetable Market in Cazneau Street was completely destroyed by fire. Both had already been damaged on the Thursday night.[109] In Silvester Street, St. Sylvester's Church was destroyed and a balloon barrage station was hit by HE at 0030 – all personnel being reported missing.

In an isolated incident to the east, Anfield Road School was showered with incendiaries. "The resulting fire was gallantly and successfully fought by the fire-watchers for a long time before a Fire Engine arrived." Most of the building was saved.[110]

For fear of repetition as much as want of information, I have passed over many bloody incidents in the Kirkdale/Everton area. The worst were Creswick Street (22 dead), Northumberland Terrace (26), Towson and Venmore Streets (70), the Fountains Road area – notably Wykeham, Newman, Morley and Freeland Streets – (100), and Hermia Street (20). Most of these incidents were the result of mines.

St. Mary's Walton, was among the churches hit. An incendiary landed on the roof and, although a fire-watcher was on duty, the Rector had to be called out to open the building. The bomb was awkwardly placed in the rafters and it was forty-five minutes before the fire service arrived, with the result that the building was gutted. The post-war reconstruction of the interior was no compensation for what had been lost. There was some understandable criticism at the loss of the building to one fire-bomb, but the Parochial Church Council was satisfied that no more could have been done in the circumstances.

Another Walton landmark was the Gaol, where the lot of prisoners and warders was not a happy one at such times. (The Gaol had already been hit in September, with some loss of life among the prisoners.) At 0030 a 500-kg bomb landed on the east wall of D block, demolishing a section of that along with the corner cells of C block. To the outside world Walton Gaol presented a front of massive Norman solidity, but the walls were actually of weak construction and the four storeys fell into the basement, killing twelve prisoners. Several 50-kg bombs followed, causing lesser damage (one landed on the ruins of K block, demolished in September), and a 250-kg bomb exploded on the third floor of I block, killing another twelve prisoners.

The rescue work was led by the Governor, James Holt, in difficult and dangerous circumstances. Chief Officer Ernest Thompson escaped by inches when a great load of masonry crashed down from one of the high walls as he supervised the release of prisoners. One rescue party working in the basement was hampered by a drenching shower of water from the broken feed pipes to a water tank. Seeing this, engineer James Halliday made his way up and clambered along the bulging and crumbling walls to reach the pipes and stop the flow. For his work now and in the previous September James Holt received the OBE. BEMs went to Thompson and Halliday.[111]

Walton also had its mines, though the casualties were mostly on the low side. The worst case was at Index Street, where 43 were killed, with others nearby at Carisbrooke Road and Peter Road. There was one at Dallas Grove, at the north end, and another just to the south of that in Walton Vale that blew the roof off the Blessed Sacrament Church.

In Bootle the dismal catalogue continued. The new St. Joan's (RC) School had just been completed and was being used for the storage of furniture from bomb-damaged premises. Fire-bombs got in among the stored items, there was no water, and the building was burnt out. Several rest centres were hit, including St. Andrew's Church Hall on the Litherland boundary where women of the WVS were clearing up after supper. Having just refused to go to shelter, all were killed along with some people who had already lost their homes. This incident does not seem to have cost as many lives as generally claimed, but the deaths of the six WVS volunteers caused particular distress.[112]

It is difficult to pick out exceptional incidents in Bootle, where the casualties occurred in small pockets scattered through the undistinguished terraces. The worst-hit area seems to have been the run of streets between Marsh Lane and Peel Road named after poets; here there were sixty killed, mostly in Southey, Shelley, Tennyson and Wordsworth Streets.

In Crosby, on the outer edge of the target, the bombs came in three distinct periods, starting with HE and fire-bombs from 2340 to 0020. It was in this spell that Waterloo Library and Museum was hit by fire-bombs and burnt out. More of the same

North Market, Cazneau Street.

came from 0107 to 0150, this time with two mines. One of these killed fourteen at Bedford Place, Seaforth. Another mine and several HE bombs fell around 0230 (BST).

Events in Litherland were on a smaller scale. Perhaps the worst incident here came when a street shelter in Bradley Road was demolished by HE, killing five.

This is a small space in which to dismiss a good deal of human misery and loss, but, as people discovered at the time, one bomb story is much like the next and the same goes for accounts of rescuers tunnelling through earth, rubble and gas fumes – so this sparse summary must stand for all.

CITY CENTRE

This raid would have been memorable in any event, but the damage to so many well-known buildings in the city centre ensured that everyone felt some personal involvement in the disaster. While many escaped bereavement in their own family circle, there can have been few who did not lose a familiar building.

Premises east of the Bluecoat Chambers in School Lane were set alight by incendiaries and the fire blown across to the former charity school, a precious remnant of Queen Anne architecture built around three sides of a small court. The fire party in the building were unable to prevent the fire from spreading to the east wing and centre block – and when the fire service came they found no water. In spite of this, the west wing and ground floor centre were saved while the rest was gutted. The upstairs hall was being used as a substitute art gallery, but by great good fortune the current exhibition of Liverpool School paintings had ended that day; all the canvases had been stored on the ground floor overnight and were so saved.[113]

Lewis's, the largest department store in the city, was hit by an HE bomb at 0014. This apparently knocked out the sprinkler system. Oil bombs and three more HE followed and soon the west end of the building was well alight and several fire-watchers dead. The admin block, on Renshaw Street, was cut off from the rest by stairs and lifts – the wind blowing from the east also contributed to the preservation of this end of the building. To the west, round the corner into Ranelagh Street, it was a different story. The contents of the furniture floor was reduced to a six-inch layer of ash and it was found afterwards that wooden blocks in the roadway had been burned to a depth of half an inch. As the fire grew in intensity, sparks and burning fragments were blown through the shattered windows and skylights of Blackler's store 130 feet away across Ranelagh Street.

The fire service was present and tried to save Blackler's at least by playing water over the building. The failure of the mains put a stop to that, and when the Fire Brigade's No. 17 pump arrived from Speke at 0055 both buildings were "a mass of uncontrolled flame on all floors." The fire raged unchecked through Blackler's, crossed Great Charlotte Street to the smaller shops opposite, and then passed over Deane Street as well.

Water was taken from steel dams in front of the Adelphi Hotel, and then a small AFS pump was used to refill the dams from the hotel swimming pool – in this way it was possible to prevent the spread of fire along Lime Street. When a heavy AFS pump arrived, No. 17 was sent further along Lime

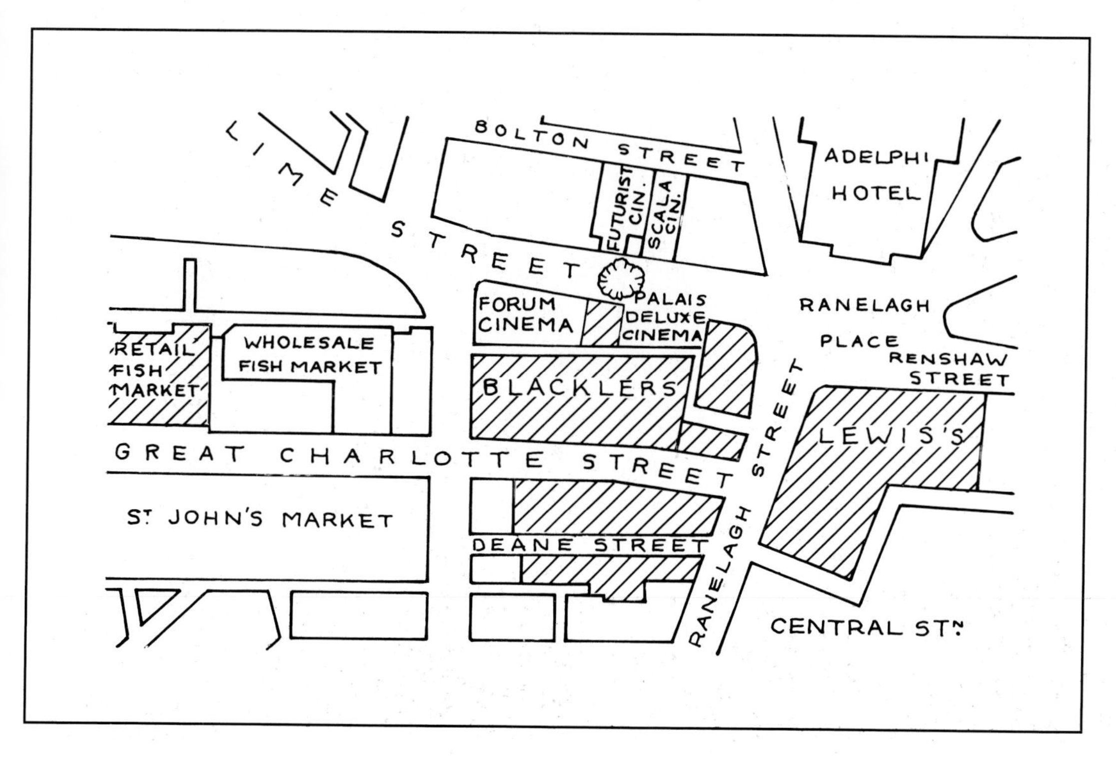

Blackler's, Lewis's, and Lime Street indicating the site of damaged buildings.

Blackler's from Ranleigh Street. The men on the right are standing by a notice that reads: "William's China Store closed for alterations."

Street to take water from a large crater – the probable cause of the water failure in this area. Blackler's and a number of smaller shops were gutted, as was three fifths of Lewis's. The structure of Blackler's remained intact, but nothing was salvaged from the goods inside. The refreshment rooms at Central Station (CLC) were wrecked by debris from Lewis's, and the unsafe condition of the end wall forced the closure of the station. Frustratingly, it was later discovered that Lewis's basement was flooded to a depth of several feet – possibly by the broken mains.[114]

Further up Great Charlotte Street, fires broke out on the roof of the Wholesale Fish Market. They were contained by the fire-watchers and later quelled with the help of the fire service before serious damage was done, but it was thought best to evacuate the shelter in the basement during the raid. This was one of the bigger ones, holding around 1,200 people and always packed during heavy raids, mostly with family groups. They had to make their way up through ammonia fumes escaping from the refrigeration plant and were apparently left to find alternative shelter in the burning city as best they could.[115]

The range of Corporation buildings along William Brown Street was under the care of the usual eight attendants or night watchmen plus eleven volunteer fire-watchers, led on this occasion by the Director of the Art Gallery. They were responsible for the safety of the Technical College, Museum, William Brown Library, Picton Library, and Walker Art Gallery; an array of mostly Victorian neo-classical buildings intended to echo the splendours of St. George's Hall, which loomed blackly over the ornamental gardens on the other side of William Brown Street. The Art Gallery had been given over to the Ministry of Food and the more valuable works sent into the country, though a large part of the collection remained in the cellars and other items were displayed at the Bluecoat or in the Libraries.

At 2330 an HE bomb behind the Gallery blew in most of the glass on that side; forty minutes later three fire-bombs landed in the Museum and were suppressed. It was at 0030 that a heavy HE (some say oil) bomb hit the William Brown Library, causing serious damage and starting a fire. No-one was killed, but the Deputy Chief Librarian was buried in debris – mostly timber – on the first floor, and two attendants were trapped in a basement passage – also partly buried by rubble from a staircase.

All three were injured and in great danger from the fire that spread rapidly in the wreckage. It took thirty minutes to extricate the two in the basement – a good piece of work in which an ARP First Aid Party assisted. The others did what they could to contain the fire while a Civil Defence Cadet[116] carried messages to the Royal Hospital and Hatton Garden. Between 0100 and 0200 the injured were given first aid and sent to hospital. At about the same time more HE bombs landed in front of the Museum and disposed of the glass on that side; then the AFS arrived, offering hope of restricting the fire to the library. At 0200 (BST) a new fire was seen on the roof of the Art Gallery, but the AFS were able to deal with that quickly using hoses already in position in the building. When the 'all-clear' went, it was clear that the William Brown Library was lost, but there seemed a good chance of saving the Picton on one side and the Museum on the other.[117]

At 0012 a heavy HE bomb exploded in the control room of the Fire Salvage Association's Chief Station at Hatton Garden, a street largely given over to various local government functions. Two officers were killed as well as the wife and two daughters of a salvageman who were sheltering in the adjoining basement. A salvageman who was helping to run a hose to a fire in nearby Johnson Street was also killed. (The 'salvage cottages' in Johnson Street were damaged.) The rest of the men and their families who were in the reinforced basement shelter and the cellar under the duty room were transferred to the shelter under the Tramway Offices till they were driven out again by a fire there. The women and children then went to the basement of the Central Fire Station opposite, while most of the men volunteered to act as guides for appliances reporting from outside the city. The Salvage Association was operating from one of the damaged cottages by noon on Monday.[118]

In Victoria Street, the Government Offices formed a block backing onto the Municipal Building in Dale Street. It provided a home for the Ministries of Health and Agriculture, the Assistance Board and the Inland Revenue Stamp Office among others. The only light one can throw on the fate of this building arises from the award of the BEM to Ernest Sidney Leatham, assistant inspector with the Ministry of Health, and Constable William Hunter.

"Mr. Leatham was on voluntary fire-watching duty with other colleagues, and was sheltering in the basement during the height of a raid when a high-explosive bomb crashed through the floors immediately above, tearing down the walls, caving in the shelter, and setting the place on fire. Mr. Leatham managed to worm his way out from under the fallen brickwork and timber and go for help to secure the release of his two colleagues, who remained trapped and injured under the debris. Police and auxiliary firemen were soon at work, the firemen fighting the fire overhead and Constable Hunter digging his way through to one man who was pinned down by beams. Despite the limited space, Constable Hunter removed the rubble, sawed through the timber and got out the casualty.

"Meanwhile, Mr. Leatham, who had already directed the firemen so that the trapped men should not be drowned by the water from the hoses, began burrowing towards the other victim, but was unable, owing to heavy obstructions, to reach him unaided. The work of rescue went on for seven hours, and while waiting for help from the rescue party, Mr. Leatham salvaged valuable papers and periodically crawled down the tunnel near to the trapped man to reassure him."[119] Throughout this work, fire raged overhead and masonry was falling. The building was a total loss. Considering the site, it is a little surprising that it remains a hole in the ground (surrounded by an elegant balustrade) and is used only as a car park – perhaps the last major 'bombed site' in the city centre.

A note on fire-watching may be apposite here. As the whole point was to catch fires before they could start there is no doubt that the best place to do it was on the roof or at least the top floor, with more men on the intermediate floors of large buildings. In larger buildings such as the Government Offices, with well-organised fire-parties, it was quite in order for some watchers to remain in shelter until called on. It seems to have been a recognised practice that watchers should wait downstairs until they had reason to believe that incendiaries had fallen – reasonable enough so long as they could reach the roof quickly. It was a risky job (though much less risky than service in a front-line army unit) and some preferred the relative safety of a shelter or basement, especially when they were most needed higher up. This is understandable and it is not for those who have never done the job to cast the first stone, which can safely be left to those who have.

Diagonally opposite across Victoria Street was the Head Post Office, occupying almost an entire block between there and Whitechapel. It was hit by incendiaries shortly before 2255. The building was defended by a well-equipped team of fire-watchers backed up by the Home Guard (believed to be a unit composed of GPO staff) and the relatively small number of people who worked there on Saturday night. On the other hand, the building had been damaged in March; there were still holes in the roof covered by tarpaulins and quantities of timber lay ready for use in repairing these. This ensured that fires were able to start at several points.

The fire-watchers had hoses laid out ready for action but these were dependent on mains pressure, which was not good at roof height. Seeing that they were losing ground, Mr. Howe, the Superintendent in Charge, hurried to a telephone and sought help from the Fire Brigade and from the AFS Station in Stanley Street. Both responded within a few minutes and soon there were half a dozen appliances at the scene including no less than three turntable ladders – a very lavish turn-out on this night, though sparse enough in the circumstances (compare the ten appliances sent here in March). At 2350 more fire-bombs fell and the fire continued to spread.

At 0130 (all times appear to be BST) Mr. Howe reported to the Chief Superintendent (Postal) by telephone only to have the line go dead during the call. This apparently marks the end of the Central Exchange (of which more later). As the fire was still gaining, he sent one of the Home Guard to ask for more help from the fire service, who replied that they would do what they could. This was evidently not much as unused appliances were thin on the ground by this time; Fire Brigade records show that a pump was sent from Allerton, arriving at 0158. Howe then made a tour of the building, noting that important records had been moved away from the fire – they were overtaken later and destroyed.

By 0300 water was dripping into the ground floor rooms and small outbreaks of fire were seen in the Sorting Office. Then came the alarming sound of small-arms fire; stored cartridges were exploding in a room on the Mezzanine floor. Howe went to investigate and found two of the staff trying to enter the room, but he thought it safer to bring in the AFS so that a jet of water could be thrown in as soon as the door was burst open. After this had been done, several boxes of hand grenades were removed. One associates these with the Home Guard, who also had to rescue rifles from other parts of the building.

As the retreat continued, registered letters and valuables in the strong room were removed and placed in a locked mail van under guard. At around 0400 an AFS patrol leader advised Howe to withdraw two of his men from the Stores. He had to order them out and, soon after, the ceiling "with its immense steel girders" collapsed. In the end there were no casualties and not a single letter was lost, though some had to be moved and covered with mail bags to protect them from water damage.

Unfortunately, Mr. Howe's report[120] then ends with the arrival of the Chief Superintendent and what followed is obscure – the Allerton pump remained at the scene till 1418 on the 4th. The basement room occupied by telegraph instruments since March "became untenable" at a time uncertain, but the instruments were all saved – again – apparently with the help of off-duty staff. (Some had to be lent to London soon after to replace losses there.)

The building seems to have been almost completely burnt out, only the Sorting Office remaining intact, and business had to be carried on from the nearby Fruit Exchange until the lower floors were restored. The upper floors were eventually removed, totally ruining the appearance of a building that had not been a pretty sight to start with.

The area bounded by Water Street, the Strand, James Street and Fenwick Street had been left substantially intact the night before, although the old White Star Building was a wreck and the Corn Exchange a smoking heap of rubble. Now it was to be virtually wiped out.

The Head Post Office, Sir Thomas and Victoria Street fronts. The Government Building is directly behind the camera.

India Buildings, Liverpool's largest office block, had already lost most of the glass from its windows along the Brunswick Street front – facing the Corn Exchange. Probably as a result of incendiaries landing in the still hot and smouldering ruins there, which it was now quite impossible to protect from this danger, the Corn Exchange fire flared up again. No bombs of any kind hit India Buildings during the night, but the fire-watchers soon had their hands full repelling burning material from across the road. Up to 0200 they were able to keep the situation under control, but then the simultaneous outbreaks of fire in curtains and furniture on all eight floors became too much for them.

Help had presumably been sought from the fire service at an early stage. What arrived was one pump with four firemen – when the building was already burning on all floors. (One of the four later recalled these events when he was Assistant Chief Officer Owens.) There was nothing they could do but try to stop the blaze spreading to too many of the surrounding buildings. The destruction involved premises across Water Street and the whole of the other side of Drury Lane. Although the fires found their way through most of India Buildings, the fireproof concrete structure ensured that it did not become a raging furnace in the way that some others did, and the structure remained intact and capable of eventual repair.

Among the offices lost were those of the Chinese and Swedish Consulates, Union-Castle line, the Inland Revenue (4th and 5th floors), and Alfred Holt/Ocean Steam Ship Co./Blue Funnel Line/Elder Dempster (7th floor). The Holt/Ocean group were the owners of the building. In their records the belief is expressed that its freedom from serious structural damage was partly due to the absence of water: "The fire brigades ignored it because of its obvious safety and therefore never really soused it." They were philosophical about the situation and quickly made a pre-planned move to houses in Ullet Road.[121]

Fred Lester was living with his parents on top of the eleven-storey Wellington Building in the Strand

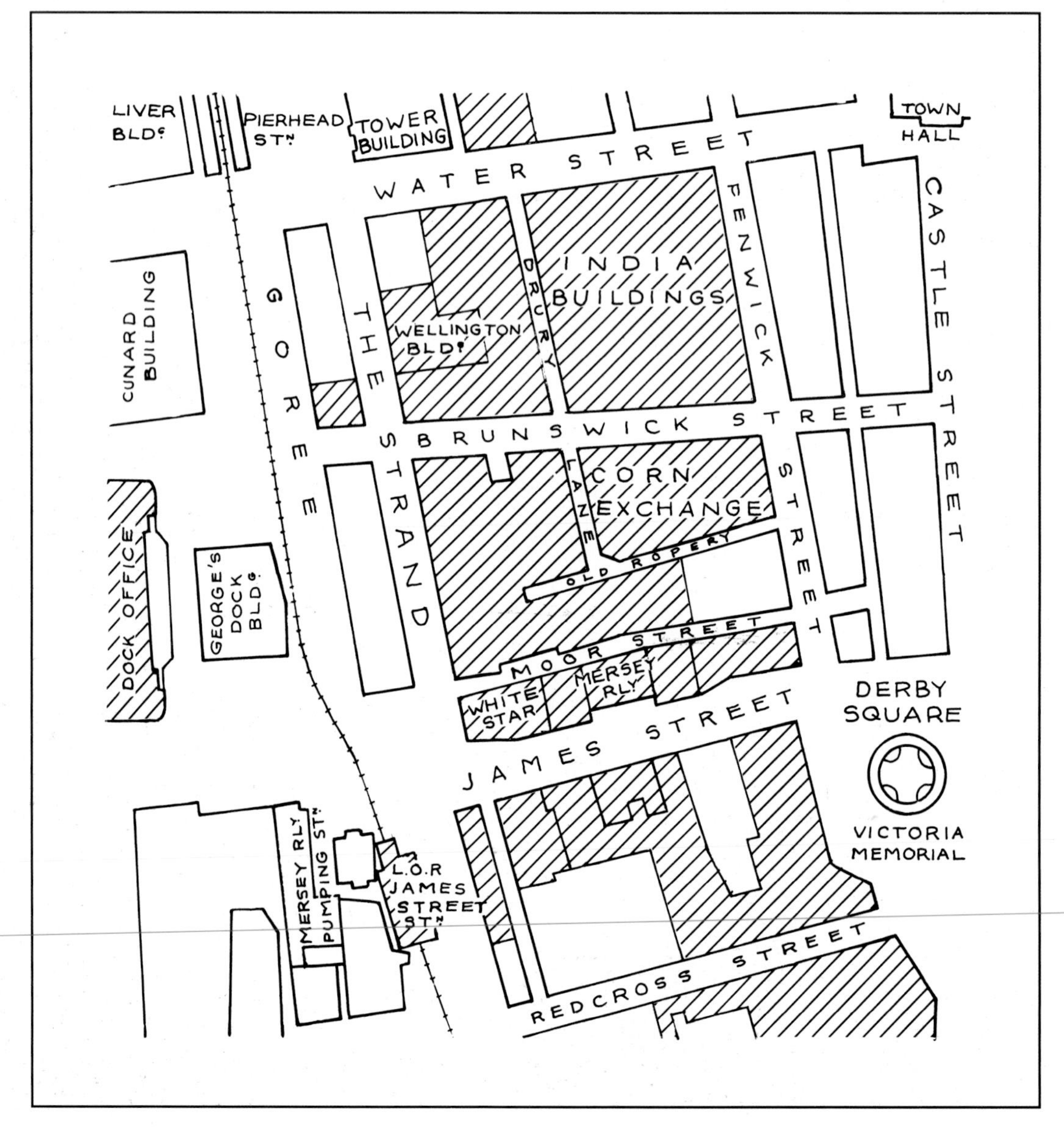

The damaged buildings around Brunswick and James Streets.

India Building on the left, Wellington Building on the right, with James Street ahead. The Mersey Railway station has been reduced to one storey.

(his father was the caretaker). He shared the fire-watching duty that night with Sam Cavanagh and William Thompson. At one point, Cavanagh had his overcoat plus an 'ARP lamp' that was fastened across his chest stripped off by a nearby explosion. That and other bombs had seen off the windows so that when the buildings behind, facing onto Drury Lane, took fire it was not long in spreading to theirs. Thompson, the eldest of the fire-watchers, saw Mr. Lester senior and his wife safely to shelter in the Liver Building and then returned.

Soon after, Fred Lester and Cavanagh – who were still trying to control the fires – heard screams for help. At first they could not make out where the cries were coming from, but after a period of frantic searching they identified the lift shaft as the source. More time went by before they found the lift, stuck between the third and fourth floors and with only the top eighteen inches visible from above. With the fire getting closer, Lester managed to reach in to open the lattice gates of the lift while lying on the floor; then the two of them had to lift Thompson out somehow through the narrow gap. Cavanagh: "We grabbed him by his shoulders, by his hair, and yanked him up and out as quickly as we could. I'm afraid we did not handle him gently."[122]

They all got out. The building was burnt out, but survived.

On the south side of the Corn Exchange, across Old Ropery, Rockliff's printing works was set alight and practically destroyed. Printing machinery crashed down from the upper floors to lie scorched and battered in the ruins. The company noted, however, that while the fire service had attended the blaze at an adjacent printing works their own establishment was spared a soaking and the machinery was allowed to cool down in its own time, which limited the damage and made it possible to restore some of the presses for use elsewhere.[123] This notion that when fires could not be put out quickly one might be better off without the fire service no doubt has a grain of truth in it, though it is a pity if the blaze then spreads to other property.

James Street was pelted with incendiaries, and fires spread on both sides aided by broken windows. The staff and fire-watchers at the Mersey Railway Station seem to have been able to cope until taken from the rear. Between the station and an array of high warehouses including Rockliff's paper store was Moor Street – only twelve feet wide. The warehouses burnt so fiercely that it was assumed they contained oil. When a wall collapsed, the burning rubble smashed through the back windows, which had been intact, into the wood-panelled booking hall. That and several floors of offices above were gutted. All the lifts were at the lower level; they were damaged by water and falling debris, but fortunately the fire did not spread to the lower parts of the station, where large numbers of people were sheltering. The subway to Water Street was also used for this purpose, but the exit under the corner of India Buildings was rendered unsafe by the fire there and debris falling into the street. Although the railway tunnel offered an escape route if all else failed, the situation must have been frightening.

An HE bomb exploded in the middle of James Street, over the Birkenhead end of the station. This did not cause any immediate damage below, but it broke a water main which caused trouble later. Much of the rest of James Street was destroyed by fire or HE, the unbroken trail of destruction continuing to Redcross Street and South Castle Street. The offices lost in James Street included those of Moss Hutchison, Frederick Leyland & Co, the Siamese Consulate and the Overhead Railway – all in Pacific Buildings – as well as United States Lines and Yeoward Line.

This brings us to the area bounded by Lord Street, South Castle Street, Canning Place and Paradise Street. Behind the facade of shops along Lord Street it was a slightly seedy neighbourhood – one of the oldest parts of the city. Amid a variety of workshops and professional offices that did not quite rate premises nearer to the Exchange the only discernible specialities were tailoring and the paper and stationery trades.

The conflagration that destroyed most of this was one of the biggest 'incidents' of the night, yet published accounts barely do more than acknowledge that it happened, while official records add virtually nothing. The account that follows was patched together from the recollections of two men who were there, a contemporary report written by one of them,[125] and the ***Daily Post's*** account of events leading to the award of a medal.

Mr. C. A. Neil was in charge of the four other fire-watchers at the premises of L. S. Dixon & Co. Ltd, paper-makers and stationers. The head office in Cable Street connected with a warehouse behind – on Thomas Street – which contained thousands of tons of paper. Part of this warehouse and a factory on the south side of Thomas Street had been lost in March. There was also an odd out-building on South John Street that was let to various tailors.

Neil reported that bombs of all kinds were falling in the neighbourhood soon after the alert, including incendiaries on Dixon's roof. These were dealt with successfully, but it was a hectic business. At one point Neil found himself sliding down the roof, only coming to a halt when his feet reached the gutter. One of the others – 'Taffy' – was to hand, but could not quite reach Neil's outstretched hand. In the end Neil chanced the solidity of the gutter, flexed his knees, and launched himself up far enough to take Taffy's hand and be pulled to (relative) safety.

Other premises in the district were not so lucky. "Many oil bombs must have been dropped because large fires started up all around, buildings flaring up in sheets of flame almost instantaneously." A steady wind fanned the flames and burning buildings crashed to the ground as HE bombs fell in the area. It has been said that there was no HE dropped here, but this is clearly incorrect. It would have been most surprising if the Luftwaffe had overlooked such a target. It may have been bombs aimed at this area that led to the burning of Cook Street Arcade – with a considerable frontage on Castle Street – as well as the Custom House. The latter, badly damaged in August 1940 and since repaired, was reputedly hit on three consecutive nights and was completely gutted. Presumably the fires at the Derby Square end of Castle Street also started around now. Neil sent for the fire service early on: "but we were told that the position was hopeless and that they had no machine available."

This was Sam Holt's night for fire-watching duty at Burnyeat, Dalzell & Nicholson Ltd. They were ship's store dealers, concerned mainly with the repair and maintenance of ship's galleys and their equipment, housed in a variety of buildings from South Castle Street to Crooked Lane and taking in both sides of Litherland Alley. After the firm's experience of the previous night, the fire-watchers were now *ordered* to remain in shelter during alerts, making periodic surveys in case of trouble. Fortunately, this firm was not seriously attacked and came through with nothing worse than a few broken windows, but when Mr. Holt did the rounds at about one or two o'clock he found the other (east) side of South

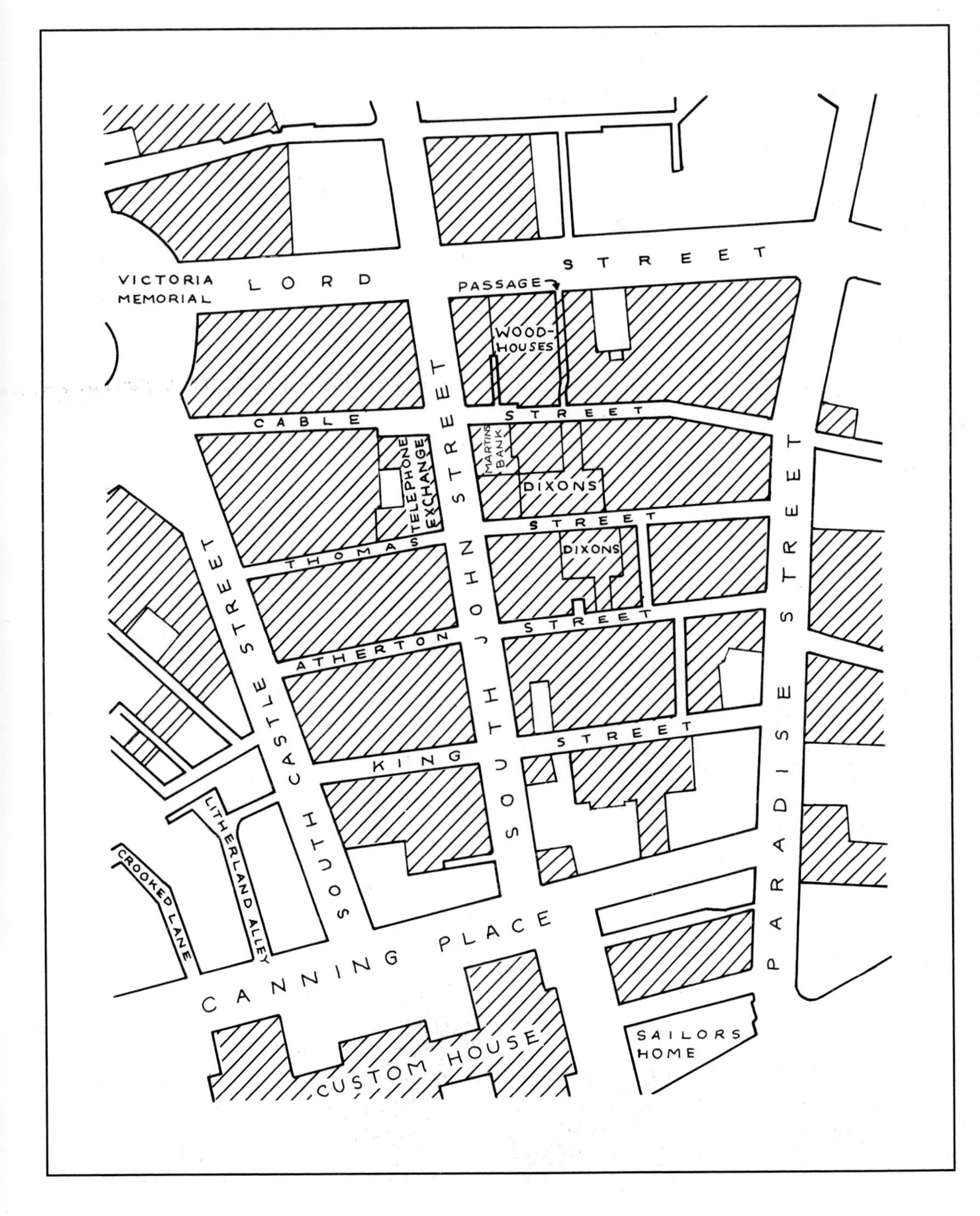

Nearly all the buildings along South John Street were damaged.

South Castle Street. Number 50, at the entrance to Litherland Alley, is the doorway of Burnyeat, Dalzell & Nicholson. An HE bomb has fallen at the entrance to Benn's Garden on the right.

The same part of South Castle Street (after some demolition) seen from King Street, by the gutted Midland Bank. The bonded warehouse of J. Chambers & Co., ship store dealers, is still functioning amid the ruins.

Castle Street well alight. Some firemen appeared and set up their trailer pump near to Litherland Alley, but the pressure in the mains was such that they were only able to produce a miserable stream of water that could barely make it across the road. The heat made it impossible to get closer.

Arguably the most important building in this area was the telephone exchange in South John Street. There were actually three exchanges here: Central, Bank, and North. It has not yet been confirmed, but it seems reasonably certain that the award of the BEM to William Ivan Darby, a telephone night supervisor, relates to this building.

"During the height of one of the heaviest raids early in May bombs had blown in the windows of the building in which he was working, and fires were raging around. With the aid of volunteers Mr. Darby took measures to secure, as far as possible, the safety of the building by tackling fires in adjoining premises. Further incendiary bombs fell about the fire-fighters, and one of them became lodged in the roof of their own building. Unhesitatingly, Mr. Darby climbed to the roof, and there, amid a surrounding inferno of flames and smoke, successfully dealt with the bomb. Conditions round about were fast becoming unbearable. Flames from the blazing buildings nearby were licking the walls of their own workplace, and there was danger, too, that the way of escape would become blocked by fire. Mr. Darby, however, re-entered the building and saved valuable equipment and records."[126]

The loss of this building can be ranked as the third of the disasters to afflict Liverpool on this night – it is a pity that more could not have been done to save it. Exactly when the exchanges had to be evacuated is not known. We have seen a reference to Central Exchange blacking out at 0130 (BST), but Mr. Neil remembers seeing the staff waiting for transport outside the building (with their headphones on) before midnight. The GPO generally kept things going as long as possible and it may be that the separate exchanges closed down at different times.

At Dixon's, Neil and his men continued to keep the flames at bay. The windows, like many others, had gone the night before so that they were open to the 'snowstorm' of sparks and burning debris that blew all around. The party was split – one man looking after the roof and top floor, one on the second, one on the first, one on the ground, and one outside keeping an eye on the South John Street building as well. When one could not cope, he would call the others in to help. "All through the night the building was constantly bursting into flame, and we must have put out dozens of fires; the place would otherwise have been gutted in a very short while."

When the 'all-clear' came, the fires were still advancing and the only thing that kept Dixon's men going was the hope that soon, surely, the fire service would come.

COMMUNICATIONS

The breakdown of communications is a subject that calls for some attention, even though little definite information can be extracted from the records.

The fact that Liverpool was cut off from the rest of the country may have had a bearing on the delay in obtaining reinforcements, but I cannot say when the Trunk Exchange or the Telegraph Office broke down. What evidence there is suggests that the need for major reinforcement was obvious well before the South John Street building ceased to function, and whenever the problem did arise it is not clear what was done to get round it. Messengers could be sent to Manchester and would presumably be able to telephone Manchester without going all the way. The Navy had direct lines to other establishments (more than 400 long-distance private circuits from Derby House) but three-quarters of these are said to have been lost at South John Street so that they had problems of their own. There were any number of wireless-equipped ships in the docks. The Liverpool Police had radio-cars and a bomb-proof wireless station at Allerton from which they had once spoken to a trawler off Norway.

It is easy to make such suggestions, but nothing could conveniently replace the facilities that had been lost and difficulties not apparent to us may have been all too obvious to those who had to cope with them. It is also as well to remember that communication is a two-way business. *If* contact with the outside world was lost early on (and this has not been established) what did the Regional and National HQs do about it? They had fewer distractions after all, and London and Manchester would have been well aware that a heavy raid was in progress on Merseyside even if they had not been warned in advance. They were responsible for directing long-distance reinforcements to Liverpool. Was the "muddle" at their end? (The story that no action was taken after the receipt of early warning of the big Coventry raid seems to be completely unfounded. I should like to make it quite clear that I do *not* wish to imply anything of that sort in Liverpool's case.)

The loss of local telephone connections was also disastrous. The 22,000 lines controlled by the South John Street exchanges were over a quarter of the total for the Liverpool area and included a high proportion of the busiest and most important. Between them they covered the commercial centre of the city as well as the north docks with a considerable area inland up to the boundary of the Bootle exchange. The dislocation extended further, as a number of the other local exchanges had no direct links with each other and could only communicate

South John Street telephone exchange with demolition of surrounding buildings in progress.

through Central. Another 5,000 lines were cut elsewhere mostly in the Bootle and Royal areas where cables were hit near to the exchanges. (This fate may have befallen some of the trunk and telegraph lines before the buildings were lost.) With the Royal Exchange covering the parts of Liverpool city centre not already accounted for by Bank and Central, this extended the disruption so that it covered precisely the worst-hit areas.[127]

The network of direct lines connecting the defence and rescue services seems to have fared little better; as with the Royal Navy's, most, if not all, were routed through normal GPO channels and lost in the same incidents. According to the Chief Constable, "All telephonic communication with the Central Fire Station, Hatton Garden, was put out of action."[128] Bootle's Control Room (Fire or ARP not specified) was also cut off at the height of the raid.[129] Liverpool's main ARP Control Centre was at the Police School, Mather Avenue, and the LFB had its duplicate Control at Allerton Fire Station nearby – it is not clear to what extent this was able to take over. Both were in a quiet area, but unable to contact the places that most needed their attention.

Dispatch riders and boy messengers were available, but they could do little to counter-act such a widespread failure. Messengers' bicycles were often mangled by near misses, craters and rubble on the roads, leaving the messengers to continue on foot; and with the messengers themselves likely to be killed or injured on the way there was no guarantee that the message would get through at all. It is recorded that one urgent message sent from Bootle to Liverpool took two hours and twenty minutes to arrive *by car* owing to blocked roads and fallen bridges. (The destination may have been Mather Avenue, but it should not have taken long to get there once past central Liverpool.)

It follows that on top of the desperate shortage of firemen and pumps it was now virtually impossible to use those that *were* available to the best advantage – simply finding out what was happening had become a task of immense difficulty. Officers at the scene of fires had to fall back on their own initiative. Some hung about waiting for water or instructions when they were badly wanted elsewhere. Some who had finished one job looked for the nearest fire with water to hand or heeded calls for help from local householders or fire-watchers; this was more useful, but could be infuriating for senior officers waiting for pumps to return to the station so that they could be sent to more urgent jobs. Everyone blundered about in the fog of war, and it was not easy to make the right decisions.

In spite of desperate efforts on the part of the GPO telephone engineers and others, communications remained a crippling problem to the end of this series of raids. Contrary to expectations, however, it is unlikely that the fact that Liverpool was deprived of reserve telegraph and trunk telephone facilities in March had any adverse effect. The telegraph service would have had to close down sooner, possibly with some loss of instruments, if it had not already been removed to the basement, and there seems to be no reason to suppose that the Victoria Street exchange could have held out longer than that in South John Street. The fact that work on replacement facilities in Lancaster House had been accelerated will have ensured that recovery after May was faster than it would have been had no damage to communications occurred in March.

RAILWAYS AND INDUSTRY

The records relating to this area are particularly patchy, so that this is by no means a complete survey of industrial damage – nor is it likely that all the most important incidents are included.

In and around Bootle there was damage to Aintree marshalling yard, a tannery, a tin works, a sawmaker's, Johnson's dyeing and dry-cleaning works, Cunard's furnishing store in Marsh Lane and Blackledge's bakery in Derby Road. Scott's bakery in Knowsley Road was gutted, the horses in the stables being let out to gallop round the town till they were herded into North Park. With so many work-horses still stabled in the city, this was a common sight during raids. At Linacre Gas Works HE bombs exploded inside two of the holders, tearing off the crown sheeting and igniting the gas. One of these was a total loss and five others were badly damaged, of which one needed 500 patches. Bootle Cold Stores' premises at Miller's Bridge were largely wrecked by HE, though it proved possible to save the 617 tons of frozen meat, butter and eggs inside.[130] (Miller's Bridge was holed where it crossed St. John's Road.)

Timber yards were fired in the St. John's Road area and at Seaforth. Joseph Gardner & Sons' timber yard at the end of Peel Road was one of the casualties – being particularly well-endowed with cranes it was used for storing heavy logs and cased equipment for various government departments. The fire-watchers did their best, but the water failed and all was lost except for the yard's petrol tank and pump. To the east, just across Chesnut Grove, more timber and coal were set on fire in Marsh Lane sidings and HE damaged the entrance to the passenger station. A UXB cut off access to Bankfield Goods Station, the signalman at Alexandra Dock Station saw a bomb block the approach tunnel, and another caused subsidence at Atlantic Dock Junction where the Canada Dock line joined.

Kirkdale Station was hit by HE at 2350. The entrance and steps to Stanley Road bridge were wrecked[131] and there were a number of casualties that would engage rescue parties for some time. The

No bread today - the wreck of Scott's Bakery, Knowsley Road, Bootle.

sequence of large goods stations at the north end – North Mersey, Langton, Alexandra and Bankfield – seems to have escaped serious damage (beyond what had been suffered in earlier raids) though all but Langton were cut off.

At Canada Goods Station, however, the timber yard on the south side was involved in the fire that swept through the large area of stored timber between Regent Road and Bankhall Lane. At about 2330 the Liverpool Salvage Association's North Station in Derby Road was reported to be in trouble with the Depot and Field well alight. (The Field was a yard used for the storage of cotton bales damaged in earlier fires.) The position in the Field seemed hopeless and the staff concentrated on saving the Depot and North Station buildings. No help was available from the fire service until a small contingent of the AFS arrived some time later. The fire in the railway timber yard spread across the road to make the situation worse and the struggle here continued well after the 'all-clear'.[132]

Further down Derby Road was one of the main works of Grayson Rollo and Clover Docks – ship repairers. This was hit by four HE bombs – one thought to be 500-kg – as well as a shower of incendiaries, and was largely wrecked. On the other side of Sandhills Lane, extensive fires were started in the yard of Sandon Goods Station. These spread to the Regent Road premises of Bootle Cold Stores through the rear loading doors. This was an eight-storey building with a storage capacity of over 300,000 cubic feet, and contained 2,750 tons of meat, butter, eggs and lard. All was destroyed in the blaze (it should be borne in mind that some of these fires burned for days). From here the fire crossed over Sandhills Lane to Gibson's paint and oil stores, and thence to Howson's ship repair works.[133]

There was more trouble at the east end of Sandhills Lane and up Commercial Road. The Trent Cold Store – 172,000 cubic feet – was demolished, and two HE bombs hit the newer part of Tillotson's paper works along with incendiaries. A thousand tons of cardboard were burnt here. As it was on the canal, one of the Corporation's fire floats was able to assist for a while. To the south, the warehouses of R. Silcock & Sons (animal feedstuffs) in Boundary Street were largely destroyed by fire-bombs.[134]

Between Tillotson's and Boundary Street was Huskisson Goods Station, occupying virtually all the space between the canal and the viaduct leading to Exchange Station. Huskisson Station, already badly knocked about, was now just about seen off completely. The main offices were destroyed, a warehouse block lost to fire, quays and cranes wrecked. The separate Victoria Yard west of the viaduct was also affected. To make matters worse, the approach to the station was crossed by the canal – a feature that had required the whole site to be excavated – and this bridge was hit so that the station was flooded to a depth of about three and a half feet, leaving wagons marooned.[135]

Unfortunately, the events of December were repeated in that some of the stop-plank barriers had been removed to allow the passage of the fire float from Tillotson's to a call further south; as a result some three miles of the canal were drained and barges left stranded.[136] These two incidents have led at least one commentator to suggest that the failure to drain the canal in advance was some kind of scandal. It is surely obvious, though, that the canal was a priceless reservoir for fire-fighters, running right through the industrial areas of Bootle and North Liverpool. It was also an essential transport link and a number of factories on its banks had production held up for want of coal in the next week. The fact that, on both occasions when they were needed, several of the stop-plank dams were not in place may be a fit subject for inquiry, though it was also the most rotten luck. As Sandon's direct link to the main lines lay through Huskisson, that station was cut off by these events. A connection to the neighbouring North Docks Goods Station was also cut by a bomb.

It appears to have been on this night that a mine landed on a warehouse at the south-west corner of Huskisson Station, wrecking St. Alban's School, Boundary Street. On the other side of the Exchange viaduct from here were the Albion Mills of Simmonds, Hunt & Montgomery, cattle food manufacturers. These premises (up to five storeys high) were hit by fire-bombs. While the fire-watchers tried to deal with these, an HE bomb struck, destroying the main water tank and releasing forty tons of water to provide an impromptu sprinkler system. The buildings would have been saved had fire not spread from an adjoining railway warehouse (possibly from oil stores under the arches of the viaduct). The works firemen and fire service kept at it, but the water ran out later and the whole place was gutted.[137]

A little to the north, warehouses in Luton and Grundy Streets – between the North Docks and Exchange viaducts – were attacked. As they contained such combustibles as dripping, hog fat, and a great many drums and casks of tallow, there was little hope for them.[138]

Fire-bombs showered down on Athol Street Gas Works early in the raid, setting fire to Nos. 1 and 2 holders along with the Social Club, fitting-shop and purifier-house. The mains soon failed, but the gas in the holders was stored over water and with this supply and a trailer pump all the fires were suppressed – only the Social Club becoming a complete loss.[139]

Between Vauxhall Road and the canal, the Distillers Company's Vauxhall Yeast Works was hit by HE, which destroyed the general stores and mechanic's shop. Fortunately, the one that landed on

Grayson Rollo's Sandhills works, with Bankhall Lane on the right.

Silcock's Dock Road warehouse. Clarence Dock Power Station is behind the camera.

the commercial yeast house hit an RSJ and broke up without exploding.[140]

Silcock's warehouses on the dock road, opposite Clarence Dock Power Station, were destroyed by HE and fire-bombs. The same unfortunate company's laboratories and warehouse in Upper William Street, alongside the branch viaduct leading to Great Howard Street Goods Station, were also destroyed by fire-bombs.[141] In view of the number of premises affected along these viaducts, it will come as no surprise that they too suffered – from fires alongside and under the arches and possibly from HE. The principal viaduct leading to Exchange and Great Howard Street had had a service of sorts restored on the 24th March, but the temporary repairs were partly of timber, which precluded the use of the heavier types of locomotive and also proved fatally vulnerable to the circumstances prevailing in this week. Just how bad the situation was could not be judged till the fires had been brought under control.

Considering its size and situation, Tate & Lyle's sugar refinery bore a charmed life throughout the raids, and it suffered no serious damage now – though it was one of the firms that relied on the canal for its coal. The Waterloo Goods Station, which was almost equally extensive, was not so lucky as several HE bombs cratered the main running lines, blasted the offices, and wrecked much of the quays and station roofs.[142] The station was also cut off by a bomb that was deflected from Fontenoy Gardens tenements to land behind the retaining wall of the short cutting between the two approach tunnels without exploding.

The triangle of property enclosed by the south end of Vauxhall Road and Marybone suffered heavily. The Liverpool Central (lubricating) Oil Company's premises north of Oriel Street were blasted by HE falling in the neighbouring cooperage, and the oil blending shop across the road was destroyed by HE. Calthrops' Lucky Star Mills were scattered on both sides of Freemason's Row with another section over Marybone. The first HE landed in Naylor Street near the boundary with James Crean's premises and hit a gas main, resulting in a flaming jet fifteen to twenty feet high. Four more HE bombs followed on or near to all three blocks of Calthrops' property. The fires that followed consumed 2,800 tons of animal feed and raw materials – groundnut cake, linseed cake, fish meal – also 300,000 unused jute sacks. The fire-watchers did their best, but the fire service was not available. At James Crean & Son's Atlas Margarine Works next door the fire-watchers were successful in dealing with incendiaries, but the gas main and fire spreading from Calthrops defeated them. Stores, offices, cooperage, packing store, boiler house, and the four-storey tallow refinery and animal oil manufactory all went – along with 200 tons of margarine and cooking fats and 400 tons of raw materials.[143]

At J. Bibby and Sons' premises south of Banastre Street, a meal warehouse was gutted along with the four-storey warehouse and sack-cleaning plant where over 400,000 empty bags were destroyed. Surround-

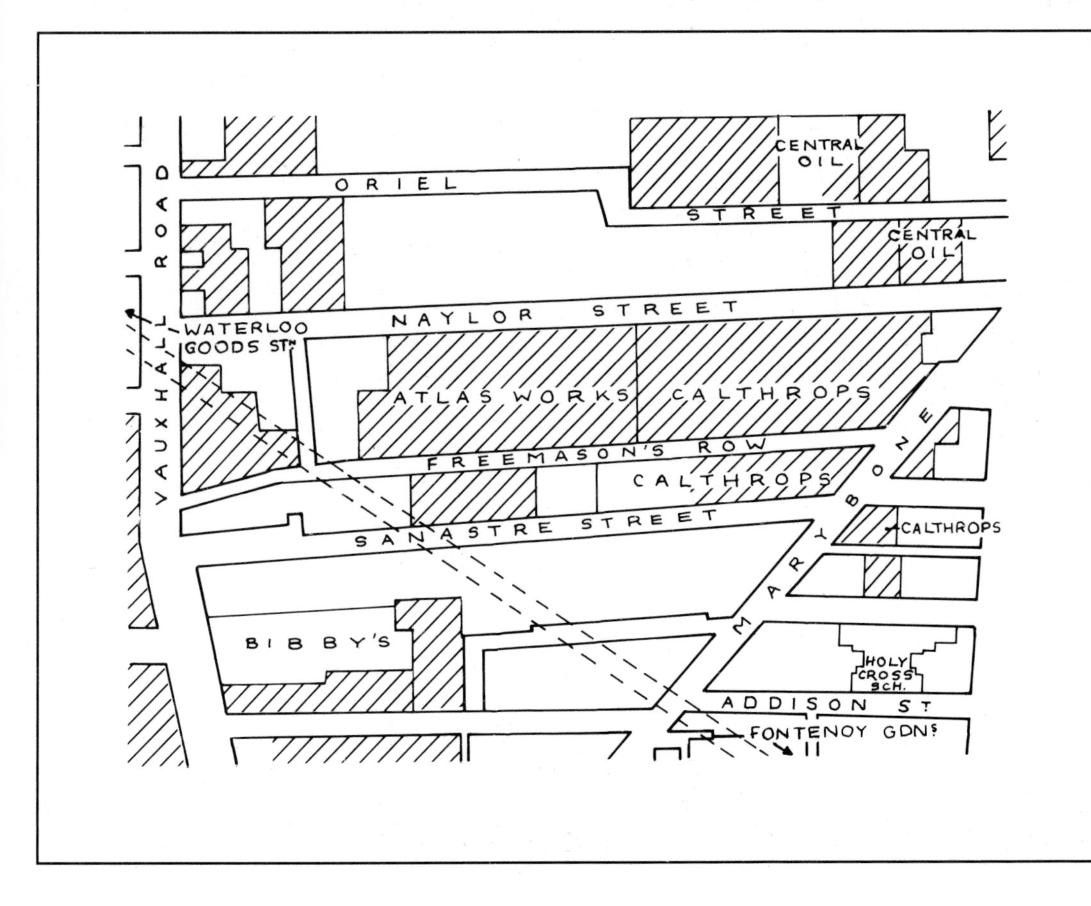

Bomb damaged buildings near Marybone, to the north of the city centre.

Calthrops, looking towards Crean's.

ing buildings were damaged by blast and falling debris, including two garages – one for petrol motors and the other for steam wagons. Most of the vehicles were saved, however, and the fact that the fire did not spread through the whole site argues efficient work by somebody.[144] (Bibby's main works were not seriously affected.)

Between this area and Exchange Station, wool and tobacco warehouses burned in Pall Mall and Highfield Street. On the other side of Tithebarn Street was the Peerless Refining Company's factory in Cheapside – the next road west of Hatton Garden. Here the factory, warehouse and offices (mostly four storeys) were completely destroyed by fire along with 400 tons of margarine and lard as well as the oils used in manufacture.[145] Palm oil ran down to Dale Street, where it congealed several inches deep.

On the other side of town, in Hanover Street, Littlewood's parachute factory was hit by HE at 2354 and totally destroyed. First reports spoke of "girls trapped", but Mr. Moores' decision to abandon the night shift had averted that although three of the five fire-watchers were killed. In the same street, Tyrer's wine distillery and warehouse and Elam & Co. – printers and stationers – were destroyed by HE and fire-bombs. A Fire Brigade pump from Speke was used here together with two AFS pumps and a hose-laying tender – the last suggesting that water was brought from some distance.[146]

The area between Hanover Street and Slater Street was dotted with a variety of light chemical works, including the scattered warehouses and laboratories of Evans Sons, Lescher & Webb (now Evans Medical) – notable as the first British commercial manufacturer of sulphonamides in 1936. The bulk of their premises, including the head office in Hanover Street and the export department (just restored after its destruction in December), were reduced to piles of rubble.[147] Much of Goodlass Wall's paint factory in Wolstenholme Square was destroyed by fire – again, HE and fire-bombs. A pump from the Central Fire Station and two AFS units were here, but the fire burned till well into the next afternoon. Leyton Paper Mills in Henry Street, on the other side of Duke Street, were also badly damaged.

There was much more going on than has been mentioned, especially among the warehouses and smaller industrial premises. Some light is thrown on these by John H. Hindley, then a corporal in the King's Regiment – one of the soldiers brought in in March to protect the warehouses. Those looking after the north docks were based at Aintree Racecourse, and those looking after the south at Huyton where they had taken over part of the new housing estate at Woolfall Heath.

The latter housed the Infantry Training Corps. From here, men of the Middlesex Regiment under NCO's from the King's Regiment travelled into the city by tram every evening. Corporal Hindley's party were based at Tabley Street, off the dock road just north of Park Lane Goods Station. The NCO's would detail the men to the various warehouses in the area – four to each – where they would take to the roof on the sounding of the alert.

On this night they were kept busy; HE fell in Pitt Street after 2300 and there was more round Cleveland Square and Park Lane. Corporal Hindley was in Park Lane when he heard a stick of bombs coming his way. He ran for it, jinking into Tabley Street and then into Upper Pownall Street to get clear. On the way he passed a courting couple cuddling in a doorway and shouted to them to take cover. He was still running when the blast of one of the bombs came round the corner and lifted him into the air. He injured his leg on landing, but was able to bind it up and go back to see what had happened. All the glass in the pub on the corner had

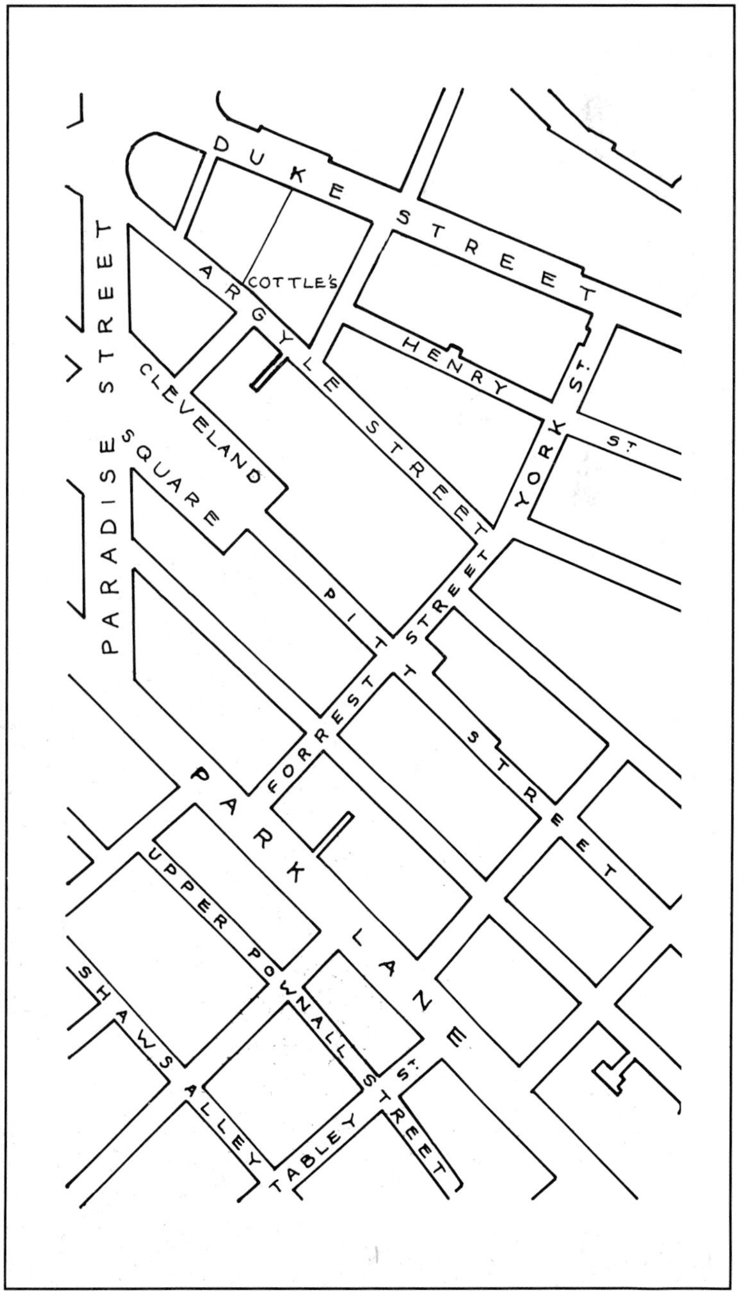

The streets around Park Lane, to the south of the city centre.

J.Crean & Son's Atlas Works, from Naylor Street.

gone and the two in the doorway were still there – on their feet, but dead.

As the raid slackened off, the men were brought down to do what they could. Some helped the firemen – of whom there were a number about, though apparently not in Park Lane – while others were organised as rescue parties. When a bomb on Pitt Street failed to explode, Corporal Hindley got men to go round warning anyone they could find in the neighbourhood to get clear. It went off later while Hindley and others were digging someone out nearby, but fortunately the blast, which demolished three houses, went straight up.

At 0340 an HE bomb hit Cottle's bakery, between Duke Street and Argyle Street, and started a fire. (Cottle's was then a well-known name locally – rather like Sayer's today.) Corporal Hindley was told there were people trapped in the basement shelter and took three men to see what he could do. As the entrance to the shelter was unreachable, they resorted to pulling the floor up in the office overhead – the only part of the premises not already in flames. On finding concrete underneath, they attacked it with picks; but before long the fire was threatening to cut off their own escape and they had to leave. (Three bodies were recovered from Cottle's, where rescue work continued as late as the 16th.)

No damage was reported at the few southern goods stations or the sprawling junction and marshalling yards at Edge Hill – though staff at Wavertree Gas Works had to deal with several showers of fire-bombs. There was, however, one more major railway incident.

What to do with train-loads of explosives was a constant problem for the railways. They would be sent to the docks for loading. If it was not possible to accept them before nightfall they would have to be taken away again. Locomotives and men had to be found to remove them. Sidings – especially sidings miles from anywhere – were scarce, and the train would be wanted at the docks again first thing in the morning. This is how the LMS came to have a train made up of wagons, each containing ten tons of bombs or shells, (some say mines) parked at Breck Road Sidings on the branch to Canada and Alexandra Dock Goods Stations.

Exactly what happened here is hard to establish. There are plenty of published accounts, one or two of them based on reports made at the time and the rest on interviews with those involved – years after the event. Apart from one peripheral Fire Brigade report, none of the original records has come to light and the available accounts are confusing and contradictory. It is chastening to have to confess that the more information one finds on this incident, the harder it is to say what happened with any confidence, though the bare outline is clear enough.

West of the running lines, and connected to them at both ends, were the four 'Old Sidings'. Further west was the coal yard, and then the six 'New Sidings' which ended in buffers on the south side of Townsend Lane. The sidings were crowded, the ammunition train being (probably) on the old siding adjacent to the running lines. They were well away from the docks, in what was a relatively quiet area, but a stray plane passed across them at about midnight and dropped its load in just the right spot.

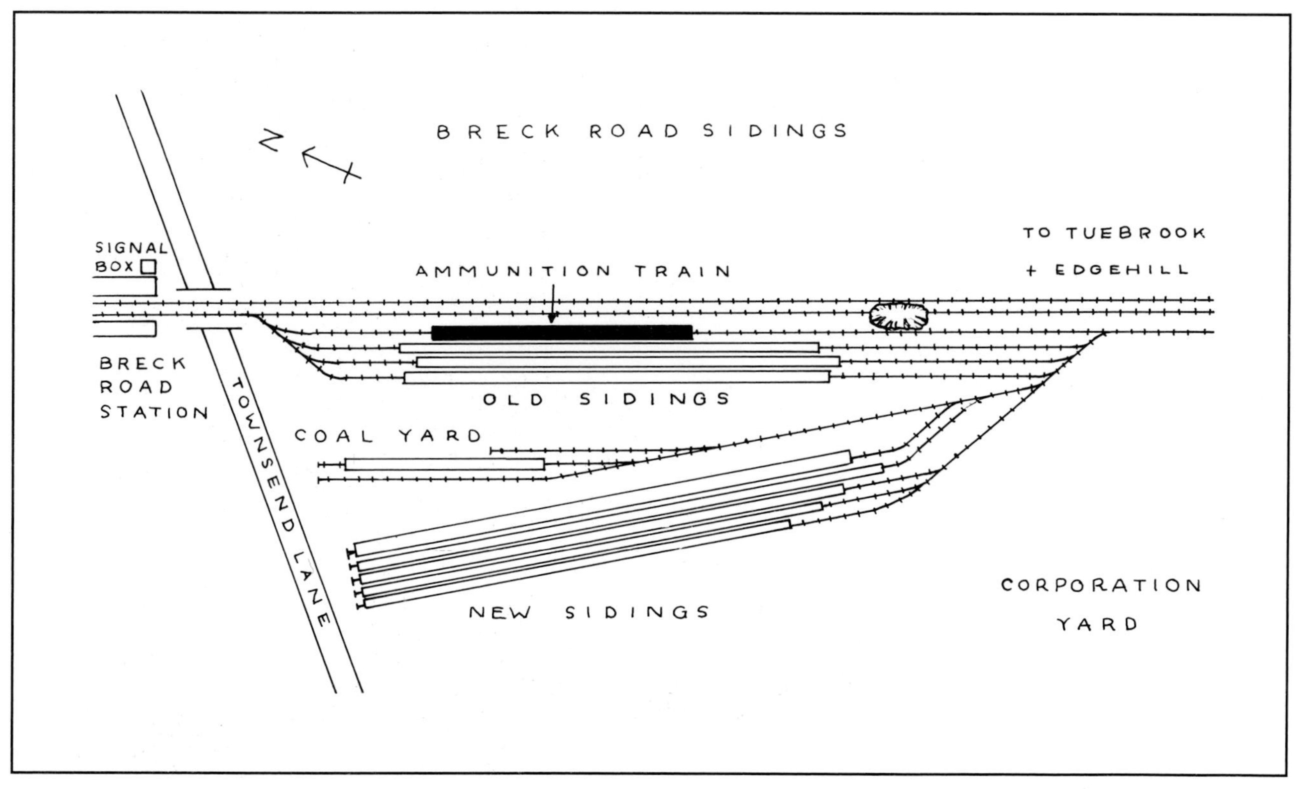

Peerless Refining Company, from Cunliffa Street.

(That this was intentional is not perhaps inconceivable, but it is extremely unlikely.) A large bomb cratered the running line to the south of the train and some incendiaries fell in the area.

On the north side of Townsend Lane was Breck Road Station. Signalman Peter Stringer was out on the steps of the station box when the bombs fell. He was thrown down the steps and tumbled on down the embankment. Shaken, and with an injured leg, Stringer climbed back to the box to find that the telephone was dead. He tried a public call box outside the station, with no more luck, before setting off for the nearest fire station. He then met an ARP cyclist messenger who volunteered to take the message on. After alerting the wardens to evacuate houses in the area, Stringer made his way to the next box to the north to pass on the news before returning to his own. It is notable that *no* account makes any reference to fire-watchers at the sidings.

At 0020 Sergeant Elymer Ankers had been sent from Derby Lane Fire Station to Breckside Park Corporation Depot with No. 11 pump. On arrival at the depot, on the west side of the sidings – south end, Ankers found that the problem there was a fire-bomb that had already been sorted out by the staff with only trivial damage resulting. Events in the sidings then forced themselves on his notice. (The way in which Ankers, in his report, treats an exploding ammunition train as a mere footnote to a failed fire-bomb is quite splendid.)

Seeing that the continual explosions made it impossible to get near the fire, Ankers decided to try moving some of the wagons clear. "I uncoupled the first truck and all hands attempted to move it." It wouldn't budge. This would certainly have been difficult with a fully-laden wagon – the train was in a dip, so it was uphill either way – though one wonders if laymen operating in the dark thought to check if the brakes were pinned down. Failing that, Ankers sent a man south to Tuebrook Station to request the services of a locomotive. He then turned his attention to the houses east of the sidings – around Worcester Drive and Pennsylvania Road. These were battered by the blast and debris from successive detonations, with soot being shaken down the chimneys and fires breaking out in many places. An Inspector came to take charge and two AFS pumps arrived, one of them being used to supply water from the brook. (The Chief Constable had been right in regarding this as a good site for an emergency water supply.) With these and stirrup pumps they managed to prevent the situation from getting completely out of hand, though a number of houses suffered serious fire damage. The wardens, meanwhile, were going round getting people out of their houses and Anderson shelters and moving them to safety.

When the news got up the line to Edge Hill a small band of men volunteered to go to the scene. Five of them, including goods guards George Roberts and Peter Kilshaw, crowded onto the footplate of a shunting engine and set off. Along the way they met a large goods engine with a brake van and asked if they could borrow it. The crew and goods guard Jim Rowlands agreed – so long as they could come too. (Among those who received awards in connection with this incident were Ankers, Rowlands and Kilshaw – BEM, and Roberts – George Medal.) They pressed on, stopping at signal boxes on the way to check for obstructions, until they came at last to the sidings where fires were burning on all sides.

They discovered the crater on the line when Rowlands fell into it and had to be hauled out. Seeing that there was no chance of getting near the ammunition train fire they considered moving some of the ammunition wagons to safety, by running past the train if necessary, but decided that it could not be done. So, they had to settle for saving some of the other wagons in the sidings, which mainly contained food – tins of Spam and corned beef have been mentioned.

Tuebrook Box, which controlled entry to the sidings, was unmanned at this hour, but Kilshaw broke in and worked the points while the others, led by Roberts and assisted by another goods guard who lived nearby, attended to brakes and couplings. A second engine also arrived to assist in drawing wagons clear of the fires. While they worked, the ammunition continued to go off in large and small quantities, hurling substantial fragments of timber and scrap metal all around. Plainly the explosion of a wagon-load would either throw the next wagon some distance or blow it to bits, scattering the contents. Much unexploded ammunition was in fact distributed over the surrounding country, but most would have gone a shorter distance to explode piecemeal as the fires caught up with it. In either case the process would have been repeated as the fires reached the next reasonably intact wagon. Every half hour or so another wagon-load would go off, the successive craters forming an irregular trench along the running lines. The larger explosions caused superficial damage over a wide area and were the probable cause of the Corporation depot being badly damaged by fire.

At dawn, there was no improvement in the situation.[148]

THE DOCKS

From what has been said already it will be understood that it was hard for those in charge to keep on top of what was happening down the line of docks. This was a pity as there was a good deal happening there.

According to a report presented to the Watch Committee a month earlier[149] there were now twenty-five sector posts and seven auxiliary fire stations along the dock estate in Liverpool. The provision of one large trailer pump for each sector post and one mobile pump for each auxiliary station is unlikely to have changed much since it was noted the previous October.[150] Whether anything had yet been done to provide towing vehicles for the dock trailers is not clear, and anyway the point is academic as on this night few of them needed to go far in order to find work. The ships – at any rate the larger ones – had hoses manned for their own defence and could turn these on neighbouring sheds when not too much engaged with their own problems. For the most part though, ships looked to the port for protection rather than the other way round. When, as now, the docks were heavily involved, the need was for large and speedy reinforcement from the city or from further afield. To what extent the fire service *was* able to send help into the docks is not known, though from what has gone before one can make a shrewd guess. There is no doubt that while firemen inland stood about helpless for want of water, ships and sheds surrounded by water burned for want of firemen.

To start with the newest and best docks at the north end, Gladstone Graving Dock was occupied by a Bibby Line vessel – now the armed merchant cruiser HMS ***Worcestershire*** (11,402). Her fire party was active in dealing with incendiaries from 0125 (DST) and the log also records the explosion of a delayed-action bomb on the quay at 0330 (DST).[151] Palm oil and latex tanks were set on fire, but the only real trouble in Gladstone occurred at North 1, where an HE bomb fell right through the stern of the ***Talthybius*** (10,254) to explode in the water under a gaggle of tugs tied up behind – the ***Moose***, ***Bison*** (274) and ***Wapiti***. (The ***Bison*** was the Canadian Pacific tender) All three were damaged and began to make water. Pumping operations started at once, the ***Wapiti*** being assisted in this by another tug, the ***Sloyne***, and all remained afloat when morning came. The ***Talthybius*** was also leaking, but in her case the damage was relatively slight.

The next dock, Hornby, was not seriously troubled except for damage to the lock to Gladstone, but Alexandra was a different story. Lever Brothers' barge ***Glitto***, loaded with resin in North 3, was set on fire by three incendiaries and sank. At the east end of this branch the Union Cold Stores were hit by HE; damage to the cold store was not extensive, but rubble fell across two elevator barges, the ***Hornby*** and ***Orrell***, which were comprehensively "burnt out, crushed and sunk."

All the sheds on the south side of the branch were gutted, the fire spreading to the elderly and decrepit Greek steamer ***Nadin*** (3,852) moored at the east end. Her crew had to abandon ship, and when the mooring ropes burned through she began to drift round the dock spreading alarm and despondency. Those on board the ***Brittany*** (4,772) – on the north side – had enough to do coping with incendiaries and burning debris from the sheds without having to keep an eye on the ***Nadin's*** wanderings; they were thus slow to spot the fact that two lighters were burning under their stern and cooking the ***Brittany's*** defensive ammunition. Any danger of an explosion was averted by the Second Officer, Mr. Orde, who volunteered to go down and flood the magazine. Next morning the ***Brittany*** looked "a sorry mess" with her mooring ropes burnt away, paint blistered, and the woodwork of lifeboats, decks and superstructure badly charred. In spite of all this, she took no serious damage.[152] The ***Nadin*** fetched up at the east end of the branch, completely burnt out above the weather deck.

The sheds along North 2 were extensively damaged and the French steamer ***Cantal*** (3,178), at North-West 2, caught fire from them at about 2300. Her future was doubtful for a while, but she proved to be repairable. Also at North 2 there was fire in one of the sheds next to the ***Pinto*** (1,346) which had 500 tons of dangerous explosives aboard. To make the situation more interesting, there was a cargo of army stores in the shed, including more explosives, as well as railway wagons containing ammunition on the side away from the quay.

The men at the scene were two police constables – Percy Green and Fred Spicer. They first advised the Pinto's master to find a safer berth, not easy in this area, and cast off the mooring ropes, then tried to control the fire until the water ran out. (They would have been using a hose attached to the mains, rather than a pump with suction equipment.) When that failed they started moving stores away from the flames, manhandling barrels of burning resin, piling ammunition and drums of kerosene onto hand trucks and using "an electric bogey" to pull them clear while masonry and burning debris fell about them. A party of police sergeants and constables then came to their aid, led by Inspector Thomas Morton Skelton. Thus reinforced, they dragged guns and limbers out of the shed and pushed the loaded railway wagons to safety, saving a good deal of valuable equipment as well as preventing any serious explosions. Green and Spicer were awarded the George Medal and the others were commended – except for Skelton, whom we shall meet again at Canada Dock. (All these men were from the Liverpool Police Force.)[153]

There was more damage to the sheds at South 2. Alexandra 1 contained the wreck of the ***Silvio***, sunk in December; there was now further damage by fire and blast to the south sheds. On the west side of the dock one shed was damaged and the ***Roxburgh Castle*** (7,801) was hit by an HE bomb that exploded in – or possibly under – the No. 3 hold. The first three holds were flooded and she was left with her bow firmly on the bottom. 2,500 tons of general cargo were submerged in water and fuel oil, and there is a report of "12 motor cars more or less wet."

The ***Trentino*** (3,079) had berthed that day at North-West Langton Branch Dock with a cargo of general goods. The sheds to either side of her were with hit by HE and incendiaries, the latter also falling across the shed in the middle and the ***Trentino***. While the other sheds were gutted in spite of the efforts of the fire service, the ***Trentino's*** crew were able to save theirs as well as dealing with what landed on the ship.[154] The Great Western Railway's depot on the south side of the Branch Dock was largely demolished and the floating crane ***Hercules*** (652), which would have been moored by the entrance to the branch, had her jib shaken and loosened by blast.

There was more damage to sheds on the west side of Langton Dock proper, where the ***Eastern Prince*** was berthed after leaving Canada Graving Dock the day before. Her crew coped successfully with HE and incendiary bombs as well as the shed fires, and her owners felt that this was a sufficient answer to the Royal Navy's complaints about their conduct in December. More HE bombs landed around the graving docks, causing damage in No. 1 lower. The ***Marton*** (4,969) was damaged in No. 2 lower, but HMS ***Belmont*** – one of the four-funnelled 'Town' class destroyers acquired from the US – was unscathed in No. 2 upper. Both remained at risk from a heavy (c. one ton) UXB in the roadway north of the middle gates. The bridge over the 90-foot passage between Langton and Brocklebank was badly damaged and stuck in the 'on' position, which means that it was closed to ships.

Of the thirteen sheds around Brocklebank and its single branch, four were burnt out or demolished and all the rest more or less seriously damaged. Those at North Carriers' Dock also were damaged by blast. Tied up at the east end of Brocklebank Branch Dock was the ***Enid Blanche***, a small Thames

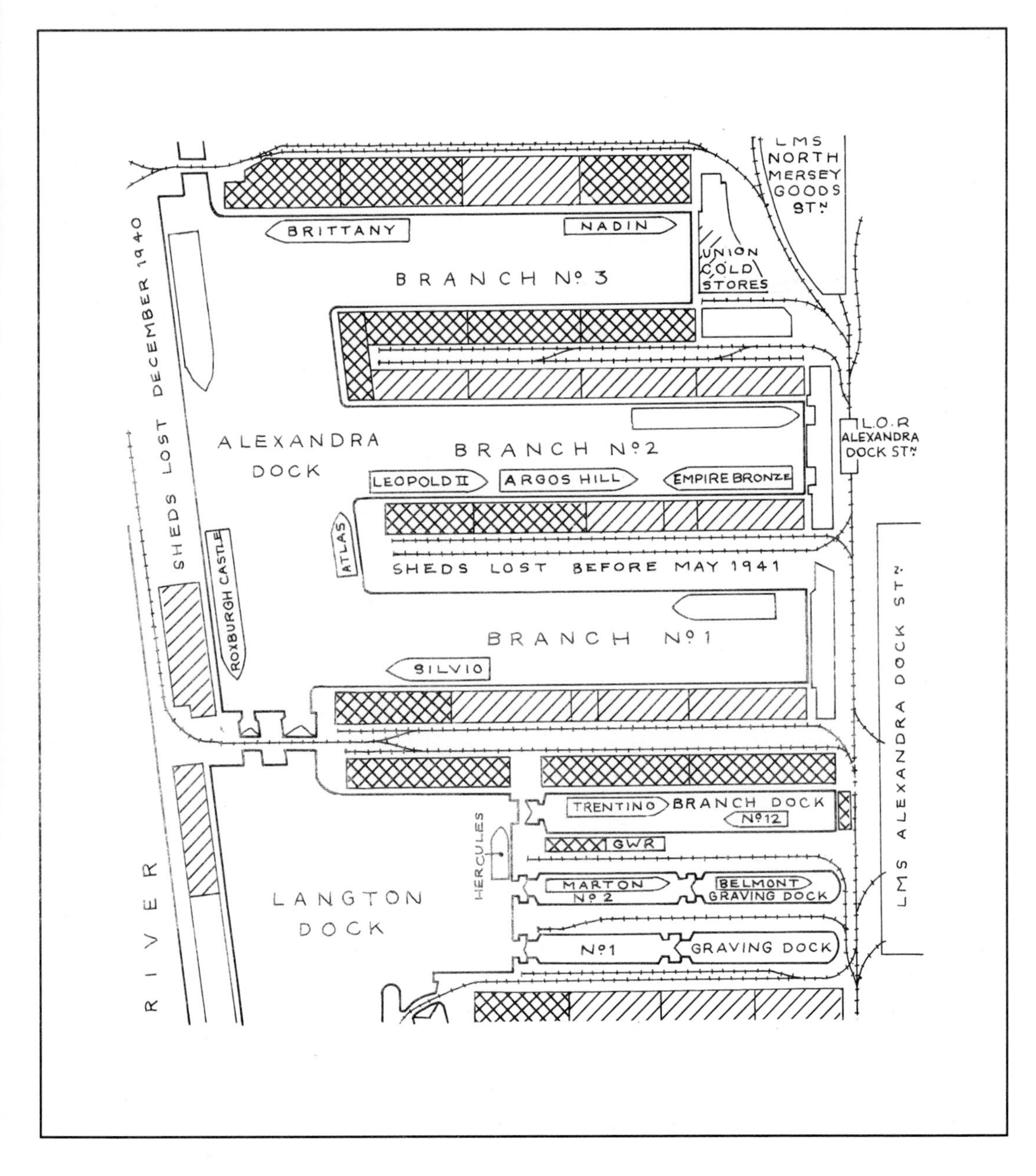

Alexandra Dock, showing which buildings were damaged and those destroyed.

tug sent to reinforce the overstretched Mersey fleet. Her fate went unwitnessed, but she was found sunk the following afternoon "and it was assumed that a roof of a shelter on the quayside had been blown on to the deck of the vessel."[155]

In Brocklebank Graving Dock lay the luckless ***Europa***, on which repair work was proceeding apace; the damaged plating at the bow had been cut away, leaving a large, but neat, hole. (She had been moved here after a brief stay in Canada Graving Dock, where some accounts put her in May.) She was first threatened by incendiaries that started fires all around her, and then hit by an HE bomb at 2330 Between 0030 and 0130 she was hit by two more HE bombs, and with the last a fire was started. (It was reported that aircraft were "flying low and machine-gunning everywhere.") There were officers and crew aboard, but with the ship under repair they had access only to one hose from the shore – and that burst. "As no fire brigade was available from the shore owing to the unprecedented fires which were raging in the city, it was impossible to save the ship." They turned up at 0600, too late to prevent the complete destruction of the ***Europa***; according to one report she burned for three days, and even the papers in the ship's safe were reduced to ashes. It appears that the dock was dry at the outset but was then flooded – either through the gates being damaged, or deliberately in an attempt to counter the fire. As a result, the shores collapsed and she sank leaning against the north quay.[156]

Canada Dock has some claim to be considered the worst hit by direct enemy action. Canada 3 was lined along its north side by coal hoists, which came through relatively unscathed though put out of action by lack of power and the cutting of railway connections. Having loaded in Alexandra Dock, the ***Domino*** (1,453) had coaled that day and was now berthed at South Canada 3 ready to sail for the Mediterranean next afternoon. Soon after the raid started fire-bombs fell across the ship and the shed on her starboard side. Those on the ship were dealt with, but the shed was soon in flames. The crew turned their hoses on this, and a party was sent inside; they also played water on the side of the ship, but their best defence was the breeze that held her in to the quay while blowing the flames away to the south. (References to wind strength and direction can be confusing – probably through large blazes distorting the picture locally.)

More fire-bombs had to be tackled on the ship and at 0030 the wind changed, posing an immediate threat to the ***Domino***. The moorings were cast off in the hope that she would drift to safety, but even as this was being done the shed wall collapsed onto the vessel, setting her alight from stem to stern. She drifted slowly, the crew doing what they could until their pumps were over-run by the fire. At around 0200 the ***Domino*** came back to the Coal Hoist Quay, "where the members of the local Fire Brigade at once commenced to pump water on the vessel from an engine but the fire had now obtained so great a hold that the flames could not be brought under control." The crew went ashore, with no casualties, and the firemen poured water onto the ship with little effect through the night and well into Sunday.[157]

Two sections of the shed at South 3 were gutted and the third damaged by blast – the fourth and last was remarkable as the only one at Canada *not* reported as damaged by the 5th May, but only because it had been demolished in an earlier raid. At the east end the flat ***John***, containing 50 tons of ships' ashes, was hit by fire-bombs and burnt.

The large wooden sheds north and south of Canada 2 were almost totally destroyed by fire and blast. On the south side, east end, was the Norwegian ***Bra-Kar*** (3,778), a curious motor-ship with minimal superstructure, three masts, and no discernible funnel – she looked like a sailing ship after a rough passage. She had already discharged 5,000 tons of cargo, leaving only 800 tons of spelter and canned goods still aboard. Her troubles started when a bomb – evidently a large one – exploded on the quay and stripped off all the hatch covers. This made it impossible to counter a shower of incendiaries that fell later, and by 0300 the ship was on fire fore and aft – an HE bomb hit the stern but failed to explode.[158]

The sailing barge ***Oyster*** was moored to the ***Bra-Kar***, with the barge ***Luce*** moored to her in turn. The ***Oyster*** reported a series of explosions on the Norwegian ship after she caught fire – "In a short time there was an explosion on the ***Oyster*** and the nose of a shell was found in the hold. This had made an 18-inch hole in deck. Hatch covers and beams blew off."[159] It sounds as though the fire had reached the ***Bra-Kar's*** magazine. As a result of the explosion on the ***Oyster***, the ***Luce*** caught fire and drifted off to sink later in the middle of the dock. The ***Oyster*** was taking in water, and, although some auxiliary firemen attempted to save her by pumping, she too went to the bottom after a few hours. It may be that they were trying to kill two birds with one stone, drawing water for fire-fighting from the barge rather than the dock. The steam barge ***Traffic***, carrying boxboards, was also burnt out and sank at East Canada 2. Meanwhile, the ***Bra-Kar*** continued to burn, settling slowly by the stern.

Berthed to the west was the ***Baron Inchcape*** (7,005). She had brought 9,000 tons of oilcake, peas, lentils and grain from India, unloading of which had started on the 2nd. Her crew dealt with the incendiaries and damage aft from HE was only slight, but she was left with one unexploded bomb on the deck.

The north sheds at Canada 1 were mostly demolished by HE and the wreckage burnt. The ***Lobos***

The tug *Enid Blanche* on the Mersey in April 1942 apparently freshly painted and certainly with nothing grey about her. Photographic evidence suggests that even some ocean-going ships were still in peacetime colours.

(6,479) survived this at the east berth where she had just started loading for Valparaiso. The ***Elstree Grange*** (6,598), repairing at the west end, was set on fire when a parachute mine landed on her and exploded amidships. Four of the twelve men aboard were killed along with two men on the quay. There were also two men injured and Able Seaman George Wheeler volunteered to go back onto the burning ship to bring them off.

Within an hour of his work at Alexandra Dock, Inspector Skelton arrived to lend a hand accompanied by PC Harry Gannaway and War Reserve Constable Sidney John Gardler. They threw ropes to Wheeler who lowered the first man down the side of the ship so that the others could pull him ashore while shells exploding in the burning ammunition locker spat murderous fragments about. A naval officer went on board to help Wheeler get the second man down and Wheeler then searched the forecastle to make sure there was no-one else about before leaving the ship. Skelton organised the production of makeshift stretchers from wire mattresses, and the police then carried the injured man to an ambulance through the burning shed with wreckage falling around them. (The George Medal was awarded to Wheeler for this action, and BEMs to the three policemen – a bar in Skelton's case.)[160]

The ***Elstree Grange*** was completely burnt out, though she remained high in the water with her funnel heeling over to starboard and her masts to port. The tug ***Thistlecock*** moved in to shift her away from the ***Lobos*** and subsequently claimed salvage on the grounds that this had saved the latter. The owners – PSNC – did not agree.

The ***Waiwera*** (12,435), which had nearly finished discharging a vast quantity of food and wool at the south quay, probably escaped damage at this stage together with the sheds alongside. It is difficult to be sure for reasons that will become apparent.

All the sheds on the west side were damaged by blast and fire, the ***Collegian*** (7,886), at the south end, suffering slightly from flying debris. At the next berth to the north was the ***Tacoma Star*** (7,924) with the Dutch steamer ***Salland*** (6,447) moored outside her – both awaiting cargoes. The ***Tacoma***

Europa - Kobenhaven - in Brocklebank Graving Dock. Beyond her stern can be seen one of the Canada Dock coal hoists, the tongue shed, and Hartley's tower. The *Tacoma Star* is still at her berth behind the first davit on the left.

An array of burnt-out sheds at South Canada 3 - the *Domino* seems to have been removed.

Star had returned from China by way of Capetown bringing eggs – mostly frozen – along with some ginger and peppermint. The eggs had unfortunately been sent to one of the cold stores whose destruction has already been noted. At 2330 the *Salland* was hit aft by an HE bomb that caused the No. 5 hatch covers to fall into the lower hold and started a fire in dunnage wood. The crew spent the best part of two hours putting this out while dealing with many incendiaries as well.

In the meantime, the *Tacoma Star* was hit by a bomb that crashed through the Second Engineer's cabin (and the Second Engineer's pillow), ending up in "No. 5 'tween deck bunker" without exploding. This was at around 0100 The master of the *Salland* then ordered all his men to seek shelter ashore in case this should prove to be a delayed-action bomb. In fact it went off half an hour later, but was not noticed at first among all the other explosions occurring locally – it was not till 0330 that the master of the *Salland* ordered his men back aboard to find several fires burning that were soon put out. They also found one crewman dead and another injured. The *Tacoma Star* had had a good part of her starboard engine blown into the dock and was settling slowly by the stern.

Moored at the tongue, east of the river entrance, was HMS *Maplin* (5,780), formerly the RMS *Erin* and now one of the four naval auxiliaries fitted out as Fighter Catapult Ships – the precursors of the CAM ships devised to provide convoys with limited air cover. Like so many others she had been slightly damaged in the December raids, but work on her conversion was now complete and she had come in that day from her trials. She was painted pale strawberry pink, which must have enlivened the other-

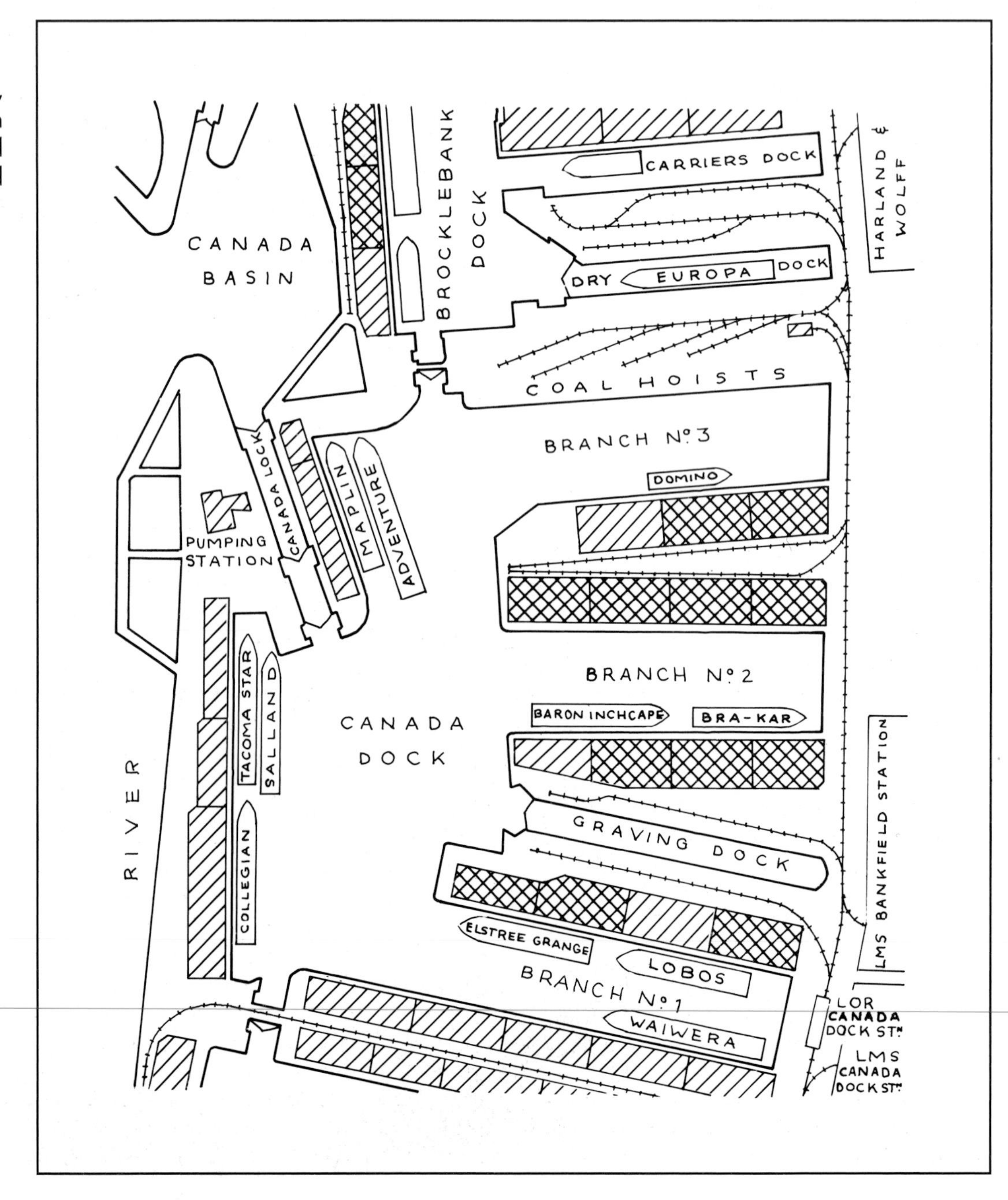

Canada Dock, with the location of shipping and damaged and destroyed sheds.

Denis Foss's surreptitious snap of the *Elstree Grange*, perhaps not up to Stewart Bales standards, but of a priceless record all the same. The legend on the gable end of the shed proclaims the allocation of berths to the Royal Mail Lines and PSNC whose *Lobos* appears faintly at the far end.

wise grey scene. HMS ***Adventure*** (displacement 7,260), moored alongside, was the Navy's largest minelayer and had been under repair since January. Her log records a near miss off the port quarter at 2300, "causing damage and small holes in ship's side." At 0230 a party was landed "to extinguish fires in adjacent warehouses and in two Merchant ships." (The ***Salland*** and ***Tacoma Star*** were the nearest. David W. Large, then an acting petty officer on ***Maplin***, reports that her crew helped to tackle the ***Europa*** fire until the fire service turned up.) More fire parties were landed by ***Adventure*** at 0345 "to render general assistance in extinguishing fires." ***Maplin's*** men shared in this work, some of them supplementing the hoses with buckets lowered into the dock and others beating the more accessible fires with lengths of wet canvas (a technique learnt in dealing with fires on Table Mountain, Cape Town), An attempt was made at combining ***Maplin's*** and ***Adventure's*** hoses to tackle fires over a wider area, but Royal and Merchant Navy hose connections did not match. With the 'all-clear' hands were employed "rigging collision mat over port side aft."[161]

The pumping station on the other side of the entrance lock – a bizarre Gothic extravaganza built by the dock engineer Jesse Hartley was put out of action. Also in Canada Dock three sailing barges came to grief; the ***Barnacle*** and ***Pike*** were lost to fire after being hit by incendiaries, while the ***Silverdale*** was reduced to a total wreck by incendiaries and burning debris. Another bomb in the passage to Brocklebank blew one of the gates away and so damaged the floor of the passage that water was able to leak out to the river. This leakage increased with time, causing a serious loss of water from the dock;[162] the source was not immediately apparent as the 170-ton gate lay over the hole.

East of Canada 1, the Overhead Railway was hit again and another span of the structure wrecked.

Like Canada, Huskisson Dock had three branches, but the sheds were of very solid construction in brick, steel and concrete – two-storey except for the continuous single-storey shed round No. 2 branch and a length of three-storey shed at South 1.

At North Huskisson 3 there were three vessels discharging sugar: the ***Clan MacWhirter*** (5,941), the Dutch Steamer ***Moena*** (9,286), and the coaster ***Ary*** (642) which had sailed from Newport (Mon.) (sic). The larger vessels at least were successfully defended from incendiary attack by their crews, the ***Moena***,[163] under Captain Ruytenschildt, being exceptionally well prepared. She retained her full crew on board, including Chinese and Javanese contingents, and the scuppers had been boarded up so that the decks could be flooded. I have come across no other reference to this simple but effective device, which accounted for a number of incendiaries. It also freed more of the crew to prevent fires from getting out of hand in the sheds and in the unmanned lighters waiting alongside to take off some of her sugar. (Three of Burton & Son's barges – ***A.E., Eric Burton*** and ***June Burton*** were reported to have suffered serious fire damage from incendiaries in

North Huskisson. The ***Bongo***, also one of Burtons' and carrying sugar, caught fire and sank in North 3. The ***Clam***, one of Rea's sailing barges, was burnt in the same branch.)

Dutch reports tell of smoke and sparks blowing across the ***Moena*** from the burning timber yards inland as well as the stench from tins of Canadian salmon that were exploding in the sheds across the dock – also of the hellish racket of crackling fires, collapsing sheds, droning aircraft, falling bombs, anti-aircraft fire and the mournful hooting of ships seeking assistance.

The sugar theme was continued by the ***Canemola*** and ***Brimolco***, which had returned to the east end of the branch for more molasses from the tanks of United Molasses over the dock road. ***Brimolco*** at least remained overnight. The only other vessel of any size in this branch was Brocklebank's ***Mahout*** (7,921), still loading explosives at the south quay; she had HE bombs and small arms ammunition in holds 2, 4 and 6. Led by Chief Officer Scoins, the officers and Lascar crew did good work tackling the many incendiaries that fell on the ship. Fires also broke out in the shed by No. 4 hatch, and the Third Mate, D. L. Campbell, was sent with a shore party to help the shed watchman with these. The Lascar Deck Serang, Ismail Mohamed, distinguished himself in this work, taking a hose up to the upper floor. Oil drums and a broken gas main fuelled the fires, but they were extinguished by the time the raid ended, with a couple of watchmen staying in the shed to keep the smouldering embers damped down with the ship's hoses.[164]

To start with, the story was much the same in Huskisson 2, though here there was only one large vessel. Along the north side were the ***Kenfinch*** (113) – a former Clyde puffer now used for trading up the Weaver Navigation with chemicals, ***No. 11 Pneumatic Elevator*** (295), ***No. 20 Hopper*** (703) and the Belgian trawler ***Van Orley*** (352). The last two were in the hands of Charles Howson & Co, converting to a salvage boat and an anti-submarine trawler

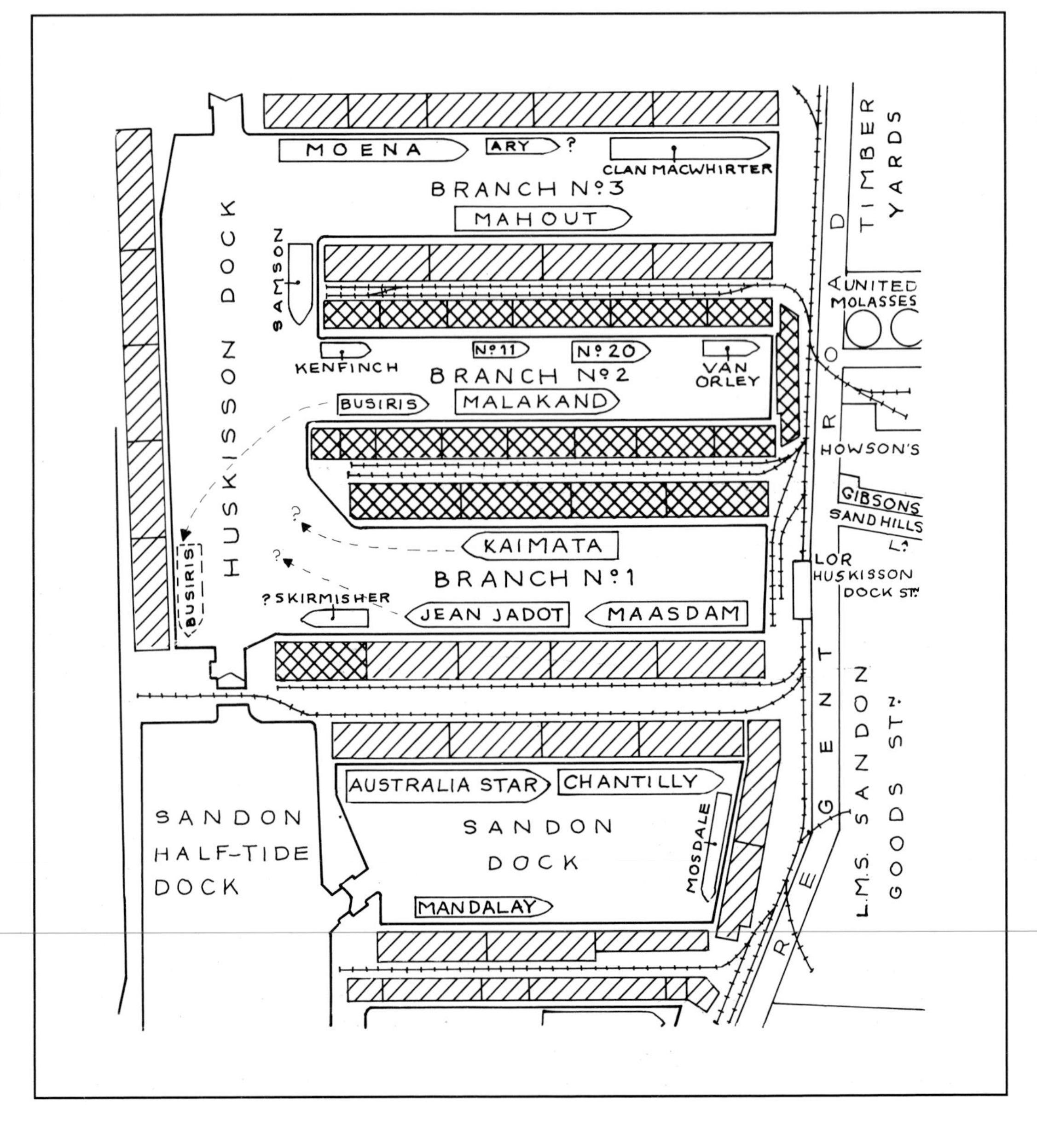

Huskisson Dock; ship movement, damage to sheds and the extent of the devastation caused by the *Malakand* are shown.

respectively. The barge ***Overdale*** was still on the bottom from December.

Towards the east end of the branch were ***Nos 2 and 3 Camels***, the flat ***Ellesport***, the grain elevator barge ***Walton***, and some other unidentified barges. Fire-watchers at the east shed had to deal with a shower of incendiaries at 2345. Soon after midnight the shed was completely demolished by a parachute mine that killed one of the fire-watchers and left only a portion of the south wall standing.[165] The ***Walton*** was hit by incendiaries and burnt out.

Confirmation is lacking but the ***Busiris*** (943), having discharged her coal, appears now to have been at the south quay – west end. Her crew had only incendiaries to cope with. To the east was Brocklebank's ***Malakand***[166] (7,649), now in the care of Captain H. C. Kinley, a 43-year-old Manxman who had left the sea in the last war to join the Royal Flying Corps,[167] with ten other shore-relief officers and a Lascar crew of 61. She had a thousand tons of HE bombs in holds 1, 3 and 6.

At around 2300 a partly-deflated barrage balloon snagged the ***Malakand's*** foremast. As it descended to flop onto the No. 1 hatch one or two flares drifted low over the ship and then a shower of incendiaries fell, two landing astern and one on the deck three feet from the hydrogen-filled balloon. H. G. Allan, the First Mate, had been pulled out of the Atlantic two months earlier after being torpedoed; this was his first job after reporting fit for duty a day or so before. As he rushed forward with others to smother the bomb with sand the balloon was flapping about in the wind. Suddenly it swept over them, caught fire, and exploded into a sheet of flame that reached the crow's nest and set the hatch-cover on fire. Allan was hurled across the hatch and half-way down the fore-deck to land with his helmet missing and his hair on fire. The burning hatch-cover was tackled with hoses, extinguishers and buckets, and extinguished within fifteen minutes.

The men hardly had time to congratulate themselves before two HE bombs landed on the adjacent shed. This stood six feet from the edge of the quay, the walls largely made up of sliding iron doors; access for goods by rail or road was by the dock avenue between the sheds. In addition to the usual watchmen (presumably augmented in view of the fact that shed doors had to be left partly open) the sheds were protected by fire-watchers drawn from the Dock Board and shipping companies. The sheds south and east of Huskisson 2 – stretching over 500 yards – were patrolled by twenty-two of Moss Hutchison's men,[168] who were already finding it hard to cope with the rain of incendiaries. The addition of high explosive made the job of the men in the section affected quite hopeless, and the contents were soon burning fiercely.

The fears expressed earlier regarding shed fires were fully realised. With the wind against them, the crew of the ***Malakand*** could not contain the new fire and before long flames from the "upper half" of the shed – presumably the roof, as these were single-storey sheds – were shooting across the ship's upper works "like huge jets from Bunsen burners", setting the starboard lifeboats and wooden decks alight from the bridge aft. The heat and smoke soon made the bridge deck untenable.

As there was little more they could do, Kinley sent the Lascars ashore to take shelter. Mr. Cullen, the 3rd Officer, went along to supervise and to seek help from the AFS station at the end of Huskisson 1.

Captain Kinley considered his options. If the ship were cut adrift now, the wind would take her north to spread the fire on the other side of the dock. The fire had taken hold of the ***Malakand*** amidships so quickly that it no longer seemed possible for anyone to get down to the engine-room to scuttle her – the popular notion that all ships have 'sea-cocks' that can be quickly opened for this purpose is mistaken. With the boats on the port side – away from the quay – catching fire, and the shed fire rapidly approaching the one gangway, towards the stern, Kinley gave the order for the remaining officers to abandon ship. (According to Lloyd's this happened at 0030[169] – the Captain puts it rather earlier.)

As they left, they advised the men on the vessel next to the ***Malakand*** to get the hell out of it and Allan cast off the moorings to give point to the suggestion. (The ***Busiris*** was moved during the night,[170] ending up at the south-west corner.)

There were two AFS sector posts at Huskisson, one of them on the west side where another had been approved in March and might have been operational by now. There was also an auxiliary station on the east side that doubled as the headquarters of the North Docks Division. This did not involve the same status as the other divisional HQs and it seems that the station would have been equipped only with one mobile pump to supplement the single trailer at each of the two or three sector posts.

Kinley hurried to the fire station at North-West Huskisson 1 – presumably the auxiliary station. There was no-one there, but the man in charge was soon found at the scene of a shed fire. He was Section Officer John Lappin of the AFS, a master stevedore who had seen service with the Royal Navy at the Dardanelles.[171]

Kinley explained the position, with special reference to the Malakand's cargo, and "Lappin immediately 'phoned from his station to his Headquarters, and asked for assistance, stating the facts as I had given them." Clearly, this was done from the auxiliary station, which had a direct line to the Divisional HQ at Westminster Road, who would have informed the Central Fire Station. They were told that few pumps were available. Kinley also learnt at this stage that the fire-float ***Morag*** was in Huskisson, but had already capsized and sunk when a large bomb fell alongside.[172] Perhaps because of the discouraging response from the fire service, Kinley also informed the Naval HQ (FOIC) in the Liver Building (the auxiliary station had an exchange line as well).

So far as one can gather from the brief reports available, Lappin had only *one* "small portable pump" – "which we helped to fit with hose and it was later started. It developed some defect after about 20 minutes." At 0100 an AFS "mobile pump" arrived. It had been driven through the burning city from Speke[173] at the extreme south end and was certainly welcome, though hardly what was needed. The new crew soon had several branches in action, "but it all made little or no impression on the shed fire and it was impossible to get near the ship."

At least one other pump was directed to Huskisson at about the same time. George Eglin, later a well-known writer on the ***Liverpool Echo***, was one of a party standing by with a van and trailer pump outside St. Helens Fire Station. According to Eglin's account[174] his party did alternate fortnights standing by at St. Helens and living in at Gladstone Dock, Bootle. On this night they were told to report to Bootle Fire Station as the first bombers arrived, set off along the East Lancashire Road, and came over the ridge to see the line of fire resulting from the first two hours of the raid. St. Helens is eleven miles from the centres of Liverpool and Bootle as the crow flies – the ridge would be topped after driving about five miles. Regrettably, Mr. Eglin offers no explanation for what appears to have been one of the slowest turn-outs on record. His time of arrival ties in with what follows. The known problems with reinforcements suggest that the starting time might be wrong and that an appliance waiting for the call in a nearby town did not get it until after midnight. Or, of course, they may have had a breakdown or run off the road in the black-out.

At any rate, they reported at Bootle for instructions and were handed a message form advising them to proceed to Huskisson Dock where an ammunition ship was on fire. Thinking that this, perhaps, was a job the local men might have tackled, they set off south to Liverpool, hindered along the way by fallen tram-wires. While negotiating a tramcar on its side at the junction of Derby Road and Strand Road,[175] they were overtaken by a cyclist messenger with a change of orders. To their immense relief, they were now directed to a fire in Effingham Street, Bootle. On arrival, they found that it was at a warehouse "piled high with beans."

This may not have been as silly as it sounds, as the Navy had not been idle. A salvage boat was kept on stand-by at all times at the Liverpool Landing Stage, a couple of miles south of Huskisson. On this night it was the ***Salvor***. William Clarke, engineer, remembers Captain Brock shouting down to him through the engine-room skylight at midnight or soon after: "Bill! There's a bloody ammunition ship going to blow up in Huskisson Dock. We're going in to scuttle it."

They cast off and bore north on the fire-lit river, past a scene that one should perhaps refrain from calling a Brock's benefit. At Sandon Dock, the southern entrance for Huskisson, they found that the tide, though rising, was still too low for the dock gates to be opened. Brock was unimpressed and told Clarke: "Put her nose against the gates. Push your way in."

Privately, Clarke thought this was "bloody mad", but he had a go. When attempts at biffing the gates open were foiled by the weight of water behind, Brock jumped ashore and made his way to Huskisson along the river wall to find out what the situation was. He had just reached the west side of Huskisson when a large explosion occurred in No. 2 branch and he narrowly escaped being struck by a flying shed door.

Captain Brock was some 300 yards from the ***Malakand***. To reach the scene on foot he would have had to walk over half a mile round the dock (supposing that the way was clear) while the ***Salvor*** stood by in the river. Seeing that he was too late anyway, Brock returned to his ship and soon found other work to do on what was to be a hectic night for the *Salvor*.

If the time given for this incident is reasonably accurate, Brock had made a terrible mistake. There were a few minor explosions on or around the ***Malakand*** during the night, and one quite serious one when the ship's own magazine blew.[176] One can only speculate on what went wrong here, but this does seem the most likely explosion for Brock to have seen. It is by no means certain that he had been given full details of the ***Malakand's*** cargo and there is reason to suspect that he had other things on his mind (see later). By all accounts Brock was an extremely brave and capable officer, in fact exactly what the situation called for, and it would be wrong to offer any criticism in the absence of fuller information. Mr. Clarke understands the explosion seen by Brock to have been the first of the major ones, but this cannot be so if his recollection of the time is right. As it is, the ***Salvor's*** visit is the only known action to be attributable to the Royal Navy (see a similar intervention four nights later) and entirely justifies the failure to send fire service reinforcements, which would otherwise be hard to excuse in spite of the need for them in other parts.

The men in the dock avenue were not affected by the magazine explosion and knew nothing of the ***Salvor's*** visit. The fire service had doubtless been informed of the Navy's initiative and turned its attention to other problems. Whatever the cause, the few men at the scene were left to cope as best they could. They were split into three parties: Captain Kinley assisting the firemen at the bow end (towards the shore), Mr. Allan at the stern, and another officer, Mr. Exley, amidships.[177] But between them and the ship lay the shed, eighty feet wide, in which the fire was totally out of control. By the time it became clear that one fire-appliance was all the help they were going to get, the telephone lines – direct and exchange – had failed.

At around 0100 Mr. Scoins on the *Mahout* was anxious for the safety of his own ship and sent his Third Mate into town to warn the authorities of the danger. The distance was two miles, but Campbell had gone only one when he met a quartermaster off the *Malakand* who had been sent on a similar errand. He had found the dock road impassable and was returning to report. Campbell was persuaded that there was no future trying to find a way through and they returned together, sheltering under the Overhead Railway if anything came too close.[178]

How long this took is uncertain. According to Kinley's account it was at three o'clock that he and Lappin made their next move – which ought to mean two hours after midnight. Logically, it should not have been long after the return of the quartermaster. What happened was that Kinley and Lappin resolved to go to the Chief Officer of the Fire Brigade to point out "the urgency of the assistance" requested earlier. They went by car with Lappin driving, but how long the journey took is anyone's guess.[179]

This information, with its clear suggestion that no help had yet been received, was published in 1943 without arousing any noticeable comment then or since. Many people who were in Liverpool that night see nothing remarkable in it, but it does seem striking that *both* of the men in command should have left with the battle at its height. Not knowing what was going on outside their small area, except that all hell was breaking loose, they were clearly anxious to press their own claim to priority.

While they were away it is likely that another section officer in the AFS was left in charge – Noel Landau. Born in Shanghai in 1908, he had come to England at the age of 15, without family or friends, and become a successful builder – a man active in public life and Jewish affairs. At the outbreak of war he was Commandant of Bootle AFS. His translation from this post to the relatively humble one of section officer in the Liverpool AFS is a minor mystery, but it provided Lappin with an exceptionally able lieutenant.[180] One obvious possibility in view of Landau's background is the general round-up of aliens, many of whom were whole-heartedly on our side, but I have no information on this.

Whenever they got there, the arrival of Lappin and Kinley at Hatton Garden must have caused a stir if the foregoing account of the reason for the failure of fire service assistance is correct. They spoke to Chief Officer Owen, Kinley asking him "if means could be provided to sink her from the off-side by either cutting holes or even a shot in the engine room." The dramatic second alternative was evidently considered impractical and Owen agreed to send "a special tender with oxy-acetylene burning apparatus", which sounds like the Brigade's special appliance van. A sergeant was detailed to arrange this and the two men returned to the ship, having been unable to contact the Dock Board or the Navy from the control room. Back at Huskisson, the struggle was continued with the equipment to hand – there is one report of a policeman helping out with a bucket. No further help arrived before the 'all-clear' sounded.

What was known of these events elsewhere in the dock is uncertain. Huskisson 1 was Cunard territory, but the only Cunarder known to have been in the area was the Company's Liverpool tender, the *Skirmisher* (582). This venerable craft, which had fetched and carried for her more famous sisters on the Mersey since 1884, was probably the oldest vessel of any size in the port. One report puts her in No. 2 Branch, where Cunard had a berth on the north side, but she may well have been in 1. Two ships under Cunard management were loading at South Huskisson 1; the Dutch ship *Maasdam* (8,812) stayed put, while the Belgian *Jean Jadot* (5,783) was moved to the west quay to escape a shed fire. During the night, the *Kaimata* (5,269) was moved from her berth at North Huskisson 1 "for safety" – from what not specified. These moves were made without the help of tugs (unless the *Skirmisher* was called on) and while manoeuvring to tie up alongside the *Jean Jadot* the *Kaimata* rammed her and dented some of her side plates.[181]

The floating crane *Samson* (522) seems to have kept out of everyone's way at the short quay between North 2 and South 3.

There was a direct hit on the machinery pit by the passage from Huskisson to Sandon Half-Tide Dock, leaving bridge and gates unworkable for several days. The 80-foot lock from Sandon Half-Tide to the river was also put out of commission, though fortunately not the adjoining 40 and 100-foot locks. The *Mosdale* (3,022) was damaged by HE in East Sandon Dock, while the French liner *Chantilly* (10,065), at the north quay had a bomb fall through her deck and out again through her side. The *Chantilly*, the *Cantal* already mentioned, and the *Charles Plumier* lying in South-East Queen's 2 were all French ships that had recently been caught taking contraband of war to France and accordingly seized as prizes – they were not, as one might suppose, Free French volunteers.

One shed was demolished at South Wellington, the debris falling onto the Belfast boat *Louth* (1,915) which was unloading there, and all those at Nelson were damaged along with others at Salisbury and

Collingwood. The roof of Clarence Graving Dock pumping station was "lifted by blast" and the power station built in the old dock was hit by HE and fire-bombs without the supply being interrupted. The shed at the east end of the Trafalgar Branch Dock was gutted and there was severe HE damage at East Victoria. In the north-east corner of West Waterloo Dock the small tug ***Bonita*** was practically destroyed by a direct hit and the ***No. 33 Hopper*** (718) on the west side was holed aft and developed a list to port. A warehouse was set on fire at the south end and debris thrown across the barge ***Crosshouse.*** There was a large fire in the sheds at Prince's Dock and also at Riverside Station – the Board's passenger station on the west side of the dock.

South of the Pier Head there was relatively little trouble. There were serious shed fires at Canning Half-Tide, Salthouse, Duke's and East Wapping Basin, the sand barge ***Richard Abel*** being damaged by fire in the last. Two ships at North King's 2 were badly damaged by near misses. The ***Clan MacInnes*** (4,672), loaded with 1,550 tons of copper and 4,350 of sugar, was left in a sinking condition at the west end, though it proved possible to keep her afloat with pumps. The Greek steamer ***Mimosa*** (3,071), to the east, also had her hull buckled amidships and her back broken and started taking in water fore and aft.

The roof of a shed at South King's 1 was shattered and a couple of sheds at Queen's 2 were damaged. The ***New Columbia*** (6,574), at South Queen's 2 reported that: "an aerial torpedo went over her after deck and struck a shed which was set on fire. The door of the shed fell on to the vessel and damaged her rails" – there were also many holes punched in her side.[182] Precisely what flew over this ship is a matter for conjecture. Ordinary marine torpedoes dropped by aircraft might be called "aerial torpedoes" but I doubt if any of these were used on Merseyside. The glider bombs used by the Germans against shipping, with considerable effect, would also fit the description, but they did not appear until a couple of years later.

At Brunswick, the only trouble came from an HE bomb that blocked the bridge at North Brunswick passage. On the east side of Toxteth Dock the two-storey sheds at the south end were hit by HE and set alight; they contained cotton, gum opal, copper, bark, tin ore, hides and rubber. An LFB pump from Essex Street was called out at 0043, that and four others being occupied at the scene till 0740.[183] The Belgian steamer ***Roumanie*** (3,563), in ballast, was hit by incendiaries as well as catching fire from the sheds and was reported burnt out. She was found to have suffered scattered damage to her upper works, but nothing serious below – a fact that may be attributable to the presence of Inspector Reanney, an expert on ship fires, who was in charge.

A large bomb fell in the middle of the avenue on the river side of the sheds at West Toxteth without exploding. Someone – it is not clear who – instructed the officers on the two Elder Dempster ships moored here to get their crews away. The ***Edward Blyden*** (5,003) was duly abandoned, but the officer in command of the ***Mary Kingsley*** (5,021) did not think the doubtful menace of a UXB on the other side of the shed justified the abandonment of his ship to possible incendiary attack. Fire-bombs did in fact fall on the sheds and the ***Edward Blyden*** later and were duly dealt with. It is possible that the shed fire-watchers, who had retreated from the UXB, would have acted if the ***Mary Kingsley's*** crew hadn't, but Elder Dempster wrote to the Dock Board[184] claiming that the sheds would soon have been ablaze if all their men had followed the instructions given to them. It was agreed that unless the Board or the Admiralty said otherwise, warning of the proximity of a UXB should not be taken as an instruction to remove essential fire-watchers from ships.

On the other side of the river, the tanker ***San Fabian*** (13,031) was hit aft at Stanlow on the Manchester Ship Canal and seriously damaged. (The large oil refinery there was almost completely ignored by the Luftwaffe.) At 0230 the ***City of Wellington*** (5,733), which had crossed the river from her former berth at West Huskisson on the 1st, was slightly damaged by incendiaries at Vittoria Dock.

Apart from all this there was a great deal of superficial damage to the docks: electrical power was cut off, hydraulic pipe-lines shattered and, as elsewhere, roads through the estate blocked by debris and UXBs.

Ships in the docks generally had little opportunity to reply in kind, but two informants recall a notable exception – an unidentified cruiser of the ***Dido*** class. Her berth is disputed but most likely she was in Birkenhead Docks. Periodically she would fire a couple of ranging shots and then follow up with a broadside from her ten dual-purpose 5.2-inch guns. The shore-based AA batteries, with only 3.7 and 4.5-inch guns, could produce nothing to match these tremendous salvoes, which apparently had ships on the Liverpool side bouncing in the water – most heartening. Whether this was the reason for so few bombs falling on the Birkenhead side is a moot point.

There were always ships at anchor in the river and the numbers could be considerable after the arrival of a convoy. In the last two days over thirty ships had entered the Mersey, of which a good few were still awaiting admission to the docks or the Manchester Ship Canal. There were one or two others that had entered the river with a view to an early start next day as well as more or less permanent residents such as the Conway. Most of them were disposed in two lines running through the narrow neck of the Mersey.

The crews, many with families in the area, looked on appalled as the raid developed. To a young apprentice on the ***Princesa*** (of the Freetown convoy – SL 71) it seemed that: "Just about every building from one end of dockland to the other was on fire." Unease became personal when it was seen that, far from being protected by the blackout, the ships at anchor were on a well-lit stage. The temptation proved too much for the enemy.

To the ***Princesa's*** apprentice, "It most certainly seemed as if the total contents of the bomb racks of the Luftwaffe's aircraft...was distributed among the units of Convoy SL 71...Illuminated by the dockland fires, and reflection off the waters of the Mersey, those ships might just as well have been lit by floodlights. Before long, of course, chaos abounded. I do not know how many ships were hit, or how many were set on fire. I do know that several, blazing fiercely, having broken from their anchored positions, drifted helplessly in among other ships, resulting in at least one instance in a collision, the burning vessel setting fire to the ship it struck. Others ran aground after narrow misses, their steering having either been knocked out or rendered virtually impossible by the glare of fires, explosion of bombs and ack-ack flashes."

The ***Moena's*** report of ships bellowing for assistance will be recalled. It is to be regretted that official confirmation of these events has proved elusive, probably because the damage was mostly spectacular rather than serious. The consequences of running aground, for instance, would have been slight on a rising tide with high water not due till around 0600 (DST). Two casualties can be identified, however.

The ***Baronesa*** (8,663), a refrigerator ship dealing in frozen meat and due out the day before, was ready to leave for Buenos Aires only to have a heavy bomb explode near her starboard quarter at 2315 She suffered damage around her propeller shaft and had to be dry-docked for repairs.[185] The ***Silversandal*** (6,770) was waiting to dock with a cargo that included ammunition as well as aircraft on the deck. Bombs exploded within fifty feet of her on either side and she began to list to starboard as water flooded into the forward deep tank, but she was able to control the situation with her own pumps. There were several other vessels that *might* have been involved, but no positive information has come to light concerning them.

One vessel – and apparently only one – was in a position to offer practical assistance. It is pure conjecture, but if the confusion described above began to develop as the ***Salvor*** was making for Huskisson it would have been frustrating in the extreme for Captain Brock to have to sail by without doing anything to help. In such a case, a reluctance to spend time simply confirming that there was no longer anything for him to do at Huskisson would be entirely natural.

The attack on shipping at anchor was surely a mistake on the part of the Luftwaffe, which had more densely-packed fleets to go for in the docks on either hand – with less chance of bombs being wasted if they failed to hit the intended target. To the men on the river it seemed that it was an act of idiocy on someone's part to have put them in that situation – a notion that received some support from the fact that with the 'all-clear' most of the ships were sent to anchor at the Bar until provision could be made for their reception.

On the 22nd May, the Ministry of War Transport issued advice to all ports suggesting that so far as possible ships should not be concentrated to form large targets and that they should be moored away from possible fires ashore, preferably at least a thousand feet apart and not in straight lines. Liverpool's response was that there was not a lot to be done about this on the Mersey. The docks were in line anyway, though they might try to reduce the number of ships double-banked at the quays. They certainly did not want to put more ships in the river, which would be impossible without reducing the recommended distance apart and presenting an easy target. There was also the risk from mines – already amply demonstrated – and the fact that most ships sunk in the docks were relatively easy to salve.[186]

Later in the morning the Home Office daily intelligence report included the following re Liverpool: "At 0123, 60 fires in the centre of the City, 56 in the suburbs and 3 in the Dock area were reported to be in progress."[187] That last figure is startling, even if it excludes Bootle. One might think it had been garbled in transmission if it had not been stated later in the day that fires had been reported at East Toxteth Dock, "Collingworth Dock", and Clarence Power Station. It may be significant that the same three are referred to in the Liverpool City Engineer's list of incidents, which makes little reference to the docks – but this is not a list of fires. Whoever supplied the information, it suggests a desperate ignorance of the true state of affairs.

The last incident reported to the City Engineer was an HE bomb at No. 49 Woodlands Road, Aigburth, at 0448. The 'all-clear' followed at around 0500 (DST). Liverpool and Bootle were in a frightful state with fires raging out of hand and spreading. Casualties were obviously heavy, but no-one had any notion of the true figures. At Webster Road Mortuary, to which most of the bodies recovered in Liverpool were taken, the electricity supply had failed at 2300 and the dreadful work continued by hurricane lamps only until 1700 the following day – the windows had been blown out and were now boarded up.[188]

It had been a bad night, and the day would be only relatively better.

SUNDAY 4th MAY

The BBC in London can have had only a sketchy idea of what was going on in Liverpool. The seven o'clock news referred to the night's main attack as being against Merseyside: "News agency messages say that the raid was on a heavy scale and that large numbers of enemy aircraft attacked in waves. The raiders were over Liverpool for hours without a break and casualties and damage in a residential area are reported." The reader would have gone on to say that, "Thousands of fire bombs were dropped but were quickly put out", but this line was deleted from the script before the broadcast – presumably on receipt of further information. According to the nine o'clock news: "Reports indicate that the number of casualties is likely to be large. Much damage has been done."[189]

After a short spell of leave, Nicholas Monsarrat attempted to return to Albert Dock in a taxi. "Outside the town, a lovely sunny day; but ahead there were billows of black smoke, and soon the air was fouled by smuts, charred paper drifting on the wind, an over-all reek of destruction. As we made our way the air grew darker and darker, shutting out the sun, the sky, the corners ahead: each street we traversed, by a dozen diversions, bumping over hoses, scuttering through broken glass and ruined woodwork, passing groups of intent rescue-workers or silent onlookers, showed a more appalling destruction. Tall houses lay in the street, flames showed through empty windows and gaping rents, shops and buildings sprawled over the roadways."

Once in the city centre, where further progress was impossible, Monsarrat abandoned the taxi by a blazing building and proceeded on foot. "Across the street it was the same, and farther on the same, and all the way to the ship the same: what was not still burning lay in red-hot piles of brick and wood; what was not torn to pieces was blasted into a vile disorder. Even to the casual observer it was a frightful scene – the mounting furnaces, the thick, smoke-filled air, the huge spaces laid waste; to a man born in that town it was heart-breaking."[190]

Explosions big and small continued to rock the city for the whole day. Apart from lines to Lime Street, which remained fully operational, no trains ran – and no trams in Bootle or central Liverpool. Large areas were without gas or electricity, and water was often a problem.

At the Central Library the situation had appeared to be in hand, but soon after the 'all-clear' the wind changed. Now blowing more from the east, it sent sparks down the ventilation shafts into the basement and spread the fire along the wooden beams of roof and floors. The fire engulfed the William Brown Museum and then continued through the roof of the Technical College next door, gutting the Museum's Upper Horseshoe Gallery on the top floor. The Lower Horseshoe Gallery was saved, and was the first part to be re-opened some years after the war. (Part of the bomb was exhibited near the entrance. One remembers passing it by at first in the belief that it was only an old clay pot.) Little more than the facade of the original Museum and Library building remained. 150,000 books were lost, along with a great deal of the Museum's collection – though the most valuable exhibits had mostly been removed to safer places.[191]

Some of the Library's most treasured possessions were stored in the basement, which was flooded. One of the first people to go through when it was safe to do so noticed a large volume floating about with the covers swollen and water-logged, and casually placed it above the water-level. It turned out to be Audubon's ***Birds of America***, one of the rarest and most valuable items in the collection. When dried out it was found to have suffered only slight water damage.

It was felt that the precautions taken, and the staff charged with putting them into practice, had come out of it well – though it would be a long time before the Museum and Library recovered from the blow, and frustrating gaps remain in these collections as well as that of the Art Gallery.

South of Lord Street, the fires were still spreading – meeting – swallowing up one building after another. As soon as the 'all-clear' went, Sam Holt and the others at Burnyeat, Dalzell and Nicholson came out of the shelter and found that the paint on the South Castle Street front of their buildings was blistering in the heat from the other side of the road. They had enough water on hand to spray the building and keep it cool. The burnt buildings opposite were collapsing at intervals – usually inwards. When one fell the other way a large sandstone coping block was sent skidding into Litherland Alley where Sam Holt and others were still standing guard over their firm. They had to run for their lives, one man leaping into the air to let the stone pass under him. At around mid-day Mr. Holt left to see how his father had been getting on. Holt Snr. was retired, but had volunteered for fire-watching duty at the sack works of Levy Bros & Knowles in Park Lane – on the corner of Forrest Street. Sam found him sitting on a low wall opposite, watching the place burn. (Burnyeat, Dalzell & Nicholson was open for business as usual on the Monday.)

At Woodhouse's furniture shop in Lord Street the back windows were hung with carpets (a blast precaution) and these had to be continuously sprayed with water from a stirrup pump to keep them from catching fire. By about 0700 the fires in Cable Street behind could no longer be held at bay and the shop had to be abandoned.

At L.S. Dixon & Co., spirits rose slightly when – some time after the 'all-clear' – an AFS pump was seen going into action at the telephone exchange, but they soon gave up for want of water. "Until they appeared, the South John Street area was so deserted that we wondered at times whether the vicinity had been given up as lost and evacuated." With the fires closing in remorselessly, Neil and his men had to tackle fires in adjoining buildings. These places either had no fire-watchers on duty or they had already given up and gone home. In the end they had to save their small store of water to preserve their own premises. The advancing flames leapt across the South John Street end of Thomas Street, raced through the smaller buildings there – including Dixon's off-shoot – and started on Martin's Bank at the corner of Cable Street. "At 8.00 a.m. another appeal was made to the A.F.S. to try to save the one building still intact, but we were told there was no hope as there was insufficient water pressure for the few pumps available in the area."

The end came when they saw themselves in danger of being trapped, with Cable Street and Thomas Street "well nigh impassable" – "through the fog of smoke every building in the vicinity seemed to be aflame." The only way out now was by a passage to Lord Street alongside Woodhouse's and they took it while it remained open.

Mr. Neil and another picked up the Company's van from Voss's Garage at the Pier Head and went to report events to the Company Secretary, while the others stayed, so long as there was any chance of the fire service arriving in time. "It was a melancholy end to a tremendous struggle waged with spirit and fortitude, lasting over nine hours."[192]

It seems that several things went wrong here. First, there were not enough fire-watchers on rooftops. Second – as was not uncommon – there was little or no water in the mains. It has to be said though that Canning Dock – a few hundred yards away – was full of the stuff. So long as Canning Place remained clear, there was no practical difficulty in taking water from there for use around Lord Street and South John Street, but for every pump at the fire there would have been at least one more needed to send water from the dock, and they were not to be had till some time after eight o'clock. The subsequent story of this conflagration remains obscure; the fires advanced on Lord Street and took out all but a couple of the shops there, which were probably saved by the eventual arrival of the fire service.

By the 23rd June, photographs of this area taken from the top of the Midland Bank's Castle Street branch, were being passed round a select circle. The view of the Victoria Monument surrounded by a sea of destruction, remains the most striking image of the May Blitz. The monument had been the subject of abuse, much of it justified, ever since its erection; and when the time came for post-war reconstruction, there was a move to have it transferred to another site – in a park perhaps. There were stern injunctions that sentimental feelings about a monument that had defied the worst that Hitler could throw at it should have no place in the argument. Sentiment won – and quite right too.

When affairs around Duke Street were brought under control, Corporal Hindley and another King's NCO, were given permission to go home and see how their families had fared. In Paradise Street they hurried past unsafe-looking high walls on either side of the way, and had barely reached the end when the walls collapsed into rubble across the road behind them. Further on, they passed Lewis's and Blackler's still burning. No. 17 pump here was still taking water from the crater and supplying four branches extending to the Bluecoat and to Cooper's in Church Street.

At the Salvage Association's North Depot, the men were still tackling the fire – assisted after 0900 by relief salvagemen reporting from leave. "Meantime the blazing timber stores outside North Station had become completely involved and the flame spread across the road threatening North Station buildings and flats. Men were stationed with spray branches against the front of the building in the hope that the fire could be stopped, but before the timber fire was got under control, North Station buildings caught fire and fire-fighting operations had to be transferred to the rear of the building. Our officers and men succeeded in confining the fire to a portion of the top floor and one house on

Woodhouse's furniture store, Lord Street. The tile passage to Cable Street still has a precarious roof over it. Note also the emergency water main in the fore-ground.

L. S. Dixon & Co., Thomas Street. The tower of Cooper's, Church Street, is just visible on the right.

Atherton Street. The more familiar views of the Lord Street area show a vast brickfield with a few scattered buildings still standing. Before clearance there were just acres of this sort of thing.

the floor below, although the building was very badly damaged as a result of blast from several heavy calibre HE Bombs which dropped in the vicinity." The fire had also spread to "the lofty corrugated iron North warehouse full of baled cotton," but this too was saved.[193]

At Calthrops, Naylor Street, the fire service did not arrive till the afternoon, but other places were luckier as fresh men arrived to start a new shift; some, arriving at the docks were told to pick their own fire. Charles Hughes, of Granton Road Station, was sent to Clarence Grove where he and another relieved the men who were keeping the fire down in the wrecked houses. As it was believed that someone was trapped, they were told to put water on only where smoke appeared so as not to risk flooding the cellar. In the event, a woman's body was recovered, but at least she had not been drowned.

Father Louis Coupe, of St. Alexander's Church, St. John's Road (just on the Liverpool side of the line), recorded "a terrible, frightful night" in his diary. The entire centre section of the church school had been demolished at 0208, though without damage to the crowded shelter under another part. "During the course of the night, both Fr. C. Rigby and Fr. A. Maguire were out attending to casualties in the neighbourhood, and helping to rescue people buried under the debris of their demolished houses. After a period of comparative quiet, during which the clergy helped and supplied water to control fires started by incendiary bombs, the 'Raiders passed' signal was sounded at 5.20 a.m."

Fr. Rigby and Fr. Coupe then went to see that all was well at St. Richard's Chapel-of-Ease at the Bootle end of Miranda Road, finding much damage along St. John's Road. A mine dropped at 2230 "had left the whole block surrounded by Stanley Road, Rosalind Street, Hermia Street and Celia Street, a mass of debris. The corner, Stanley Road Olivia Street, was one blazing inferno. Fr. Maguire reported similar scenes from Derby Road area, where Vincent Murphy's timber yard was ablaze and fire spreading to the adjacent property."

There were UXB's in the St. John's Road – Ceres Street – Sylvia Street area, which had to be evacuated. "About 6.20 a.m., Sunday, a weary procession of priests and people wended its way to St. Richard's, where masses were said for surprisingly large congregations." One was taken by Canon Kelly, who reported: "At about 7 a.m. I had just said Kyrie Eleison once, and before the server could reply, there was a terrible explosion which shook the church and roared for 5 seconds. No one moved – the silence was intense."[194]

A mile away in Huskisson Dock the ***Malakand*** had been burning for four hours when the 'all-clear' sounded. The men tackling the fire must have expected every moment to be their last, but the small band of firemen pressed on, helped by the ***Malakand's*** officers with a few watchmen and others. The midships party was simply tackling the shed fire. Allan's could see the ***Malakand's*** stern through the large doorway opposite, glowing red-hot – then white. It was impossible to enter the shed, but for what it was worth, they played water on what they could see of the ship. Kinley's party was doing much the same at the bow.

Sunrise heralded another fine day, spoilt only by the smoke pall over the city. In Huskisson 3, the men of the ***Moena*** had sorted out their own immediate troubles, though here and in Canada Dock, water was draining out so that some vessels – the ***Moena*** among them – settled gently on the muddy bottom. (In some docks, including these two, the water was normally maintained at an artificially high level by pumping. The high tide may not have reached this level.) At 0600 the wind changed, blowing the smoke and sparks from the timber yards and the troublesome fire in the next branch, clear of the ship. Captain Ruytenschildt then sent most of his crew to get some rest and turned in himself.

Still no help came to Huskisson 2 – no reinforcements – no tender. Lappin of the AFS remained in charge, though he and his men were now in a state of exhaustion – smoke-blackened and red-eyed. (There may have been a good deal going on behind the scenes. Dock Board rumour has it that the possibility of towing the ***Malakand*** out of the river was considered, only to be rejected for fear of her blowing while passing through Sandon Dock gates.)

Kinley had suggested several times that perhaps the time had come to call it a day and withdraw, but Lappin would not hear of it and all stayed. Considering the circumstances, one is entitled to suspect that this was a fairly vehement argument rather than a polite discussion. At about 0730, seeing that the fire to the east was dying down at last, Lappin decided to concentrate his branches to the west where it was still burning fiercely. At this point Kinley decided that he'd had enough; he could see no point in risking his men's lives any further and called them off, leaving the firemen to it.[195]

Almost immediately after, at a time between 0730 and 0745 in the morning, the ***Malakand*** exploded.

This came as a surprise to people who had not been tipped off that something of the sort was liable to happen – including Captain Ruytenschildt, who ran out of his cabin to find debris raining down in the form of mud and stones interspersed with thirty-foot deckbeams weighing two tons each. These came down, glowing red-hot, to hang twisted in the rigging and over the ship's rail. Three-ton iron shed-doors were blasted onto the ship – one of them spitting itself on a davit. The blast also sent a wave round the dock that lifted the ***Moena*** from the mud, only to let her fall back again with a jarring crash.[196] The sinking *Tacoma Star* in Canada "strained and surged heavily."[197]

H. Peters, on the *Clan MacWhirter*, was walking aft to his bunk after a hard night: "As I was nearing the wheelhouse it happened – a terrific 'whoosh' came from the next basin and the whole sky was blotted out by a dirty yellow fog...For a full minute metal of all shapes and sizes came raining down. A steel plate crashed through the engineer's cabin, just missing the sleeping occupant and completely wrecking it. In that one minute we received more damage than we had all night."[198]

Mr. Campbell, snatching some rest on the *Mahout*, found himself lifted from his bunk and held against the bulkhead of his cabin as the stern moorings gave and the ship was flung across the dock. The forward topmast and five of her derricks were blown off and all the hatch-covers displaced. A small coaster nearby (the *Ary*?) was "completely coated with shed doors" as the blast tore through the sheds.

A crane driver at S.W. Huskisson was thrown into the dock, badly hurt. Charles W. White, a dock gateman who had just come on duty, jumped in after him, despite the hail of debris that continued for some time after the blast. He managed to bring his man to the anchor of the *Busiris*, hanging at water level, and held on there till more help arrived, although the anchor was being swayed about by the turbulent water.[199] The *No. 11 Elevator*, just across the branch from the *Malakand*, sank quickly. There were three men aboard who were able to get clear and were rescued "by nearby bargemen" – they were uninjured.

In Sandhills Lane, running down to the dock road at Huskisson, men going to work in the docks and ship-repair works had limbs sheered off. (Opinions vary as to how much had been done to cordon off the biggest UXB of the night.)

There is some evidence that the bombs in No. 6 hold blew first, tossing a fifty-ton section of the stern nearly twenty yards,[200] sending the funnel inland, and gouging a hole in the quay wall. The forepart of the glowing wreck apparently remained buoyant and swung out towards the centre of the branch. The assumption on the *Mahout* was that everyone involved with the *Malakand* was now dead. Astonishingly, it was not so; perhaps because the explosion occurred low down in the ship and the quay provided shelter from direct blast. The men were, however, bowled over and subjected to a bombardment of steel and rubble that killed at least one of the firemen off the Speke appliance.[201]

Lappin, according to the citation, rallied his men and "continued to hold the situation", while Landau "attended to the removal of the dead and injured, personally rescuing many of the wounded and organising their removal to hospital in improvised ambulances."[202] Apparently he missed two. Mr. Allan was knocked unconscious and came round to find himself lying amid the debris, smothered in fine oil and with his helmet gone again. He was struck by the profound silence, though possibly this was the effect of blast on his ear-drums. Finding an injured fireman nearby, he helped him to the dock entrance where he waved down a car to take the man to hospital in Bootle. Allan then walked into town to report what had happened.

As the *Mahout's* stern swung back towards the quay, a bollard was successfully lassoed and the ship properly tied up again. The crew were also occupied in putting out a number of fresh fires. Then, to the general surprise, the *Malakand's* men (less Allan) were sighted on the quay. (It is not clear whether the Lascars off the *Malakand* had been called from their shelter, but some of the *Malakand's* crew were on the *Mahout* already.)

Campbell and the *Malakand's* third mate were soon engaged in first aid work as men with minor injuries queued up to have them washed in the scullery and then dressed in the galley. Towards nine o'clock, there was a second explosion on the *Malakand* that sent a piece of shrapnel clean through scullery and galley without touching any of the men crowded inside.

This second blast was too much for the Lascars on the *Mahout*, who broke and ran. They commandeered the adjacent coaster and steamed off rapidly round the dock. They were recovered over the next couple of weeks except for some who were killed in the raids that followed.[203] (According to Brocklebank's records, one Lascar off the *Malakand* and three off the *Mahout* were reported killed or missing) This incident was unfortunate as, had they but known it, all danger was now past. The Lascars had worked through the night, under fire, doing as much as anyone to prevent the *Mahout* from going the way of the *Malakand*.

Although the second explosion was not so bad as the first, it was quite bad enough. Once again debris was scattered over a wide area: fragments of the ship and her cargo, pulverised dock sheds and their contents. Twisted steel plates, hatch-beams and ventilators turned up in unlikely places. A Javanese seaman on the *Moena* was slightly injured, while the shed doors were blown off again onto the quay – except for the one caught on the davit. A Lascar on the *Clan MacWhirter* was killed by another flying shed door and a cart-horse three quarters of a mile off in Boundary Street was sliced in two. One of the white-hot ship's plates caught an Austin Seven passing Huskisson on the dock road, killing a man and his wife inside. When Mr. Allan came back, already in a state of shock, his attention was drawn to the burnt-out wreck by a policeman. After taking one look at the two incinerated bodies inside, he reeled away, sickened, to the *Mahout*.

Huskisson No. 2 Branch, looking east from the hole blown in the quayside. Beyond the twisted girders of the *Malakand*, the *Van Orley* is at the east quay, with the Overhead Railway and molasses tanks beyond. The sheds on the right belong to North Huskisson 1.

On the Overhead Railway at the east end of Huskisson 2, looking north to Canada Dock station, with the dock road on the right. The fire is probably one of those started on the night of 7th/8th May.

What of the promised tender? In his published account, Captain Kinley says that it "duly arrived, but the ship exploded before anyone could approach to sink her." This is odd because other reports, including an earlier one by Kinley himself, make no reference to this belated arrival. It is clear that no special appliance van came up the dock avenue at the last minute.

An explanation is offered by Jim Burke, then a seaman on the ***Salvor***– which might be described as a tender. He remembers reporting for duty at about 0800. Volunteers were called for ("You, you and you") and half an hour later Mr. Burke was one of a team, largely composed of divers, climbing the river wall at Huskisson with cutting equipment. The ***Malakand*** exploded before they were over the top, fortunately – for them – blowing mostly inland. If Mr. Burke's recollection of the time is correct (and 0800 sounds right for the change of watch) then this could only be the second explosion. No explanation for the delay has come to light, though one can imagine that if the "special tender" originally promised was a Fire Brigade vehicle, it may well have been caught in some inaccessible part of the city.

Huskisson No. 2 Branch was now a scene of total devastation. The ***Malakand*** was a pile of scrap, only a few twisted girders showing above water. Several of the smaller craft in the branch that had contrived to remain afloat were burning. The elevator had part of its tower blown away, possibly by the second explosion – one reason why ships in the vicinity suffered less than the sheds must be that the former could ride the blast. This did not apply so much when they were on the bottom. The ***No. 20 Hopper/Watchful*** was burnt out and struck by an anchor, which crashed through the engine-room skylight to land on the cylinder heads. (Similar events elsewhere resulted in quite substantial vessels being cast up on the quaysides; it may be that the fall in the water level prevented the same from happening here.)

The sheds on all three sides of the branch were totally demolished; in fact, those on the north quay disappeared altogether, leaving hardly a trace of rubble or a stump of wall. The larger sheds beyond were badly battered, especially about the roofs and doors.[204]

The Overhead Railway was severely shaken and deluged with Lever Brothers' soap.[205] (The quantities of green soap that littered the scene were noted by several observers. In one place it formed a compacted mass like a termite mound.) The top of a mast or flagstaff adorned the roof of Canada Dock Station, and a flying bollard bounced once on a rail, bending it down, with the iron track-bed beneath, into a neat 'V' shape.

Premises at 44 Derby Road, some 650 yards from the ***Malakand***, were badly damaged by debris and blast, and large sections of the roof burnt as a result. Part of the building contained a store of ammonia gas in cylinders, some of which were pierced and the gas lost. Three quarters of a mile off, No. 5 gas-holder at Athol Street was hit and set alight in numerous places, all the gas being lost. A four-ton winch landed in Stanley Park, a mile and a half away. The two sixty-foot high storage tanks of the United Molasses Company, conspicuous across the road from the end of Huskisson 2, survived, but their roofs collapsed. Debris fell on the small ship repair works of C & H Crichton Ltd. at the south end of Derby Road. (Work here was only held up for two days – by an unexploded bomb.)[206]

The ***Lobos***, in Canada 1, was among the vessels damaged by shed doors, and the ***Maasdam***, in Huskisson 1, suffered in much the same way as the ***Mahout*** with the loss of windows and hatch-covers and other superficial damage. The ***Busiris*** reported "fires and severe damage...These fires practically covered the ***Busiris***, but were extinguished by the crew before damage was done. Many pieces of iron were thrown up from the ***Malakand*** and surrounding sheds, and several of these landed on the ***Busiris***, smashing No. 1 derrick and fittings. Damage was done to beams in No. 1 hold, and all doors in the vessel were blown in, starboard lifeboat was damaged and minor damage caused around deck."[207] There were no casualties among the crew. (If these vessels *had* been evacuated, it is likely that some of them would have been lost.)

All this was directly attributable to one or other of the explosions on the ***Malakand*** and there must have been a great deal more. Attributing damage to the ***Malakand*** is not easy though, as the area concerned had already been bombed heavily that night and would be again before the week was out. An attempt was made at doing so in 1942/3 (the RAF wanted to know the effects of heavy air raids on a port and the fortuitous results of an ammunition ship exploding had to be eliminated as far as possible). The documents relating to the ***Malakand*** are not among those preserved in the Public Record Office, however, and appear to have been destroyed.[208]

It seems reasonable to list some likely candidates. The reports of damage to ships could no doubt be repeated for all vessels in the immediate vicinity; it is probable that the misfortunes of the following were mostly due to the ***Malakand***. The ***Skirmisher*** had her bridge blown off and one man killed – this may have happened during the night, but she was also skewered by a length of mast when the ***Malakand*** went up. The ***Waiwera*** was slightly damaged in Canada 1. The barge ***Emily Burton***, carrying sugar, was sunk at North Huskisson 3 by the weight of debris that landed on her. In Huskisson 2 the burnt barge ***Walton*** was further damaged by masonry and the flat ***Ellesport*** was sunk. The sailing barge ***Limpet*** had all her woodwork burnt in

Huskisson, probably in company with her sister barge ***Ling***, which was completely destroyed by fire. The floating crane ***Samson*** suffered extensive damage to her deck fittings.[209]

Sheds were severely damaged about the roofs and doors at South Canada 1, North Wellington, and all round Sandon. Similar damage occurred at the two nearest railway goods stations, Canada and Sandon. The wrecking of Grayson Rollo's Sandhills premises must have been initiated by the bombs and that of Charles Howson & Co. by the fires that have already been referred to. At the latter, the whole central block – "offices with electricians' shop over, platers' shop, saw mill and joiners' shop, compressor and motor house and smith's store and 2 blocks of stores on the South side"[210] – was completely demolished. Everything else seems to have been damaged by blast or fire, the framework of machines in the plumbers' and sheet metal shops being bent.

The timber yards that occupied much of the land to the east were, of course, already on fire. It seems that much of the surrounding area was evacuated after the explosion – some of it possibly earlier – with fires being left to burn as a result.

The casualties caused are also a mystery. The Dock Board's figure is four dead, including the two in the car: certainly an under-statement, but by how much it is impossible to say – the citation in the ***London Gazette*** (a publication not given to exaggeration) refers to "many deaths." Six have been mentioned above. Fourteen civilian deaths were reported at Huskisson on the 4th, which is substantially more than for any other dock.

A boy travelling around with a mobile canteen from Bootle, looked in at the north entrance to the dock and found a brick shelter by the Overhead Railway with the door broken. Inside were five men that he took to be dockers – all asleep. When he commented on this, a companion pointed out that they were dead – evidently from blast. The ***Malakand*** is a likely cause, but the explosion of at least one mine in the area makes it impossible to be sure. (The boy was also impressed by the sight of half-a-dozen Bedford army lorries on the dock, with all the canvas and rubber burnt off.)

The full total *may* have been more like twenty or thirty, but there is no evidence to suggest that it would be much more than that.

It is a pity that all this was not prevented, as it apparently might have been. It is also a pity that the reports and inquiry that must surely have followed have not been made public.

At the end of the week, Sir L. A. P. Warner issued the following "Instructions to Dock Masters." "Immediate steps are to be taken for all vessels in seaworthy condition in the various Docks to be in a position to be hove off the quay at least 50 feet at any time when necessary. For this purpose the Dock Masters should inform the Masters and Shore Superintendents at their respective Systems that wires or ropes should be run every night before dark and where necessary taken in again the following morning at daylight. For the purpose of heaving vessels off, auxiliary steam should be maintained through all the dark hours and the necessary complement of men for this operation to be on board."[211] It is difficult to avoid the conclusion that what could now be made compulsory ought not to have been forbidden before. Otherwise, there is no evidence for any worse culprits than the confusion of the night and the honest mistakes of men doing their best in conditions of appalling difficulty and danger.

A number of awards followed these events. They included: the George Medal, to Lappin; the BEM, to Landau, auxiliary firemen Henry Hodges and James Roach, Ismail Mohamed, and C. W. White (who also received the silver medal of the Liverpool Shipwreck and Humane Society); and Commendations to Kinley and Scoins. The Merchant Marine seems to have received something less than its due – Lappin said as much – though Allan and Exley of the ***Malakand's*** officers were later awarded the MBE for services including this incident.[212] Comparison of these awards with those arising from a couple of other incidents recounted in this book suggests that the distribution of honours is a subject as fathomless as the distribution of penalties in magistrates' courts. (Brocklebank's directors had a small silver medallion prepared for the ***Malakand's*** crew, to commemorate their conduct.)

I cannot leave this subject without alluding to some improbable stories that have been told about it. ***Port at War*** would have us believe that: "The ship took 74 hours to blow herself out." There is no hint of this in Brocklebank's records, and people who strolled round the site within that time are surprised at the suggestion. Certainly no-one on the ***Mahout*** or the ***Moena*** seems to have noticed. From the same source we learn that the blast from the ***Malakand*** plucked a rail from the Overhead and drew it back to hit the jib of the ***Samson.*** There is a genuine record of the ***Samson*** being struck by bits of the Overhead when the line was hit in December. (***Port at War*** also turns the Ellerman's Wilson Line freighter ***Silvio*** into an imaginary Dock Board salvage boat called ***Silvo.***)

A story that has appeared in print a couple of times recently has it that a foreman stevedore boarded the ***Malakand***, went below to feel the bulkhead of No. 1 hold, and came up to warn everyone that it was hot and the ship was about to explode – which it did a few moments later. If it had been possible to adapt this story to the facts recorded in Brocklebank's records, Captain Kinley's reports, and information supplied by survivors whose presence in the vicinity is on record, I should have done so, but frankly it is

Howson's, just across the dock road from Huskisson South 2 sheds. A notice directs enquirers to a temporary office in Rumford Street. Incidentally, the main building seems to have been a striking, if somewhat premature, example of "Post Modernist" architecture.

not. It is not uncommon for genuine exploits to attach themselves to the ***Malakand***, which is the name that everyone knows; the ***Samson*** incident above is an example and this may be another.

It is only fair to add that a letter to the ***Echo***[213] suggests that men "clearing up the rubble" at Grayson Rollo's works were told to run when they got warning that the ***Malakand*** was about to blow. In due course a man "dashed into the yard and shouted: 'Beat it, boys. She's going up any time.'" I am surprised that rubble-clearance should have been considered a sufficiently urgent job to be done under these conditions, and that it should have been organised so soon on the Sunday morning (there is no suggestion that rescue work was involved). It is also worthy of note that there is in this case no claim that any explosion followed. I suspect a practical joke a day or so later.

More likely to be true is Mr. Campbell's story about Captain Kinley. It seems that when he was discharged from hospital three weeks later, his first job was to take a ship up the Manchester Ship Canal. Concerned that an injured finger might have impaired his skill as a conjurer (he was a member of the Magic Circle), he stood on the bridge practising with a matchbox to get his hand in again (now you see it – now you don't). The Canal pilot was so enthralled by this performance that he nearly ran them aground.

A. W. J. Holland was fifteen at the time, living on the front at Seacombe. With the 'all-clear', the family left the air raid shelter and looked across the river to see Liverpool in flames from Formby to Garston – or so it seemed. Father left for work at 0630; he was captain of the ***Kenfinch***, now moored at the west end of Huskisson 2. At 0745 the rest of the family were sitting down to breakfast when the front window was blown in; there was no glass broken, but the whole frame was nudged a few inches inward. After a while, rumours of trouble at Huskisson reached the house and Mrs. Holland asked her son to go and see if his father was all right.

He left at nine, or half past, and caught the Seacombe Ferry to Liverpool. Finding the dock road blocked by a fallen warehouse at the Pier Head entrance to the road tunnel, he walked into Prince's Dock and made his way along by the river wall. Seeing no-one along the way, he came to the south-west corner of Huskisson at about 1030 and walked round to the landward end of Huskisson 2. The mess here was indescribable, with smoke all around, small craft burning, and oil ablaze on the water. There was no sign of the ***Kenfinch***, but he was able to pass up the north side of the branch and on reaching the end, saw her moored at the north-west corner of the dock. This meant another trek round No. 3 branch.

The ***Kenfinch***, when he reached her, was held by one rope at the bow and was down by the head, with the upper works stripped off and the hatch covers missing. The boy shinned down the rope to find the fo'c'sle half full of water and the engine room partly flooded. There was a cap and a packet of sandwiches on the fiddley, but no sign of his father or anyone else.

He returned to the quay and noticed a similar boat, the ICI packet ***Francis Poole***, moored a little further along with her stove-pipe smoking. Hoping to find someone who knew what had happened, he went to her and shouted. The only reply came from a policeman behind – hardly recognisable as such, as he was black from head to foot, caked in dirt and oil, his eyes "two red orbs in his face." The boy explained his quest, to be told that there was no-one about now and all the injured had been taken off. The constable advised him to get the hell out of it as there were unexploded bombs and shells all around.

Disappointed and none the wiser, the boy returned the way he had come to find that the ferries had stopped running. Instead, there was a minesweeper trawling the river. Along with other people he walked through the Mersey Tunnel, using the dock entrances, and had reached his own road when he met his father just setting out to look for *him*. Finding the roads blocked, Mr. Holland had never reached the ***Kenfinch***.

They learned later that Harry Riley, the engineer, had been in the hold putting a fire out when the explosion came. He was plucked out and thrown on the quay badly injured. The ***Kenfinch*** had broken adrift and been recovered and tied up by the men of the ***Francis Poole***.

It was not only in the river that mines needed sweeping; two of the three that had landed in the docks south of the Pier Head on Friday night were still there, blocking all movement till they were dealt with. Among the naval mine experts sent from HMS ***Vernon***, was Lieutenant J. S. Mould – an Australian. On the Sunday morning he was taken by Commander MS (minesweepers) to Salthouse, which contained few vessels of any consequence, to deal with the first. The technique for disarming mines in docks was crude, but had been found effective. First the mine was pin-pointed by dragging the dock with wire ropes; then a charge was exploded nearby to knock out the delicate magnetic mechanism, so rendering the mine safe for disposal whenever convenient.

On this occasion Mould had just got his charge ready to take out in a dinghy when another Australian lieutenant hurried to the scene – 'Digger' Fayne of Bomb Disposal. In appropriate language, Fayne asked Mould to desist from exploding his charge, which, would very probably also set off the bomb that he and his men were about to deal with 300 yards off. Since Mould could do no more till Fayne's bomb was seen to, he went to have a look at the other man's problem.

"Fayne took Mould through a line of railway trucks along the dockside, where the smoke of the night's fires still drifted, where water from fire hoses still lay in wide puddles and where a working party abruptly came into view. They stepped, Fayne and Mould, from between the trucks and there the men were, one hundred paces distant – five ratings and a petty officer. Fayne waved and the petty officer returned the wave and the bomb exploded.

In the frozen instant before Mould flung himself down, the earth squirted flame and smoke and debris and human bodies. The bodies hurled upwards and outwards, cartwheeling in death. One body came down over the bows of a ship and seemed even to grab at the anchor cable, the final convulsion of a life already gone."

Mould had to return to his mine. He placed the charge and detonated it from a safe distance. All went well and he declared Salthouse Dock safe for traffic. The Commander then showed him his next job, a mine that turned out to be almost in the dead centre of Canning Half-Tide. The same procedure was followed. Mould rowed out in the dinghy to recover his equipment and returned to report to the Commander that this dock too was now safe.

"Instantly a shattering explosion blasted both men flat on the dock. An immense column of water and mud cracked over their heads and rained down by the ton and it continued to fall for many seconds."

It was mysterious as well as embarrassing. An acoustic mine would have gone off when snagged by the wire. A magnetic one *might* have been set off by the charge – or conceivably by a passing ship later if the charge had failed, but there was no accounting for this. The dock was empty, so apart from the dock bottom and the gates to Albert there was little serious damage, but Mould had to advise that Salthouse be closed again.

After cleaning up, he was taken to see Admiral Sir Percy Noble, C-in-C Western Approaches, in Derby House. From his office, Mould was able to ring ***Vernon*** to seek advice (the line was either independent or a priority for repair). He was told that the only thing to do was repeat the standard procedure for the Salthouse mine and declare the dock safe. As he was ordered to proceed at once to a job in Barrow-in-Furness, Mould left the Commander MS to see to this and went north feeling not altogether happy with the situation.[214]

During the day, two more mines exploded spontaneously in the river mouth.[215] The ***Clarecastle***, bringing urgently needed supplies from Dublin, was admitted to the Half-Tide Dock, but was unable to moor at the Guinness berth in Salthouse until the 7th.

According to the records of the Mersey Railway, windows at their Mann Island pumping station were damaged by a "heavy explosion" at 0750 and the engine-room door was "blown out of its guides" by another at 0840. This was all but two miles from Huskisson 2 and surely well sheltered from blast by intervening property. It seems more likely that the explosions recorded by Lieutenant Mould were responsible.

The fourth mate on the ***Tacoma Star***, Denis Foss, had spent the night in a Bootle Hotel – the Windham, Oriel Road – with his wife until the window was blown in onto the bed. Having made fresh arrangements for Mrs. Foss, he set off for Canada Dock to see how his ship was. On attempting to cross the railway at Miller's Bridge, he was stopped by a man who advised him that it had been blown up. Foss insisted that he had to get to his ship, and the man suggested that he try the subway under Oriel Road Station. When Foss expressed doubt, the man explained that he was Kelly, the Mayor of Bootle, and ought to know. His advice proved sound, although Berry Street, to which the subway led, was "burning from end to end".

On reaching Canada, Foss had to persuade the policeman on the gate to let him past and then pick his way through the unexploded bombs to the ship, which had settled on the bottom at 0930. Most of the accommodation remained above water, if at an odd angle, and it was necessary to keep her manned, so Foss relieved the third mate. Smoke was still rising on all sides and a dirty tide-mark appeared round the dock where clean stone was exposed by the falling water. (The east bank of the river must have presented an appalling sight in the daylight, with black smoke being shovelled up from fires large and small. I find it remarkable that no photographs seem to have been taken of the scene. Unofficial photography was of course discouraged, but if anyone has such pictures taken surreptitiously from behind the bedroom curtains in Wallasey, it ought to be safe to bring them out now.

In Canada 2 the ***Bra-Kar*** was well alight and sinking slowly, stern first. In Canada 3, firemen kept pouring water into the ***Domino*** until 1500, by which time she was burnt out, smouldering, and wallowing deep in the water. Tugs were brought in to push her away from the coaling quay and back to her former berth on the south side, turning her round in the process. Around Huskisson there was a lot of patching up to be done – the crewless ***Mahout***, without her hatch-covers, would be in serious danger from any further raids. Help arrived in the form of a working party from HMS ***Reading*** in Gladstone and she was safely battened down before nightfall.

Mr. T. J. Sloan later recalled being one of a number of dockers awaiting work at Brocklebank Dock when Inspector Skelton appeared and asked for volunteers. Sloan and others went along, loaded sandbags onto a horse-drawn wagon, and then deposited them – carefully – over an unexploded bomb in a crater near to a ship under repair; this under the supervision of Skelton and a naval officer.[216] It sounds rather like the UXB by Langton Graving Docks.

In Gladstone, the struggle to keep the tug ***Bison*** afloat failed and she sank towards 0700.

Delayed action bombs continued to go off at odd times and quite often in unexpected places – there were several killed in one such incident in Fraser Street, off London Road. The wagons at Breck Road Sidings went on exploding at intervals through the day; after returning to Edge Hill, Peter Kilshaw volunteered to go back to the sidings with a fire train and continued his work as a pointsman. It appears to have been impossible to prevent the destruction of the entire ammunition train, which gouged a trench over 250 yards long that incorporated the running lines. The block of property around Worcester Drive was so badly shaken that it remained uninhabited for some time,[217] and lesser damage was widespread. It has been claimed that St. Margaret's Church School in Rocky Lane, just over half a mile away, suffered damage, in which case damage to the roofs and chimney stacks of Belmont Road Hospital was very likely caused the same way. Extraordinarily enough, it appears that no-one was killed in this incident.

Some white material was wafted a considerable distance by the wind, drifting around the streets and hanging like blossom on some improbable trees. It has been positively identified as cotton, cotton-wool, and gun-cotton; considering the possible variety of goods in the sidings, these suggestions are not mutually exclusive.

Experience at other times suggests that fresh fires must have been breaking out all day in damaged areas of the city.

In London, it was known that things were bad in Liverpool, but the failure of communications left ARP Headquarters largely in the dark about what was happening. Their records include the entry: "A ship in Husskison (sic) Dock, containing defused bombs, was set on fire and the bombs have been exploding."[218] (This subject is not touched upon at all in later reports.)

The Regional Commissioner, Sir Harry Haig, set out from his HQ in Manchester in the morning to see for himself what was going on. He was disturbed to find "large areas of the docks still on fire with no fire appliances there at all and nobody attempting to put them out."[219] (It is not clear to what extent this refers to the area around Huskisson.) Sir Harry held a meeting at noon in the Municipal Annexe to discuss the situation, at which it was noted that there were "2,000 to 3,000 homeless at present" for whom thirty rest centres had been opened. A representative from the Ministry of Information was there, and noted local resentment of "intrusion" by Government Departments. He would have liked to talk to Liverpool's "Emergency Information Officer", but that official had not been called to the meeting by the Town Clerk – who did not think that the envisaged emergency had yet arisen.[220]

In Bootle on the other hand – where the Town Clerk *was* the Emergency Information Officer – the MoI was called in at once. Mobile loud-speaker vans were sent there from Manchester: "and all day Sunday they toured the town giving the dazed populace information on cooking, billeting, and other matters."[221] For part of the time these vans were accompanied by the Mayor or an Alderman.

One thing Sir Harry was able to organise was a link between Liverpool and Manchester using police wireless, which seems to imply that this facility had not been used earlier.

Public transport was virtually non-existent. There were not many buses available to provide an alternative to the crippled tramways, and while more were called in from neighbouring operators, they were put to more urgent uses for now.

Joe Kinsella lived in Barmouth Street (off Boundary Street, near Athol Street Gas Works) – an area that had been badly hit. He and others went to Hatton Garden to press for transport to be laid on to get people out to rest centres. This arrived in the form of about ten buses with open staircases at the back – not as antique as it sounds, as this fashion was retained longer in London from where buses had been obtained to run workers to the ordnance factory at Kirkby. They eventually took everyone who wanted to go, though there was some unpleasantness when the conductor of the last bus raised an untimely objection to people standing. The bus left absolutely packed, but without the officious conductor.

Hundreds of people with children and bundles of clothing gathered around Stanley Road Hospital and in the playground at Daisy Street School, from where they had heard that evacuation would be arranged to Walton Village. They were disappointed as no transport appeared, and there was no-one there to give advice or control the situation. One by one, they gave up waiting and either returned home or hitched lifts if they could.[222]

Some made their own way out on foot – to Prescot or St. Helens – though apparently not many at this stage. The St. Helens rest centres catered for 200 that night. This unofficial night-time evacuation – 'trekking' as it was called – was frowned on by authority, but invariably occurred in places that were heavily attacked. It was by no means a local phenomenon.

Late in the day it was reported that there had been 200 incidents requiring Rescue Parties. Thirty of these were still outstanding at noon, of which nine were believed to involve the living.[223] At Mill Road, a woman was taken out alive at 0810. Rescue

Parties and the Pioneer Corps worked on till 2005, by which time thirty-five bodies had been recovered. Peculiar stress was caused at this incident by the failure (entirely understandable) to keep a record of which of three hospitals the survivors had been moved to. Anxious relatives thus had to traipse round the hospitals – and perhaps the mortuary – in the hope of finding their loved ones. In spite of this, observers noted a striking absence of hysteria.[224]

3,000 military personnel were reported to be assisting in traffic control and 400 in clearance of debris (these figures appear to have been transposed). Another 1,900 were expected by Monday evening along with 350 lorries.[225] The 5th Battalion, Suffolk Regiment, stationed at Huyton, were then on exercise around Skipton; 200 were sent back to help with clearance work on the 4th, increased to 450 on the next two days. The 260 officers and men of the 560th Field Company, Royal Engineers, were training in Croxteth and Knowsley Parks (learning to deal with parachute landings). All were brought into Liverpool on the 4th: to help generally in repairing damage, to assist the Fire brigade in repairing appliances, and to lay surface pipelines. "Worked with and helped AFS and Fire Brigade in their efforts and found them to be a magnificent crowd indeed." The Company was fully engaged in this work till the 15th.[226]

The 159th Field Ambulance – an Army unit – sent ambulances, stretcher bearers and dispatch riders, the last to maintain communications between the various hospitals inside and outside the city.[227] (2,435 patients were sent out of Liverpool and Bootle during the week.) Stretcher bearers were always in short supply, and the Army men did the work in about a third of the time taken by enthusiastic volunteers.

Thirty Mutual Aid Parties were drafted in from as far as Rochdale and Bury. One such party was put to work at Towson Street; they were volunteers and worked efficiently, but the leader expressed a desire not to spend the night in Liverpool. Permission to leave was refused, but they went anyway.[228]

In Liverpool, most of the utilities had been restored by nightfall, though gas was at reduced pressure. The restoration of the telephone services was a slow business, but some trunk lines were reported open to Lancaster House (which had itself been hit again). A start had been made on the laying of salt water mains from the river into the town – probably on a very limited scale at first. They were a nuisance to traffic and impossible for trams. Some felt they ought to have been provided earlier, but, while they might have been of some use the night before, they still needed spare pumps to push the water through them.

It was thought that Liverpool's emergency feeding scheme would be operating satisfactorily in the morning, but Bootle still had no gas or electricity for this purpose. At 0530 the Queen's Messenger Convoy in Manchester received a call for their services from Bootle. They arrived before seven – a water tanker, kitchen lorry, food store and two mobile canteens, manned by the Manchester WVS with some Manchester Transport drivers. By noon they were serving hot food and tea to the homeless, firemen and ARP workers. A similar convoy was thoughtfully sent to Liverpool. Bootle's own five canteens were in use and there were others from outside; for several days one or two came from Blackpool – at first accompanied by a van with a reserve stock of bread and butter and bully-beef.[229]

The position with regard to fire service reinforcements is obscure, Birmingham being (as yet) the only place known to have useful records. The first call to that area, at 0552, had been for three Special List Officers to go to Bootle Fire Brigade HQ. These were senior officers who had volunteered to go wherever they were needed – a facility not often used. They left at 0740. At 1211 Birmingham was told to send ten pumps and crews to Altrincham by 2000, where they were to stand by for Merseyside. Fifty more men left for St. Helens at 1910 (to relieve those who were fit to drop after long hours on duty). At 2004 five pumps and crews left for Altrincham, followed by another twenty men at 2040.[230] Similar demands were made of this and other towns and cities as the week wore on.

When night came, there were six large fires still burning as well as many smaller ones.

SHIPPING MOVEMENTS – 4th MAY

Inward	*G.T.*	*From*	*Outward*	*G.T.*	*To*
GEZINA	1828	Digby (Nova Scotia) to Garston	**PARDO**	5400	Rio Grande
MARGALAU	4541	Buenos Aires*			
NAGPORE	5283	Hong Kong*			
NIGERIAN	5423	Burutu (Nigeria)* to Manchester			
NORMANDY COAST	1428	Belfast			
STAD ARNHEM	3819	Takoradi (Gold Coast)* to Garston			

* Convoy sailed from Freetown on 8th April.

NIGHT – 4th/5th MAY

SUNSET 2146
BLACKOUT 2231
ALERT 2358-0426
BLACKOUT ENDS 0546
SUNRISE 0631
MOONLIGHT TO 0300

Sunday night's raid was a good deal lighter – 53 aircraft / 57 tons HE / 11,560 incendiaries – but quite enough to stoke up the fires that were still burning. The Luftwaffe's main target was Belfast, and Barrow-in-Furness was also visited. Many of the bombers flying to these places passed over Liverpool so that the guns opened fire about an hour before anything was dropped locally. There was scattered damage in Wallasey, where three were killed at Mostyn Street, and also in Birkenhead. Some HE fell on Aintree Racecourse and caused extensive damage to the Union Cold Storage premises nearby. Between 0125 and 0155 a number of HE bombs fell on Crosby, near to the Bootle boundary, without actually killing anyone. Bootle got off lightly, with some incendiaries and five HE bombs reported; though several of these landed on Linacre Gas Works, cutting mains, demolishing the fitting-shop and detarrer-house, and damaging a purifying house.[231]

The attack on Liverpool opened soon after 0100, with incendiaries and HE starting some serious fires around Everton. St. Sylvester's RC School in Silvester Street (next to the church hit the night before) was one of the first casualties, losing its infants and junior sections to fire. At Athol Street Gas Works, No. 2 holder was pierced by a flying fragment and all the gas lost; later in the night No. 4 holder was completely destroyed by another near miss. George Hadfield's fertilizer and vitriol works in Lightbody Street was also badly damaged. Just opposite to Canada Dock, the six-storey Bankfield Cold Store in Brunswick Place (350,000 cubic feet) was being prepared by the Ministry of Food in case other such stores were lost. Now that its moment had come, it was completely gutted – though better while it was still empty than later.[232]

The Fountains Road area suffered for the third night running when one of the few parachute mines of the night landed on Walton Lane Council School at 0140. It demolished a third of the buildings and half the remainder was gutted in the fire that followed. The Rotunda Theatre in Scotland Road was another fire loss shortly after 0200 (it seems not to have been in use *as* a theatre at this time). It had been a prominent Everton landmark and remained a useful reference point long after its destruction. The records are not always clear as to the allocation of railway damage between Saturday night and Sunday night (not to mention Sunday morning), but it appears to have been during this raid that Sandhills Station was hit and the central and east platforms badly burnt.[233]

The attack soon widened to affect other parts of the city. The worst incident was at Great George Square, where the declining splendour of a Georgian terrace was shattered by HE at 0130. The worst-affected property was being used as a boarding house for Belgian seamen, but it would be some time before the dead here were brought out and counted. Littlewood's parachute factory in Oldham Place, off Roscoe Street, suffered when the building next door to it was hit, production being restricted for a few weeks.

One of the mobile canteens from Manchester tangled with a delayed-action bomb and returned to base at 0700 "with their radiator cover blown off, their windscreen blown in, and the body of the canteen riddled with shrapnel."[234]

It was a much less hectic night along the docks, though ***Adventure's*** log[235] records the fall of a heavy bomb at 0100 on the north quay of Canada Dock that threw a large amount of debris over the ship. It also dug a considerable hole in the quay and threw a crane into the dock where it narrowly missed ***Adventure. Maplin's*** stern ropes parted and had to be replaced. The ***Euthalia*** (3,553), unloading wheat at East Brunswick, was damaged by a near miss while, further south, incendiaries fell around the oil tanks at Dingle, to be dealt with by the staff, police and soldiers. One such bomb actually penetrated a tank full of petrol without igniting it.

In Albert Dock, Nicholas Monsarrat was back on HMS *Campanula.* "Hoses were rigged, sand-buckets filled and placed, wires run out to the opposite side of the dock in case the tall building alongside should take fire." The advisability of the last precaution had been learned by experience and it was carried out in disregard of Dock Board rules unless the Navy was a law to itself in such matters. "It wasn't one of the worst raids; but it sufficed, it passed muster. We had a number of incendiary bombs on the fo'c'sle and on the warehouses alongside: some near-misses which fell in the dock made a disconcerting whistling sound. But the barrage, which had obviously been added to, was one of the most formidable things I had ever listened to; and at intervals the night-fighter boys tried their hand, the bursts of machine-gun fire being applauded by the crew. Then dawn, and a respite, and hot whisky all round."[236]

The ***Silversandal*** was still at anchor in the river; between 0200 and 0300 she was hit by a bomb that exploded on the weather deck abaft the engine-room. Four men were injured; of three who had to be sent ashore for treatment, one died soon after.[237] Fire started among the aircraft on deck and was extinguished only to break out later – the ***Vigilant*** assisted in bringing this under control.[238]

The main attack ended at 0215 and the AA batteries were ordered to stand down twenty minutes later – only to be called out again as the bombers that had passed over before returned the same way,[239] some of them still with bombs to dispose of after failing to find their primary targets. Not much was dropped in this second period – incendiaries fell in Everton at 0300 and south of the city centre soon after 0330, and there was some HE around the centre at 0400 – but over 5,000 rounds had been fired when the guns fell silent at last. Even relatively, this could hardly be called a quiet night. That the enemy should fly over a heavily defended area argues scant respect for the guns, though there was doubtless sound policy involved; when Liverpool was attacked, much of England lost sleep as a result.

All rescue operations arising from this raid were reported complete by 0900 with only six known to be dead in Liverpool. The gunners lost two men killed when a shell exploded prematurely, soon after leaving the barrel.[240]

MONDAY 5th MAY

Monday morning provided the first opportunity for the local press to cover Saturday night's raid, the ***Daily Post*** devoting a large part of its front page to the subject. The headlines were honest enough: "MASS NIGHT RAID ON MERSEYSIDE – CONSIDERABLE DAMAGE AND MANY CASUALTIES". Naturally, all the detail given concerns homes, hospitals, churches – but the ***Daily Post*** also quoted the Hun. The German News Agency stated that the raid was one of their heaviest on England and aided by "very favourable weather conditions."..."The harbour and dock installations along the Mersey were very heavily damaged and set on fire, and so also were large warehouses and industrial plants. In addition to many large and innumerable small fires one gigantic conflagration broke out the extent of which, it was declared, was greater than has ever been observed in night raids."..."The German High Command communiqué stated: 'Several hundred bombing planes last night attacked the important supply harbour of Liverpool for several hours with very good effects. In the harbour installations of the Eastern Mersey Bank, in dry docks, grain and wool warehouses, and other important military targets numerous great fires broke out.'"

These claims were not unreasonable and were passed on without comment or denial. ***The Times*** reported "Heavy Damage in Liverpool" in a very brief paragraph, and referred to the attack on the ports in its leader column. This also called for regional organisation of the fire services – part of a campaign that was rapidly coming to a head.

The increase in activity on this day – or at any rate the increase in *recorded* activity among the official classes – is noticeable; there is an air of everyone settling down to tackle the problems and get things moving again. (Far be it from me to suggest that the intervening day being a Sunday had anything to do with the time-lag.)

One action was prompt enough. At 0800, the destroyer HMS ***Viscount*** was ordered to Belfast "with any available trailer fire pumps."[241] (Another was sent from Glasgow.) At first sight this suggests that things must have been really bad across the Irish Sea, but Merseyside's fire services had, after all, drawn in reinforcements from a wide area. Belfast was not so well placed.

The Dock Board's main concern was with the potential for still worse disasters represented by several thousand tons of ammunition reposing in the holds of various ships.[242] The ***Pinto***, in West Alexandra, had 500 tons; an attempt at getting her out by the evening tide failed, but she was taken into the river on Tuesday and finally dispatched on Wednesday morning. The ***Silversandal***, with an unspecified quantity of ammunition, was still on fire in the river, but arrangements were made to get her to a crane in Birkenhead so that the aircraft could be taken off. She was not formally docked in Birkenhead until Tuesday, when the fire had been fully extinguished. The ***Mobeka***, in Queen's 2, carried safety ammunition and was not a problem. The ***Sicilian Prince***, in Birkenhead's West Float, contained a modest 60 tons and was to be got out as soon as possible.

Others were more worrying. The ***Glen Beg*** "loading in Vittoria Dock with 1,400 tons of high explosives urgently required for Singapore and Hong Kong", was due to complete loading on Thursday and could not be rushed. The ***Martand*** was in the East Float "with 1,500 tons of RAF explosives aboard" – thought to be highly dangerous. Sir Thomas Brocklebank was consulted about this vessel and strongly urged that she be got out by the evening tide; it proved possible to complete loading in time and this was done.

Curiously, there is no reference to the third of Brocklebank's trio – the ***Mahout*** – which was shunted from berth to berth for a few days. Mr. Campbell reports that one night she was berthed next to a ship of the City Line that began to loose off enthusiastic bursts of anti-aircraft fire during a raid. A message was sent suggesting that, in view of the ***Mahout's*** cargo, it was perhaps inadvisable to draw attention to the area. The other ship ceased fire and made a skilful and rapid departure through the nearest dock passage without benefit of tugs. (I am not *aware* of any other omissions.)

A committee set up to review the railway situation was chaired at its first meeting and several of the later ones by Ashton Davies, Vice President of the LMS.[243] The position that faced them would have been disastrous, were it not for the fact that the handling capacity of the docks had been reduced to a similar extent. Of the dozen or so principal goods stations along the docks, North Mersey, Alexandra, Canada and Great Howard Street were completely cut off from the main lines; Sandon and Waterloo were in the same case until certain UXBs were dealt with. North Docks and Langton seemed all right, subject to inspection, but Wapping was cut off from the dock lines by the fallen Overhead Railway – which also made it impossible to divert traffic to any great extent. Huskisson did not rate a mention, presumably because it could no longer be regarded as a principal station.

Arrangements were made for traffic from the north and east to be handled at outlying stations from the 6th: Seaforth, Walton Junction, Preston Road and Broad Green (also Stanley on the Bootle branch) with some others further out to spread the load. As many of the firms for which goods were arriving were no longer in a position to receive them, the scope for confusion was considerable. The three main passenger termini were also closed. There was still a fire burning at Exchange and damage to the approach viaduct remained an unknown quantity – it was at least partly caused by fire under the arches.

Priorities were established for clearance work, the Breck Road crater being high on the list. Two hundred infantrymen from the North and South Staffordshire Regiments were sent in to help the railway engineer's staff here.

Among the first of many officials sent north to see what was going on, was Wing Commander Hodsoll.[244] He arrived in Manchester on Sunday evening for preliminary talks with the Deputy Regional Commissioner, and drove into Liverpool the following morning.

His first impression was of chaos on the streets. There was no electricity in the city centre, so that trams were stranded in great numbers. They could not be towed away because of the profusion of parked cars – no attempt had been made to discourage private motorists from entering the city. (Apart from people coming in to work or to check on their loved ones and property, there were also a good many sightseers from outside the city.) Driving in from the East Lancashire Road: "we did not see one single policeman until we reached the main entrance to the Mersey Tunnel, where there was one traffic policeman and that was all. The result can be well imagined." (Where were the 400/3,000 soldiers?) Traffic to and from the docks was at a complete standstill.

In the centre, it was "like a bank holiday" – the streets crowded with sightseers and people who had found their offices damaged or non-existent. (At opposite ends of the social scale, the merchants of Cazneau Street Market and the Corn Exchange alike resorted to street trading.) "With the exception of Derby Square which was still burning, practically no effort was being made to keep people away. So-called barriers consisted literally of pieces of string, and although there was sometimes a policeman there, people were going backwards and forwards as they liked. The names of casualties had been posted up outside the Town Hall, the normal place for this purpose, but it was supposed to be in a cordoned off area and there were, incidentally, still bad fires raging. This caused large crowds to congregate in a place from which they should have been entirely excluded."

At noon, Hodsoll attended the Regional Commissioner's meeting at which these matters came up. "The Chief Constable apparently had little or no idea that there even was congestion going on, had obviously made no plans at all or even thought about it, and it was only when he was heavily attacked by the Regional Transport Commissioner that he was sent out, first of all to try and clear all the parking in the streets and secondly to introduce some sort of proper traffic control, if necessary with the help of the military." (Following Coventry's big raid in November, cordons were set up the morning after for this purpose.)

Winstanley then asked Sir Harry for powers to close off part of the city to traffic, only to be told that he and the Emergency Committee could do anything they liked. It is clear that this disagreeable scene still rankled when Winstanley wrote his post-war summary of these events, undoubtedly making use of reports written nearer the time. There was *no* real congestion! Dale Street was the only route to the Pier Head and had also to be used by traffic between the north and south docks. Horse-drawn vehicles slowed everything down, "giving the impression at times of a traffic block." And he still didn't think he'd had the authority to bar motor vehicles from the city centre.[245] The hapless Chief Constable was also criticised for being ignorant of the fire situation – he was after all 'Director of the Fire Brigade' as well. As the Chief Fire Officer was not present at the meeting, this subject remained obscure. Hodsoll noted that: "There was a great deal of smoke all over the city including the Mersey Tunnel and it was quite clear that the fire situation had been out of hand." It was equally clear that a lot of the damage was due entirely to this cause.

(The Flag Officer in Charge represented the Royal Navy at these meetings. In his opinion, "The outstanding fact which emerged from these deliberations was the proof that the fire-fighting service were unable to deal with the situation, and that fires could not be got under control in time to avoid their presenting targets to the enemy for attention on succeeding nights."[246] It was reported in London that: "The fire situation appears now to be well in hand and it is hoped all fires will be damped down by nightfall.")[247]

As to utilities, it was thought that electricity and gas supplies would be restored to normal in a few days; there were now large areas without gas – notably in Bootle, Kirkdale and the Scotland Road area. (The crematorium gas supply had been cut off. It was therefore "not available for the destruction of unidentifiable portions of the dead."[248] Electric facilities were eventually obtained.) Water was only lacking in a few places, but pressure was low – a problem if any more was needed for fire fighting. Many miles of surface piping had been laid, however, which would help. The restoration of telephone services was proceeding slowly, and Hodsoll observed that people seemed helpless when deprived of this service.

The food situation was not too bad, except that the destruction of bakeries had led to a shortage of bread – supplies had been ordered from Manchester. (Lord Woolton had arrived to look into this side of things. One of his contributions was to ask the Board of Trade to send emergency supplies of cigarettes for ARP workers – the shortage of tobacco after raids had an impact on morale that only smokers will fully appreciate.)

On some points the Inspector-General's report was favourable: 800 repair parties were already tackling first-aid repairs to houses, rescue work was efficient (the St. Brigid's Church incident in particular), and the meeting itself was a model of its kind with fifty or sixty people involved, all leaving as soon as their subject had been covered, and the whole thing over in about an hour. He found morale good, with only about 500 people described by a Ministry of Health official as 'windy' and trying to get out. Known fatalities in Liverpool from Saturday night were 406 – it was thought unlikely that the final figure would exceed 450. (The equivalent figure for Bootle was then 57.)

Liverpool's City Engineer reported to the Emergency Committee at a separate meeting.[249] There were 250 roads blocked and 3,600 men working to clear them, including 850 soldiers. (According to Home Security there were now 2,400 military clearing debris, with 350 vehicles, but this would doubtless cover all categories of work.) Rescue parties were still in action at nine incidents, of which those at Linnet Lane, Strand Street and Cairns Street were outstanding from Friday night. The others were all from Saturday: Hermia, Ceres and Warren Streets, Hamilton Road, Kirkdale Station and Mill Road.

At Mill Road, the work was now being done by rescue squads and soldiers, including a detachment of Royal Engineers in the morning. From 0800 to 1400 seven bodies of women and babies were recovered. Eight of the nine found from then to 2245 were men, bringing the total to 51.

The Chief Constable, having prepared his plans for cordons round the city, sought to advertise the fact in the local press – only to have his notices turned down by the censor. (He may have been able to do anything he liked, but he wasn't allowed to tell everyone about it. If he went home and kicked the cat that night, I think he might be forgiven.)

The Ministry of Information's loudspeaker vans might have helped, but apparently did not. They were called into Liverpool on this day, but were only able to give limited information on transport and notices from the Ministry of Labour owing to continuing reluctance on the part of the Liverpool authorities to make use of their services. In Bootle, where there was full co-operation, the vans were distributing sundry forms and travel vouchers and allotting billets. In Liverpool the vans were mobbed by people hoping for help and advice. "They gave what help they could, but had not nearly time or knowledge enough to deal with the situation properly."[250]

Along with a message of encouragement and sympathy from the Emergency Committee, that evening's ***Echo*** carried the Lord Mayor's appeal to the public "to avoid all unnecessary use of motorcars in the area." And that was all anyone knew until they tried driving into town next morning.

During the morning, at South Canada 1, the ***Domino*** turned over on her starboard side and sank at the quay. The ***No. 33 Hopper*** was reported still listing in West Waterloo; she turned over and sank soon after. The fighter-catapult ship ***Maplin*** has been mentioned. The RAF had chosen this day to set up the Merchant Ship Fighter Unit at Speke Airport – to provide the crews to fly the Sea Hurricanes that were the RAF's contribution to this project. Being at the south end, this operation was probably little affected by the raids. The catapult for training purposes arrived on the 8th and was in use by July. An RAF Hurricane was less fortunate, flying into a balloon cable at Runcorn in the afternoon. This one was not equipped with a lethal device and the fighter was able to land at Speke.

The theatrical event of the evening was the "Grand Gala Reopening" of Bootle's Metropole – a theatre/music-hall that had been closed for some time on account of war conditions. Billy West and his Harmony Boys led the cast of "Rations Unlimited" and there were spotlight prizes and surprise items to celebrate the occasion.

"Happy Go Lucky" opened at the Empire with Wee Georgie Wood, Tessie O'Shea, Rawicz and Landauer, and the John Tiller Girls among others.

It was announced that members of the AFS and ARP in uniform would be admitted free of charge for the week – though it may be doubted whether many found the time or the energy to take advantage of the offer.

In Litherland, all entertainments in connection with War Weapons Week were cancelled until Thursday.

That night rather more than 500 people from the worst-hit areas proved to be windy (or sensible). Transport difficulties had probably limited the 'trekking' movement at first, but large numbers were now walking out of the city; some to Rest Centres in Prescot and Huyton, some to find safety in the open fields. Their pessimism was not misplaced.

SHIPPING MOVEMENTS – 5th MAY

Inward	*G.T.*	*From*	*Outward*	*G.T.*	*To*
AGATHA	3369	Preston to Stanlow	**BARON RUTHVEN**	3178	Sydney (Nova Scotia)
TAHCHEE	6508	New York to Stanlow	**DALEBY**	4640	Lagos ex Manchester
			HIGHWEAR	1173	Cardiff
			PARTHENON	3189	Takoradi
			PINTO (per Lloyd's)	1346	Gibraltar
			RUNA	1575	Gibraltar ex Manchester

NIGHT – 5th/6th MAY

SUNSET 2148
BLACKOUT 2233
ALERT 0003-0407
BLACKOUT ENDS 0544
SUNRISE 0629
MOONLIGHT TO 0330

The main target on this night was Clydeside, with Belfast and Hull hit as well. Again, many of the planes over Liverpool were just passing to or from the first two of these. 27 bombers with 34 tons of HE and 6,228 incendiaries claimed to have attacked Liverpool – guided by fires still burning from earlier raids – and 2,528 rounds were fired by the guns.

Incendiaries caused a fire at Brotherton's Dye Works, Bromborough, at 0015; there were some small fires in Wallasey, and a few HE bombs fell on Birkenhead from 0045 to 0101. There were three reported killed here, and fires were started around the docks including one bad one at a fat warehouse in Cathcart Street and another at South Vittoria Dock. In West Kirby, at 0125, a house was damaged and two people injured by an AA shell.

On the Lancashire side one HE and a load of AA shells fell on Crosby, causing no casualties, and a UXB was noted at Aintree Racecourse – near Becher's Brook. Otherwise, the only areas affected were Liverpool city centre and points south, where there was a steady drizzle of HE and incendiary bombs for two hours. The first bombs were scattered from Islington to Abercromby Square from 0022. Places hit here included T. J. Hughes's store in London Road, St. Silas' Church in Pembroke Place, the Royal Infirmary – where one ward was badly damaged – and the Nurses' Home in Mulberry Street.

The Emido Flour Mills in Glasgow Street, just inland of Prince's Half-Tide Dock, were seriously damaged by HE at 0130. At about the same time trouble started around St. Nicholas' Church at the Pier Head, caused by incendiaries, oil bombs and – possibly – HE. The church had lost its roof in December; the remains were now burnt out, spelling the end for one of the city's most valuable links with the past. The nineteenth-century tower apart, the building was now a mere shell and was later demolished. The replacement was to be in somewhat half-hearted Gothic, but, like the Irishman's rifle, it remains the one surviving building that can be seen on the earliest views of the seminal fishing village. Fires at St. Nicholas' Building and Hargreaves Buildings only involved the roof timbers and upper floors, and all were out or under control by 0450.[251]

In the south docks there was fresh damage at South Canning, Duke's grain warehouse, West King's, Coburg Dock Yard, and the Brunswick Dock nitrate sheds, where fire broke out again after a hit by HE. An HE bomb landed behind the high brick retaining wall above the Park Lane end of Wapping Tunnel, blocking the line below with earth and rubble and so cutting off the goods station there at both ends. There were also fires at chemical works in Park Lane and Hardy Street (off St. James Street). At the half-finished Anglican Cathedral, incendiaries fell on a wooden shed containing stonemasons' and carpenters' equipment at about 0130. Four pumps were sent, including one from Featherstone, and the fire was out by 0330 – the shed was lost.[252] Further problems were created for the railways when the double-track tunnel leading to Crown Street Coal and Mineral Depot was pierced by an HE bomb that brought down twelve yards of the arch.[253]

The Bluecoat Building suffered more damage when the west wing was showered with bricks and girders from the adjacent premises, but the worst-hit area was around Renshaw Street, Bold Street and Duke Street, where serious fires were started. St. Luke's Church at the top of Renshaw Street was completely gutted; all the glass was lost, though it was noted that the flames provided a living, if temporary substitute. The shell was left just as it was after the war, as a memorial. (This has not prevented frequent threats of demolition. It seems a pity that the building has been cleaned and the rusting ruin of the clock replaced – a personal view.)

In Duke Street – at the end of Colquitt Street – the premises of the Liverpool Gas Company were hit by incendiaries at 0045. These were dealt with by the fire-watchers, but an HE bomb fell soon after and fire took firm hold. There was no water in the mains, and the Cornwallis Street baths just behind had been emptied in previous raids. As a result the

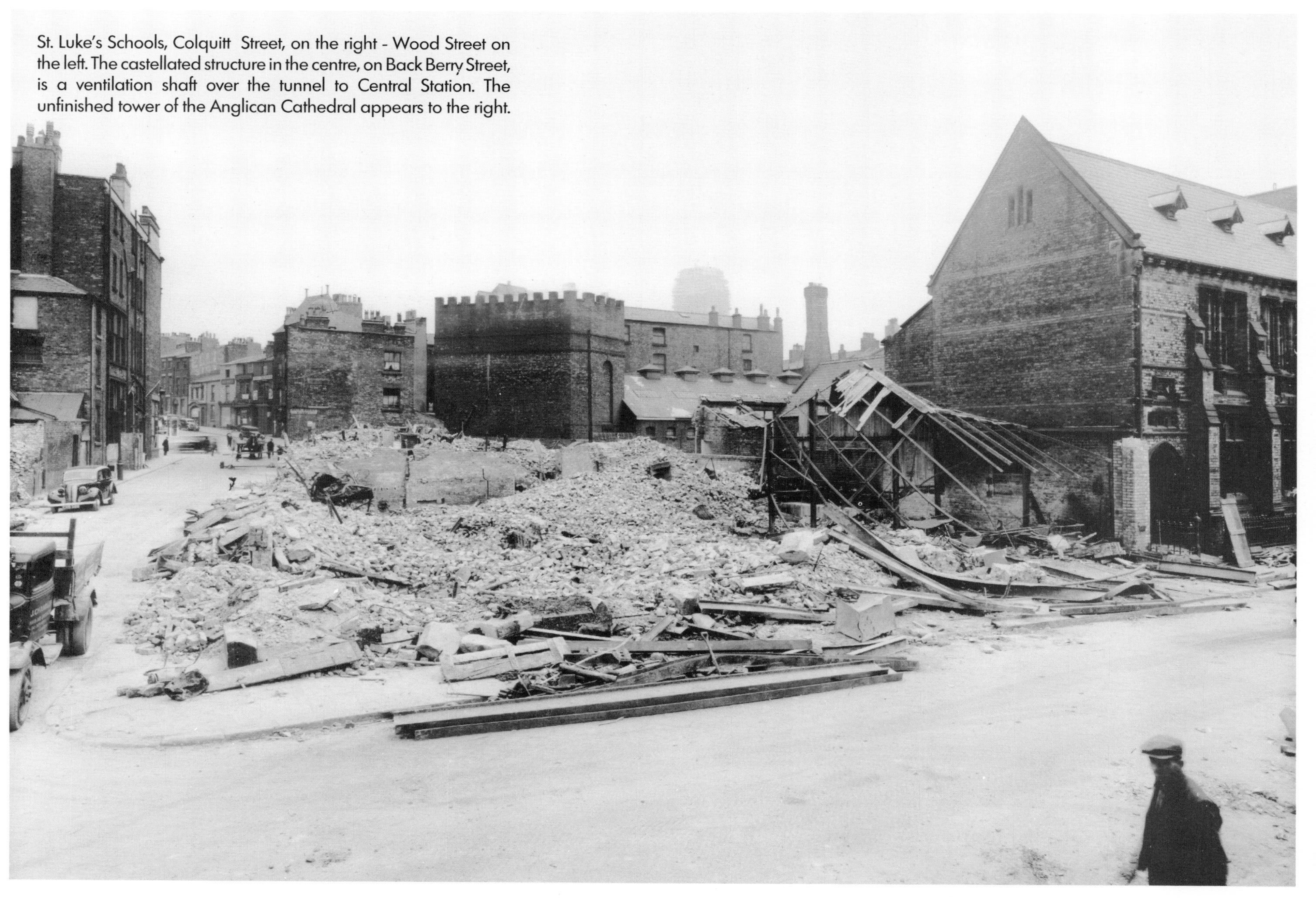

St. Luke's Schools, Colquitt Street, on the right - Wood Street on the left. The castellated structure in the centre, on Back Berry Street, is a ventilation shaft over the tunnel to Central Station. The unfinished tower of the Anglican Cathedral appears to the right.

main offices, associated buildings, and neighbouring shops were totally destroyed.

At 0200 the Central Fire Station learnt of a fire at the former St. Luke's Schools in Colquitt Street, threatening the new automatic Royal telephone exchange. This was as yet unfinished – the schools were being used by the GPO for mail. (Whether this was an emergency measure since the damage to the Victoria Street Post Office is not clear.) Constable Thomas Jones was promoted to acting sergeant and sent out with No. 17 pump (full-size) and an AFS crew from Lytham St. Anne's. They arrived at 0205 to find the fire spreading rapidly and no water in the mains. Jones's first thought was the baths. Failing that, he went to Salthouse Dock a good half-mile away, obtained two more pumps (from Woolton and Granby Street), and was thus able to get one branch working at the schools. This shows what could be achieved, but also how bringing water from a distance ate up the pumps. The single branch was enough and the fire was under by 0250; one wing of the schools had been destroyed, but the exchange was safe and no mail was lost.

Jones was then reinforced by two more pumps manned by men from Wolverhampton and Hinckley as well as supplies of hose. These enabled him to man four branches at other fires in the area. One was at the F. L. Calder College of Domestic Science on the other side of Seel Street from the schools – this was seriously damaged. Property on the south side of Duke Street, between York and Suffolk Streets was completely destroyed – including another manufacturing stationer, a lifebelt manufacturer, and a marine optician. Seeing that the situation there was hopeless, Jones concentrated on saving the property to either side managed to restrict damage at Legge House, over the road, to the roof. Jones's team also tackled fires around Wolstenholme Square and Parr Street, where the works of a printers' ink manufacturer was saved, but another factory was destroyed. All these fires were out or under control by 0900.[254]

It is clear that Constable Jones and his men had done a magnificent night's work, but there is another side to this. It was not a heavy raid, and the Liverpool fire service now had access to large-scale reinforcements. The fact that Jones and his small party had to take on so much, shows that the defences were wilting under the repeated attacks. There was evidently a good deal more happening in this area, as elsewhere, but one can only add that two soldiers brought a piano out of a bombed store in Bold Street and struck up a chorus of 'There'll Always be an England' amid the flames, in which others joined.

Of the many fires started, two or three big ones were still burning when morning came. Casualties were light and rescue work was completed quickly.

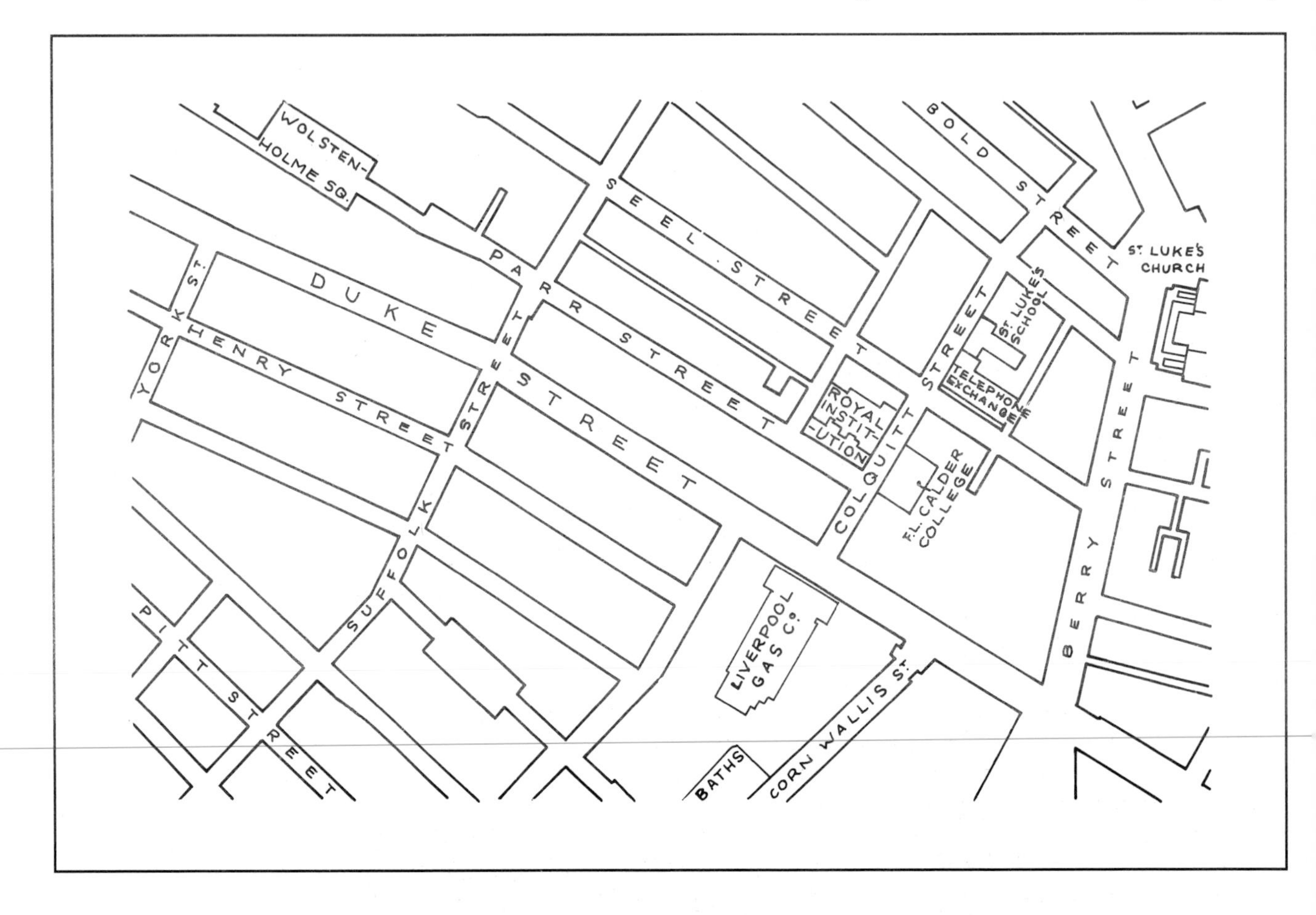

Duke Street, just to the south of the town centre.

TUESDAY 6th MAY

During the night eighty miles of hose had been brought into use and the new salt-water mains had proved their worth. 300 pumps had now been brought in to reinforce the local brigades. Even so, Sir Harry Haig was alarmed by the fresh outbreaks of fire after he had thought they were being brought under control; accordingly, he "asked Home Security to send up someone who could take executive charge of the Liverpool Fire Brigade."[255] The man selected was Commander Firebrace, whom we have met already. He was in Liverpool soon enough to see the car at the end of Huskisson 2 with the bodies still in it – apparently on the afternoon of the 4th. (Strange, the way this features in so many memoirs.)

"After the second night (sic) of the Liverpool blitz, the Regional Commissioner applied to the Home Office for assistance. Having received certain Ministerial instructions, and having arranged to be followed by a team of London and Outer London officers, chosen by myself, I set off; we went to render Merseyside all the help we could, in any way we could."[256] That phrase – "certain Ministerial instructions" – seems to leave a lot unsaid. One would very much like to find a copy.

Unfortunately, Firebrace was to find that the help he had to offer was unwelcome. When Sir Harry sent his deputy to tell the Liverpool Emergency Committee that Firebrace was on his way,[257] the response appears to have been that this was unacceptable interference in Liverpool's affairs.

One fire still burning from Saturday night was that on the ***Bra-Kar*** in Canada 2. At about 0900, burning oil leaking from the ship was caught by the wind and a stream of fire issued from the branch. The flames licked round the ***Collegian*** and spread on south to the Canada-Huskisson passage. Captain Ruytenschildt on the ***Moena*** – still at North Huskisson 3 – was woken with the message: "Captain, the water round the ship is on fire again!" The crew did their best to ward it off from the stern, using foam and floating beams, while the four-inch ammunition from the magazine at that end was transferred to the shed for safety and covered with sacks of sugar.[258]

Elsewhere, someone remembered the ***Mahout*** and her (reputed) cargo of 3,000 tons of bombs. Everyone in that area now knew what a ship-load of ammunition could do and the exodus was general and rapid. The Fire Brigade was called and sent two pumps from Westminster Road, followed by the air crash tender from Speke. The last worked for two hours, supplying foam, and the situation was under control by 1345[259] apparently without serious damage other than to the gates of the dock passage. The ***Collegian*** had to be dry-docked on the 9th to see that she had come to no harm.

The Chief Constable's cordons were brought into play that morning in a sequence of three concentric rings:

Outer: Queen's Drive.

Middle: Lambeth Road – Everton Valley – Walton Breck Road – Sheil Road – Holt Road – Sefton Park Road – Ullet Road.

Inner: Boundary – Great Homer – Soho – Stafford – Seymour – Rodney and Parliament Streets.[260]

All motorists without urgent business were turned back at the first line. Those who got through were advised at the second that they would not be allowed past the inner line. In the centre there were 'no parking' notices on all the lamp-posts and police jumping on everyone who had passed through all the hurdles – or who simply happened to live in the central zone.[261] A system of passes for display on the windscreen was quickly introduced.

On the same day, the Railway Executive Committee decided to have notices posted at the booking offices of stations in towns around Liverpool: "In view of the situation in Liverpool the Government strongly request passengers not to travel to the city unless they have important reasons for doing so."[262] Taking these measures in conjunction with the fact that it was impossible for outsiders to contact friends and relations in Liverpool by telephone or telegraph, that even letters were not getting through, and that any news of what was really happening was known to be censored, it is not surprising that wild rumours began to circulate in which the prosaic possibility of traffic jams played no part.

Tuesday's ***Daily Post*** contained a long list of notices of new addresses inserted by bombed-out firms, from which an astute German intelligence officer with a copy of Kelly's Directory might have learned much. The Customs, MDHB, T & J Harrison, Union Castle and United States Lines were all now crowded into the Cunard Building. The LOR had moved its offices from the train in Pier Head Station to Tower Building.

The local warehouse keepers were called together to discuss the situation. Jarvie, the Regional Port Director, asked for a list of inflammable goods with a view to getting them out of the dock area as quickly as possible; cotton, jute, rubber and timber were the principal items.[263]

Rescue work was still going on at Mill Road, where fifty men of the Royal Engineers were now working. Nine more bodies were found, bringing the total to sixty. All were sent to Webster Road, where the electricity had failed again at 0100 and was not restored till 1700.[264] (Volunteers from the 15th Battalion, King's Regiment, at St. Helens were sent to help there.)

Clearance at the docks was under way, but greatly hampered by UXBs – especially at the north end. The railways also faced increased disruption, with only the southernmost station at Brunswick (CLC) able to take wagons from the docks – and then only from Dingle oil sidings and points south of Wapping. The fall of the tunnel at Crown Street had cut off the original terminus of the Liverpool & Manchester Railway. There was in fact another tunnel, dating from 1829, but that was single-track and so small that it was believed no steam locomotive had ever worked through it. (Originally rope-worked, it was now traversed only by horses shunting the odd coal wagon.) It was discovered, however, that Bank Hall Shed had some diminutive steam shunters that could be squeezed through – just – and one of these was borrowed to maintain a service of sorts to the Crown Street coal merchants. Other traffic was diverted.[265] (The Bank Hall engine must have been one of the former Lancashire & Yorkshire Railway 0-4-0 saddle-tanks, which were ten feet nine inches high at the funnel. As the tunnel was only twelve feet high in the centre *before* allowing for track and ballast, one wonders if an example with worn tyres was selected.)

The MoI vans were now able to add Ministry of Pensions notices to their Liverpool repertoire. "Again, vans were besieged by people wanting information. To make any progress at all, it was necessary to use the loudspeakers to tell people that they had had all the information available from the van; that there were people in the next street who had not heard the announcements; and that the van would come back if there was any further information to give them." With some difficulty, the Emergency Information Officer found the Town Clerk and persuaded him to provide Corporation information from Wednesday. The Personal Service League lent staff to accompany the vans and answer questions, most of which concerned the chances of getting out of Liverpool for a night's rest. Some were able to hitch lifts on the MoI vans themselves, which returned to Manchester each night.[266]

That night's ***Echo*** gives a convincing picture of the public reaction to events (among those spared the worst at least). "'Something like this was bound to happen sooner or later' was the general feeling... There was, too, the purely sentimental regret, which will recur more sharply later, at the disappearance of much that was familiar. Streets and corners, shops and vistas which one had known since childhood, altered; familiar places of refreshment wiped out. All day long the crowds went by, gasping perhaps as they saw a familiar building a mere shell with charred walls or a shop presenting a truly extraordinary sight with every bit of masonry and glass gone from the ground floor, exposing the shell of the building resting entirely upon its steel supports." (This last was probably Blackler's.)

It was a fine spring day, with the usual complement of people catching a bit of sun and fresh air at the Pier Head and feeding the birds. (The weather was good all week – unfortunately.) Many were impressed by the sight of the Victoria Memorial, untouched amid the ruins. One old man mused: " 'I wonder what she would have thought about it?' 'We are not amused,' grimly quoted another bystander, while a third added: 'And if there was one thing in Liverpool I'd have been glad to see go, it was that – yet there it is.' "

Late in the day, HMS ***Viscount*** returned from Belfast. Another Naval visitor was the aircraft carrier ***Furious*** (Displacement 22,450), which slipped into Gladstone Dock at 2045 and moored at the north quay. She had been in the thick of it in Belfast on Sunday night, though only hit by one bomb that exploded inside a hangar. The damage could be repaired in 48 hours, but not in Belfast as Harland & Wolff's works had been among the casualties there.[267]

The ***Daily Post*** also made the significant comment that: "There is in all conscience plenty to be done in perfecting our fire defences." In fact it was reported in London (presumably via Manchester) that at 1838 the fire situation was well in hand – "and it appears that previous reports were exaggerated."[268] (In a desperate endeavour to kill fires before nightfall, the Fire Brigade, on at least one occasion during the week, opened all the doors and windows of a burning warehouse to make it burn faster – a successful ploy.) As things were now looking better than they had been, Sir Harry did not press Firebrace's services on Liverpool and the Emergency Committee agreed that he should act in an advisory capacity.[269] Whether his advice would now be needed remained to be seen.

SHIPPING MOVEMENTS – 6th MAY

Inward	*G.T.*	*From*	*Outward*	*G.T,*	*To*
BOLBEC	1345	Barry to Irlam	**MARTAND**	7967	Middle East?
DELIUS	6065	Avonmouth	**SOUTHGATE**	4862	Father Point
KILKENNY	1320	?			
LONGFORD	1913	?			
SAN EMILIO	8071	Curaco to Manchester			

NIGHT – 6th/7th MAY

SUNSET 2150
BLACKOUT 2235
ALERT 2353-0407
BLACKOUT ENDS 0542
SUNRISE 0627
MOONLIGHT TO 0400

Clydeside was the main target again and most of the aircraft that came near Liverpool were going to or from Glasgow, though this time it was noticeable that a high proportion passed to the east or west – perhaps the guns had impressed them after all. Twenty-seven aircraft claimed to have bombed Liverpool, but the bomb-load is not known. 3,541 rounds were fired and fighters were allowed to operate over 12,000 feet from 0045 to 0210. The searchlights were blacked out when the sky clouded over at 0200.

There were a few bombs on Seaforth at 0040 and on Birkenhead and Wallasey soon after 0100, with little effect; otherwise the attack was heaviest around Liverpool city centre and the docks. Bootle came through unscathed and Liverpool north and east of the centre was little affected – though the east was singled out for a bombardment of faulty AA shells, one of which killed a sow and three pigs in Yew Tree Lane. No mines were dropped, but anti-personnel bombs were reported. The first incident recorded by the Liverpool City Engineer was a fall of HE in the Mill Street area of Toxteth at 0015, all other incidents coming in the period 0030 to 0230. There was a serious fire at Wilson's Flour Mills, Mill Street, which was successfully confined to the garage and engineering shops, and Mill Street Police Station was badly damaged. The fire there was put out by the AFS but broke out again an hour after the 'all-clear' when it was quickly suppressed.

At Moses Street, between Mill Street and Park Road, an off-duty constable, James Tarbuck, was dealing with an incendiary on a roof-top when an HE bomb fell nearby and demolished two houses. Tarbuck was thrown to the ground, injuring his left kneecap, but went to the wrecked houses and organised a volunteer rescue party that managed to extricate all the ten people trapped inside before the official rescue party arrived. "An hour later, when Tarbuck heard of an unexploded bomb in another street, he organised parties to evacuate the district. His action was all the more noteworthy by reason of the fact that he was not in uniform and that his leadership impressed his followers by the sheer force of example." He was awarded the BEM.[270] A little to the west, Brunswick Goods Station suffered serious damage when it was hit in several places,[271] and the nearby Brunswick Gardens tenements were hit at the same time.

There were more bad fires in the centre. The Custom House was set alight again and left a bare shell with glass from the skylights melted and hanging down in bizarre shapes. The fire-float ***Silver Foam*** in Wapping Dock supplied water to the scene, where a turn-table ladder from Salford was among the appliances used.[272] At Bent's Brewery in Johnson Street (next to the Salvage cottages) the upper floors of the north wing burned, but the blaze was contained by the AFS and pumps from the Central Fire Station. This was noted as a fine piece of fire-fighting. In Hatton Garden there was HE on the Parcels Post Office next to the Fire Station, and another bomb set a gas main alight outside the Tramway offices. One outside the offices of the Liverpool, London and Globe Insurance Company in Dale Street caused serious damage there as well as blasting the Town Hall opposite, where the Council Chamber was rendered unusable for a while. Before the night was over, all the roads between Dale Street and Tithebarn Street were blocked.

More HE landed round the Pier Head and Landing Stage, and Riverside Station was hit again and rendered unfit for use. St. Catherine's Church, Abercromby Square, was gutted (though the classical facade survived until the University demolished it). This blaze required the evacuation of Oxford Street Heart Hospital during the raid; it was attended by pumps from Durning Road Fire Station, Newton-le-Willows and London. To the north of Exchange Station, an engineering works in Charters Street was gutted.

After getting off lightly for a couple of nights, the docks were at centre stage again. A shed at South West Wellington was damaged by HE as were others at Bramley-Moore. The Finnish steamer ***Anneberg*** (2,537) in the latter dock got a bomb on the bridge, causing damage to the chart-room, master's cabin and passenger accommodation; she also

Offices of the Liverpool and London and Globe Insurance Company, showing signs of blast damage. The Town Hall is off to the left. There is a water pipe running along the gutter opposite with a crude arrangement of sandbags to allow motor vehicles to enter High Street.

Stanley Dock, north side, in 1942. The far end of the warehouse was demolished in one of the earlier raids. Barges present include *Ellesmount*, *Joan*, *George*, *Alice* and *Mary* - a previous editor, wishing to concentrate on these, has scrawled "shade out" across the upper part of the negative.

suffered splinter damage on her port side. The ***Anneberg*** had other problems, being "under guard and detention for some time" before she was allowed to leave Liverpool on the 19th June. The circumstances of this detention are obscure, but before she could leave British waters, Finland had entered the war on Germany's side and she was commandeered. At South Stanley, two barges loaded with pulverised coal, the ***Ellesbank*** and ***Grosvenor***, were sunk by HE – the former "smashed to pieces."

To the south, it seems likely that it was on this night that warehouses on the south and east sides of Albert Dock were hit. The demolition of a large part of one corner on the east side resulted in the most spectacular air-raid damage to be seen in recent years (it was only made good in the 1980s). Shed roofs were damaged at North King's 2 and sheds and cargo burnt out at South King's 1. The ***Clan MacInnes***, presumably still at North King's 2, was shaken violently by another near miss and suffered further damage – her port side was reported to be "crinkled."[273] More sheds were damaged at South Queen's 2 and South Queen's 1 – also at Coburg, especially the south side. The pumping station at Queen's Graving Dock was put out of commission, and the ***Adda*** (7,816), loading NAAFI stores and mails (and later passengers) for the West Coast of Africa, suffered fire damage at North Queen's 1. The ***Industria*** (4,861) was damaged at North Queen's 2, but was able to sail to Glasgow on the 11th for a couple of weeks in dry dock before continuing her voyage to West Africa. Sheds at East Harrington were gutted and three vessels moored on that side were also damaged by fire: the ***Asiatic*** (3,741), the barge ***Cragdale***, and the Greek steamer ***Moscha D. Kydoniefs*** (3,874), of which more in a moment.

At the extreme south end of the system, the approach to South Dingle oil jetty was hit by two HE bombs and all oil pipelines broken. Burning oil poured from the pipes and forty yards of the jetty were involved in the fire. A report of a balloon set alight by a blazing petrol dump presumably relates to this incident,[274] and it must have been at this time that the tanker ***San Emiliano*** (8,071), moored at the jetty with a full load of petrol, was slightly damaged by a near miss. Several AFS pumps arrived along with No. 11 from Derby Lane Fire Station and used foam stored on the site – the Speke foam tender was sent but not needed. The salvage boat ***Vigilant*** also put in a brief appearance with foam, but it was over three hours before things were brought under control here at 0445.[275]

In Birkenhead there was trouble on the south side of the West Float. HE bombs landed on the quay at Ilchester Wharf and the ***Panaghis*** (5,187) – under repair – was damaged by splinters; there was also fire damage at Cubbins Slipway, involving the barge ***Barbell***, and at the Vacuum Oil Company's premises (lubricating oil and grease) where several oil tanks were damaged. When the south end of Wallasey Landing Stage (used for goods and cattle) was hit by HE, flying debris wrecked the upper works of the passenger ferry ***Marlowe*** (606) moored alongside, and also caused damage to the luggage ferry ***Bebington*** (732) – possibly awaiting the call for use as a fire-boat.

While there were a good many incidents involving casualties, including two more AA gunners killed by a premature shell-burst, there was nothing outstandingly terrible. There were six or seven killed in the worst incidents, such as those at Moses Street and Brunswick Gardens.

In 1942 a claim for salvage was heard in the Admiralty Court[276] that throws a bright, though confused light on events surrounding the ***Moscha D. Kydoniefs*** – abbreviated to ***MDK*** in the judge's summing up, which seems a useful precedent.

The ***MDK*** was moored at East Harrington – north end – with her port side to the quay. She had most of her crew aboard under the chief officer – Greeks except for some Portuguese stokers – and had just taken on 2,000 tons of coal for Lagos. Moored outside her was a smaller vessel, the Norwegian steamer ***Sollund*** (941). Incendiaries fell early in the raid, starting fires in the sheds on both sides of the dock. Those on the east side were soon fiercely ablaze and posing the usual threat to vessels moored there. Seeing that the fires to the west were being successfully put out, the master of the ***Sollund*** decided to move his ship across the dock. The Greeks helped in casting off the ropes and the ***Sollund*** was tied up on the west side at around 0135. The Norwegians still had to cope with burning material from the east, but they were now relatively safe.

The Greeks on the other hand were fighting a losing battle and Mr. Oftedal, chief officer of the ***Sollund***, was sent across in a boat to offer assistance in getting them away from the quay. He was given a rope that he brought back and made fast to a bollard on the west side; then the Greeks cast off their bow ropes and hauled themselves some distance into the centre of the dock. They stopped there – probably because the fires aboard would have put property on the west side at risk – and dropped the starboard anchor. At this point four or five of her crew were seen to jump ashore from the stern with their belongings – the Portuguese according to the Greeks. Not long after, Mr. Oftedal saw a boat being lowered amidships and what seemed to be the rest of the ***MDK's*** crew abandoning ship and pulling away across the dock.

The fire in the east shed was growing in intensity, the flames still sweeping across the Greek ship, but the master of the ***Sollund*** thought that something might be done to save her. He sent Mr. Oftedal across again with five volunteers from the Norwegian crew. Oftedal climbed on board first to see how things lay. He found the hatch covers, both sides of the boat deck, and the crew's quarters aft on fire. Coal "in the bunker hatchway on the deck" was alight, and of twenty barrels stowed on the starboard side of the No. 1 hatch, over half were burning and leaking oil across the deck.

There was no doubt that the ***MDK*** was in grave danger, but Mr. Oftedal did not think the situation was hopeless and he called his men aboard. Two went below to start the pumps only to find insufficient pressure in the boilers; they set about raising steam while the men on deck used buckets and threw burning debris overboard, plying axes where necessary. After about half an hour there was enough steam to get a hose working, and also to pull the bow further across the dock. The anchor cable had to be paid out while this was done. According to the Norwegians there were three lighters floating round the dock on fire, one of which caught under the ***MDK's*** stern.

At around 0430, the ***MDK's*** steward came aboard to lend a hand, and an hour later all the fires were out except that in the crew's quarters. At 0700 she was taken the remaining distance across the dock and moored outside the ***Sollund*** while damping down operations continued. This, at any rate, is the Norwegian story. The owners, master and crew of the ***Sollund*** duly claimed salvage, a claim completely denied by the Greeks. They said that the ***MDK's*** crew (apart from the Portuguese) had never left the ship and that the ***Sollund's*** men had come aboard, uninvited, when there was no longer any danger.

The judge, Mr. Justice Langton, preferred the Norwegian version of events – though he was prepared to believe the Greek chief engineer's claim that he had stayed aboard, taking shelter below – a story that would hardly be creditable if his shipmates were fighting fires on deck. He was, however, at pains to say that the Greeks had pluckily stuck by their ship until a time when they could be excused for thinking that the situation was hopeless.

Counsel for the Greeks also raised the interesting point that there were others fighting fires and saving valuable property in Liverpool that night. Was it fair that this particular group should be singled out to receive a substantial reward? The judge felt that it was not for him to query the law that treats ships as being different in this respect from factories and warehouses – the law of the sea was devised to cope with situations that were rare on land before the blitz. He awarded a sum of £1,500, recommending that most of it should go to the ***Sollund's*** crew, rather than her owners.

Wednesday 7th May

The minutes of the Liverpool Emergency Committee for this day, record that Sir Harry Haig attended with the Ministry of Home Security's offer of Commander Firebrace's services, which was accepted. He was to take charge of the Liverpool and Bootle Fire Brigades during the emergency, with a view to "the coordination of all the fire services." What actually happened was not as harmonious as this suggests.

According to Sir Harry, after the experience of one night in an advisory role "Commander Firebrace informed me that this arrangement would not meet the situation, and that it was necessary for him to be placed formally in executive charge."[277] What the problems were is not stated, but Firebrace's memoirs fill out the picture a little. "The strain on the fire defenders, however gallant they may be, of a city under nightly bombardment is very great. When they are not actively fighting fires they are engaged in preparing for the next night's battle. They grow more and more fatigued as raid follows raid. I actually saw one Liverpool fire officer collapse in the main Control Room. Without any warning he gave a stifled cry, and immediately lost consciousness – sheer exhaustion of mind and body."[278] It is also clear from other sources that Firebrace felt he and his London colleagues could manage things better.

Knowing how the Emergency Committee felt about letting an outsider take charge, Sir Harry went to Liverpool to put it to them personally. Finding them still of the same mind, he told them that he was anxious to maintain public confidence in the Committee; that being so, it would be better for them to appoint Firebrace themselves rather than his "taking action over their heads."[279] Faced with this ultimatum, the Committee reluctantly agreed. Accordingly, Firebrace was put in command and two London officers were attached to each main fire station.

It is impossible to say who was right in this dispute. Firebrace had more experience in the handling of large forces than anyone in Liverpool, and it was undoubtedly desirable that reliefs and reinforcements should include some senior officers. On the other hand, there is reason to suspect that the shortcomings of the LFB in Firebrace's eyes arose from things being done *differently* in London – not necessarily better – and there is no obvious sign of improvement after the take-over. The nearest thing to a statement of the Emergency Committee's point of view surfaced at the June Council meeting, when Alderman Hogan warned of "an ever-growing tendency towards local government by Regional Commissioners," which he feared might be retained after the war.[280]

Some outside help was more welcome. Workers on the night shift at Pilkington's glass works in St. Helens were constantly interrupted by short alerts as flights of bombers passed over on the way to Liverpool – a nuisance, as the glass-making process cannot easily be suspended. Starting with the sheet-glass works on the 7th, men volunteered to go to Liverpool to give what help they could during their free time (the men who went seem all to have been members of the Home Guard or Rescue Parties). At the end of the second day the Plate Works asked why they hadn't been invited. Ravenhead glass works followed; then the collieries and other local firms. By the eighth day up to 300 men a day were making the trip.[281] On Wednesday the work at Mill Road was given over entirely to Pilkington's men, who found one more body.

Nineteenth-century railway competition had provided ten separate links between the Liverpool docks and the main lines, with a great number of possible variations in case of isolated blockages. With the damage to Brunswick, all were now closed. Sappers clearing the Overhead Railway were concentrating on the breach at Canada to give a clear run on the dock lines below from Gladstone to Canning; this would enable them to restore access to all the north docks as soon as the first main line link at that end was functioning. It was still not possible to examine the arches of the Exchange viaduct "owing to bombs and fires." Goods that could be got to Langton Station by road were being taken out on the 7th, and the use of outlying stations was proving effective.

At Breck Road men were still clearing butter and other perishables from stranded and damaged wagons. It was reported that they would start clearing wreckage from the edge of the crater on Thursday. Someone suggested that coal on the site might be used to fill in the hole, until it was pointed out that if there was one thing the Dock Board was not short of it was rubble. Sir Lionel Warner agreed that the Board would take the responsibility for supplying this in whatever wagons were available, to be handed over at Canada Dock Goods Station as soon as the railway engineers were ready to accept it. There was a stranded locomotive at the station that could be steamed for the purpose. The trouble at Atlantic Dock Junction had apparently been sorted out, but the line to Alexandra was still blocked.

Meanwhile, Lieutenant Mould had been having trouble at Barrow with another mine that blew up when it shouldn't have. He arrived back in Liverpool, seriously worried, and reported to the Commander MS in the Liver Building. The Commander explained that he had fired two more charges by the Salthouse Dock mine in the approved manner before declaring the dock open again. (It seems that men from the minesweeper HMS ***Restrivo*** – under repair in Bidston Dock – were called in. They may well have assisted Mould on his first visit as well.) Mould was trying to explain his unease when the room was shaken by a major explosion not far away.

Together they ran to the window to see the 200-foot plume of water falling back on itself somewhere to the south. Fearing the worst, they hurried out to Salthouse "and found a scene of new destruction, a wrecked warehouse, fragments of a barge, and the bodies of two seamen." It was 0935. Salthouse South Shed had gone, along with the steam derrick barge ***Kileenan*** and her load of coal. The ***Kileenan*** had been reduced to scrap even more completely than the ***Malakand*** and all aboard – Master, Mate, Engineer and two coal-heavers – were killed.

A good while later, it was discovered that mines were being dropped with time fuses*in place of* the magnetic mechanism – of a type that could stop for a while only to be reactivated by any slight disturbance of the water.[282] What had happened was bad enough, but it might have been a lot worse if these three mines had fallen in more important docks than Albert, Salthouse and Canning Half-Tide.

It appears to have been on this day that the unexploded bomb at West Toxteth (from the Saturday night) went off while a Naval bomb disposal squad was working on it. There were a number of casualties, including some killed. This may have had a bearing on the decision of the Naval authorities to advise the crew of the ***Marton*** in Langton Graving Dock to leave the ship that afternoon on account of an unexploded bomb only thirty feet away from her[283] – presumably the one first noted on the Saturday night. Saturday's long shadow extended to other docks: during the day the ***No. 20 Hopper*** sank in Huskisson and the ***Bra-Kar*** in Canada. It was thought that the latter event might have been precipitated by the explosion of the magazine, though this may have occurred earlier – it will be remembered that she also carried an unexploded bomb towards the stern.

While the lighter raids and the reinforcements that had arrived certainly brought some relief, damage during the week tended to be cumulative. As each night fell, there were more damaged roofs, more wrecked buildings, and more piles of shattered timber and exposed combustibles that were difficult – or even impossible – for the fire-watchers to protect. Blocked roads and fallen bridges – damaged water mains and telephone lines – the general strain and exhaustion among the defenders: all worked in favour of the enemy. Many firemen went for days without taking off their uniforms; short of food and rest, crowds of them were to be seen sleeping on St. George's Plateau. The toll of damage and wear-and-tear on fire-fighting equipment was considerable; the grounds of the Police Training College in Mather Avenue were used for repair and maintenance of pumps[284] (with help from the Royal Engineers), the worst being cannibalized to keep the rest going.

A young girl living in the Grove Street area, near the University, saw St. Catherine's Church the day after, with a fireman on a ladder silhouetted by the sparks and smoke. She also, most improperly, viewed the raids from the top floor while left unsupervised and remembers that the corner of Oxford and Grove Streets was a regular site for one of the mobile AA guns that used to alarm people by turning up unexpectedly. The mobile smokescreen generator was another device that passed her way in May – whether it had any useful effect is doubtful. She was particularly impressed by the line of fire appliances parked nose to tail along Grove Street – the overspill from the School for the Deaf in Melville Place to the east, which was one of the three reporting centres for reinforcements. (The others were at the Students' Union and at Simpson Street near Queen's Dock.)

In Middleton, to the north of Manchester, five men of the local AFS were chosen to go to Liverpool and joined a hundred others piling into buses at Oldham Fire Station. They were going as relief crews rather than reinforcements, so that cars with trailer pumps awaited them at the Blind School. The Middleton party did not need a local guide as their driver was a Liverpudlian.

This being the first Wednesday of the month, Liverpool Council assembled for its regular monthly meeting – in the Municipal Annexe, Dale Street, as the Town Hall was not fit for use. One side-effect of this was that the public were excluded for lack of room, which may have seemed a happy accident to some. It is most unfortunate that no detailed record of this meeting is traceable, so that we are left with the account in the next day's ***Daily Post***, to which only a few details can be added.

The Lord Mayor, Sir Sydney Jones, opened the proceedings with an address in which he paid tribute to the courage of the city's people "I feel personally very proud today for the way in which the city has carried on." In due course, the minutes of the Emergency Committee were read. These would have included the appointment of Firebrace, stressing that this was for "the present immediate emergency" only, as well as details of places where rescue work was continuing. There were twenty-eight of these. Of those identified, four were outstanding from Friday night, fourteen from Saturday, two from Sunday and four from Tuesday.[285] Mr. Saltmarsh then criticised the arrangements at Webster Road Mortuary, where he said only twenty-eight men were employed. "A general discussion followed, and various suggestions were made towards the further improvement of the civil defence services."

Alderman Shennan replied for the committee. "The criticisms made, he declared, were untimely and unnecessary, and to his mind they had a political flavour (cries of dissent)." The staff at Webster Road had now been augmented by personnel from First Aid Parties and many additional workers had been brought in from outside to help with rescue and clearance operations. He gave the casualty figures to date, which he thought were unlikely to be increased to any great extent. The figures were not quoted, but were probably the same as those reported in London the day after;

Night – 1/2 .... 20 Killed
2/3 125
3/4 850
4/5 4
5/6 15
6/7 32
Total - 1046[286]

The increased number for Saturday night over the figure quoted on Monday is startling.

After covering road clearance and tram services (there were none between Liverpool and Bootle, and other routes were terminating up to a mile short of the city centre), Shennan passed on to the emergency meals arrangements, which had been a marked success. "From a food angle the Council will need have no anxiety." "There was an interruption at this point and Alderman Shennan retorted, 'That statement is true – right up to the hilt.'" Water supply was almost normal and billeting of the homeless was being efficiently handled, with all forms of empty property being requisitioned as necessary. "There was no room for private motorists in the city. 'It may be that in a day or two they will be compulsorily prevented from coming into the city.' he added." Alderman Hogan concluded for the committee, saying that they could add no more to their report, "because they did not know where they were themselves. During the raids and until just before that meeting the Emergency Committee had been almost in continuous session and they still did not know where they were." Honesty of this order is refreshing, though not perhaps encouraging.

The Council then proceeded to a warm debate on the question of Sunday opening of cinemas (for the duration), which was approved by a substantial majority. During the meeting, an MoI loudspeaker van parked outside and had to be asked to move on as it was rendering debate impossible.

The Bootle Council meeting was held on the same day. Alderman J. S. Kelly, the Mayor, thought the Council services had borne up well, but hinted that some Councillors were not pulling their weight. Alderman Simon Mahon wanted the women and children to go while deep shelters were provided for the men.[287]

It was reported that that night's performance of ***Patience*** at the Royal Court was attended by "a very fair house" in spite of the conditions outside. (The presence of the D'Oyly Carte company in Liverpool seems a fair English counterpart to the Berlin Philharmonic's playing ***Gotterdammerung*** as the Russians closed in.)

SHIPPING MOVEMENTS 7th MAY

Inwards	*G.T.*	*From*	*Outwards*	*G.T.*	*To*
DUCHESS OF BEDFORD	20123	Troopship*	**BLYTH**	1108	Rochester
LEONIDAS N. CONDYLIS	3923	Barrow** to Manchester	**MAGICIAN**	5105	Calcutta
LYCAON	7350	Hong Kong and Singapore	**MARGOT**	4545	Buenos Aires
PORT MONTREAL	5882	New York	**NOVA**	1382	Reykjavik ex Runcorn
SANTIAGO	3864	Rosario** to Manchester	**ROSLIN CASTLE**	7016	Buenos Aires ex Eastham
			SICILIAN PRINCE	3489	Iceland
			TUDOR QUEEN	1029	Belfast

* Canadian Pacific - the largest passenger liner known to have put in an appearance during the week - then engaged in the carriage of troops to the Middle East via the Cape. She was later renamed Empress of France and survived till 1960.

** Convoy sailed Freetown 8th April.

Night – 7th/8th May

SUNSET 2151
BLACKOUT 2236
ALERT 0002-0425
BLACKOUT ENDS 0540
SUNRISE 0625
MOONLIGHT TO 0430

The seventh night proved to be the second worst. Some attention was paid to Bristol and the Trafford Park area of Manchester, but Merseyside was the main target. "The weather was cloudy and overcast, smoky and dark at the start of the raid"[288] so that the search-lights were suppressed again. As a result of weather reports sent back by the first waves of bombers a large part of the force was diverted to Hull, which 72 crews claimed to have hit.[289] In fact the skies cleared over Liverpool so that before the raid ended the moon, now nearly full, was shining brightly.

The crews of 166 aircraft claimed to have delivered 232 tons of HE and 29,064 incendiaries to Merseyside, including a high proportion of heavy bombs and mines among the HE. This was made up of 44 1000-kg bombs and 18 large mines, 47 500-kg bombs and 8 small mines, 455 250-kg bombs, and 547 50-kg tiddlers. There were also half a dozen oil-bombs, and at least one bomb-mine is referred to in a German source. It will be seen that 90 tons of the HE bomb contingent was made up of thousand-pounders and above.

The available records for this night are not good, but there are enough references to parachute mines falling in the area to suggest that, in spite of the poor visibility to start with, this was one of the Luftwaffe's more successful nights and that Bootle especially can be thankful that the raid was not completed as planned. It was heavily concentrated in the two hours from 0030. For most of this period the guns were restricted again, though managing to fire 3,064 rounds, and it was a better night for the fighters with three successes in the Merseyside area alone.

There was scattered activity across South Lancashire. On the Cheshire side three HE bombs landed on Great Sutton at 0132 and two on Bromborough at 0215. Six more on New Brighton caused extensive damage, apparently without killing anyone. Otherwise, the attack was distributed in much the same way as on the Saturday night with a shift to the north. The main weight of it fell on Bootle and North Liverpool, which perhaps explains the small number of outstanding incidents recorded relative to the seriousness of the raid. With the best will in the world, Everton, Kirkdale and Bootle contained few places of interest to people who did not live or work locally.

Casualties were also down a lot. Trekking was a nuisance to the authorities and a real problem for the rest-centre volunteers in outlying areas; it could also lead to loss of property when there was no-one around to deal with small fires quickly. On this night, however, there can be little doubt that it saved the staff of mortuaries and hospitals a good deal of unpleasant work. The areas hit hardest were precisely those where unofficial evacuation was greatest, and the numbers involved were considerable.

Crosby was showered with HE, mines and fire-bombs from 0040 to 0150, the worst incident occurring when a back-passage shelter in Seaforth Vale West was hit at 0125 and thirteen killed. Twenty minutes later, five mines landed harmlessly along the shore. At 0045 another mine had killed eight at Rawson Road. A number of HE bombs fell at 0250, with modest results.

Litherland was similarly treated. A rubber dump was set alight here (always something of a fireman's nightmare), and the most spectacular incident of the night occurred at Bryant & May's match factory – reputed the largest in Europe. At 0100 this was hit by incendiaries that were dealt with promptly by the twenty fire-watchers on duty, though fires were started in adjoining buildings. Several HE bombs then hit the premises, starting a fire that was at its height from 0300 to 0400 and destroyed most of the factory, only one of the five main buildings being saved.[290]

Bootle General Hospital had been moved from its home near the docks to the relative security of the Isolation Hospital in Linacre Lane, next to the cemetery. Here it was housed in a collection of lightly built huts or pavilions with room for only 130 beds, of which up to forty were kept available for raid casualties. This was thought adequate in view of the facilities offered near to hand by Liverpool. In the first hour of the raid sixty serious casualties were brought in. While some patients remained in their beds, others were placed underneath the beds on stretchers or mattresses with only another mattress and the light roof overhead for protection.

Then, within half an hour, the hospital suffered a rapid series of hits. A bomb fell on the east end of Pavilion 7, which contained the First Aid Post, and demolished it. Luckily, the patients and staff inside were at the other end and the only casualties were a nurse and stretcher bearer slightly injured. Incendiaries followed, one of them starting a fire in the joiner's shop that was soon put out, while the others were scattered across the grounds. As these were being dealt with other bombs fell in the area, some of them large – one landed without exploding twenty yards from the point where casualties were being brought in. Finally, a very large bomb, possibly a mine, fell at the edge of the grounds near Pavilion 7 blasting windows and doors and stripping slates from the roofs.

When the dust settled, the situation was chaotic – with the blackout curtains stripped away it was not even possible to use torches. Fortunately, mattresses were an adequate defence against the light debris that had been tossed around and there was only one more casualty in spite of everything. There was also a striking air of calmness that is often the thing that impresses people recounting similar incidents at hospitals. It seems to communicate itself from the staff to everyone else involved. Ambulances were still bringing in the night's victims. The injured were given what shelter was available and the dead laid on the grass outside, but it was obvious to MrCooper, the Superintendent, that the place had to be evacuated.

"Electrical, gas and telephone services had long been interrupted, but with that hope which springs eternal in every breast a visit was made to the telephone room. The light of the moon, its coldness now enriched with the glow of many fires, revealed the operator still sitting patiently in front of her 'dead' switchboard, windows gone and debris all around. Just at that moment providence intervened and an indicator dropped. A thoughtful operator at the exchange asked if the hospital had any messages.

"Contact was made with Control and transport requested for evacuation. Before the conversation could be completed the board again became 'dead'. For a second time fortune favoured us, as on leaving the telephone room there unmistakably was a solitary bus coming along the road. This stopped in response to signals and once again the kindness and helpful spirit which seemed to prevail on these occasions was in evidence as the driver immediately agreed to take a bus load of patients to the nearest hospitals."[291]

A fleet of ten-stretcher ambulances appeared at about 0300 and within a couple of hours everyone had been taken to Walton or Fazakerley with no further casualties arising. With the exceptions of Pavilions 6 and 7, which were too far gone, Bootle General was functioning again within six weeks. Additional ambulances for Bootle were requisitioned from the regional pool, but did not arrive till the following afternoon owing to bad communications.

The damage in Bootle was widely scattered. The ARP headquarters in Knowsley Road was wrecked, with the loss of all the equipment prepared in case of gas attacks, and the Broadway Cinema next door was demolished. The stores of the Mersey Cable Works were also burnt out in this area.

The mortuary (formerly the baths) in Marsh Lane was destroyed by a fire in which 180 bodies were incinerated. Nearby, the library, hall and Junior Instruction Centre were burnt and Salisbury Road and St. James (RC) Senior Girls' Schools damaged by fire. Marsh Lane Station was hit, the buildings and platforms burnt, and debris thrown down to block the newly-reopened Langton branch where it passed underneath. (This branch was also cratered by HE.) The LMS goods yard north of the station was extensively damaged.

Merseyside Food Products' margarine works by Linacre Gas Works was so badly damaged that production ceased soon after, while R. Rolph & Company's Langdale Mills in Stanley Road (animal feed – ground-nut meal, rice meal, etc.) was hit by HE and incendiaries, leading to a dust explosion that completely demolished the place.[292]

Also in Stanley Road, a little to the south, the freshly-reopened Metropole Theatre was destroyed by fire. There was a large basement shelter under the Co-op, to the north of Langdale Mills, and many of the patrons went in there; others in Anderson shelters locally were advised to leave them on account of the spreading fires and again were directed to the Co-op shelter. The shelter – "brightly lit and cheery" – was thus more than usually well filled when a heavy HE bomb landed on the billiard hall next door, on the corner of Ash street.

James Kenyon, a lorry driver at the gas works, was sitting on a box at the rear of the shelter when there was a call for volunteers to deal with incendiaries outside and a number of those near the entrance responded. "A few minutes after they had gone I heard a terrific explosion and a great blast swept through the shelter, bricks and debris from the building above crashed down, and to add to the confusion the lights went out and we were plunged into darkness." As at St. Brigid's earlier in the week the bomb had blown away one of the walls of the shelter, allowing the concrete roof to fall on that side. There was a moment of panic – "People were screaming for help, and trapped persons were moaning pitifully."

Senior Warden Grundy found himself stumbling over dead bodies in the dark near one entrance. He had to attend to a Shelter Marshal,

A pictorial definition of the word "gutted". Part of Bryant and May's Litherland establishment.

Rimrose Road, Bootle.

whose face was badly cut; then, "He called to all the people that if they were quiet and orderly they would all be safe. His steady confidence reassured them, and they filed out in an orderly manner."[293]

Mr. Kenyon, who was clear of the damaged area, sought the emergency exit only to find that the grid on the other side was covered with burning timber. It was still possible to push it out of the way though, and those who were able to made their escape this way. In all, there were over thirty killed in and around the shelter (including some who had gone out to tackle the incendiaries) making it the worst incident of the night.

Elsewhere, Mr. Collins, the Chief Fire Officer, was himself bombed out and had to help his wife and daughter out through an emergency exit before returning to the fray.[294] As he appears to have lived next to the Bootle Fire Station in Strand Road, which is conspicuously absent from the next directory of the area along with most of the 'firemen's cottages' adjoining the station in Irlam Road, it is likely that these were hit at the same time. There is a surprising absence of information on this.

Bootle Town Hall and the area round it were badly hit. The boys' secondary school and technical school on Balliol Road – now used as a billeting and information centre as well as a headquarters for mobile canteens – were completely burnt out, and the adjacent baths severely damaged. Substantial parts of Oriel Road Station were demolished. Harland & Wolff's premises, over the road from Carriers' Dock, were hit by eight HE bombs of which two failed to go off. The damage here was extensive, though it was possible to resume production in less than a fortnight.[295]

The work of Mrs. Lilian Illidge, Air Raid Warden and grandmother of 46, is worth re-telling as it provides a rare and graphic picture of the sort of thing that was happening in many districts of Merseyside. She was on duty at her post in Cinder Lane when, at 0012, an HE bomb went off at the corner of Monfa and Annie Roads, just south of the Litherland boundary. Warden Illidge went to the scene, where a fire had broken out in demolished houses, and was asked by the police to call the fire service. Finding the telephone at the nearest post out of order, she ran to Orrell Lodge Fire Station. She then returned and helped in the recovery of several trapped people, only to have Police Sergeant Smith tell her to: "Get the hell out of here – this is no place for a woman." After helping with the removal of the injured by ambulance she returned to her post – to assist in tackling incendiaries in Cinder Lane and Thornton Avenue. It was then that a mine landed in Annie Road, demolishing houses there and in Patricia Grove.

Mrs. Illidge arrived at the same time as a fire engine, and heard someone calling weakly for help. Following the sound and feeling about in the dark, she came upon the coat of a man lying under the rubble of his garden wall – Mr. Poulson. In clearing the rubble off she found one of his arms rolling about loose and wrapped it in a curtain, then she called two wardens who got Mr. Poulson onto a door as a makeshift stretcher and took him to an ambulance. When he asked what had become of his wife and child, Mrs. Illidge went to investigate and found them safe in their Anderson shelter. She then returned to the wreckage of another house where rescuers were trying to reach Sergeant Smith's family. Finding that there was an opening too small for any of the men to get through, Mrs. Illidge volunteered to crawl in and was able to bring out Smith's eighteen-year old daughter with a baby: the others were recovered by a hole made on the opposite side. They had been saved by sheltering under the stairs.

Going to fetch water for them, Mrs. Illidge found Sergeant Smith lying dead on the pavement and brought this to the attention of a constable before going on. When the Smiths and others were brought out by the Rescue Party, she helped in getting them to the wardens' post and looking after them until ambulances arrived – questioning them to find out who was unaccounted for in the shelters. She also had to tell them about the Sergeant. While going to check some of the information given to her, she came across another body – a man with no head or feet. Seeing no-one else around, she laid the body on a loose piece of tin from a window and covered it with a curtain before getting help to carry it to the post. In a spare moment she made tea for the firemen and Rescue Party with her daughter's help.

The more humdrum duties of a warden – providing help and advice for people looking for relatives, making sandwiches and so on – occupied her through the day and she was not finally able to relax until the next night's 'all-clear' sounded. She was later awarded the BEM. There were seventeen killed in Annie Road and Monfa Road – most, if not all, by the mine. That apart, this was a *quiet* area.[296]

The picture in north Liverpool was much the same. In Walton, the gaol was hit again by one of the larger HE bombs, E block being reduced to a heap of rubble and the whole gaol shaken to its foundations. Surprisingly, there seem to have been no casualties, though two prisoners from G block made use of the confusion to escape and were thought to have been buried until they were seen outside soon after and recaptured.[297] The gaol was now such a mess that the remaining prisoners were transferred elsewhere – it may be that some had gone already. The platform and buildings at Walton Junction Station were damaged and the south end of Walton Hospital was hit by two HE bombs, leading to the evacuation of the infectious ward.

St. Alexander's Church in St. John's Road, Kirkdale, had escaped on the Saturday night. On the following night a delayed-action bomb fell behind the presbytery, to explode at 0630 on the Monday morning. "The whole of the sacristies and the Sacred Heart Chapel had been completely destroyed, leaving four bays of the main roof hanging unsupported; the wall had gone, too; the Predella of the High Altar was lifted at a precarious angle and the Altar Rails buried under bricks, but, not a single vase of flowers on the Altars (decorated for the First Sunday in May) had been disturbed!" From Sunday, the area round the church had been evacuated on account of the unexploded bombs in the vicinity – about eleven of them – and now, on the Wednesday night, the shattered church was set alight and the roof fell in with the 'all-clear'.[298]

Rolling stock at Kirkdale carriage sidings was set on fire, seventy-five carriages being affected, and seventy yards of the adjacent main line was damaged. A bomb in this area brought down twenty-five yards of Spellow tunnel, through which the branch to Canada and Alexandra Dock goods stations passed.[299] At Canada there was more damage to goods sheds, and the passenger coaches used as offices since the December raids were destroyed by fire and HE. It was probably here that the Middleton AFS party finished the night putting out fires in trains of coal wagons; they had already spent some time pumping foam into a ship lying on her side.

Where Stanley Road crossed the CLC line to Huskisson and Sandon goods stations, two thirds of the bridge was demolished, blocking the line below with a great mound of rubble.[300] Another section of Stanley Road was scattered over the lines leading into the LMS Bank Hall engine shed. These blows were peculiarly disastrous in view of the detours needed in order to find an alternative road crossing; it was not to be expected that the extra mileage would be devoid of additional blockages. Further south, there was extensive damage to the Distiller's Company's premises in Juniper Street, Lambeth Road School, and the British & American Tobacco Company's factory in Commercial Road.

In Everton, St. Martin's Market was hit for a third time and suffered more damage: "a portion of the wall being demolished and the roof blown off, it being impossible for the building to continue to be used as a market."[301] Serious fires raged at stables in Dickson Street and a cooperage in Gildart's Gardens, the railway viaduct appears to have taken more damage, and houses, churches and schools were involved, but no outstanding incidents arose.

In the centre, an HE bomb fell down a lift shaft in Tower Building. The LOR had moved in here a couple of days earlier, lost its windows the previous night, and now had its new offices wrecked in turn. The large provision warehouse of Morris & Jones, 11 to 17 Sir Thomas Street, burned for several hours from 0230. The six appliances here included a turn-table escape from Macclesfield and AFS pumps from Ilkeston and Congleton.[302] A fire at the Municipal Annexe in Dale Street was put out by fire-watchers, and there was more trouble in Pembroke Place.

To the south and east, the only incident of note recorded is a mine on Daffodil Road, Wavertree.

Again it was the docks and shipping that took the brunt of the attack. The Wallasey ferry-boat ***Royal Daffodil II*** (591) was hit by an HE bomb on the starboard side of the engine room and sank at Seacombe Landing Stage. Otherwise, it was the Lancashire side, especially the north end that got it.

The ***Mobeka*** (6,111) was damaged at North East Queen's, but evidently not badly as she sailed next day. After being knocked about in Wellington Dock as already noted – and then having her forward funnel damaged by the ***Malakand*** explosions – the ***Louth*** moved to West Prince's on the 7th. Here, for the second time, she was showered with debris from a near miss, but she was a tough little ship and came to no serious harm. In Salisbury, HE and fire-bombs caused slight damage to sheds and to a couple of coasters, ***Stormont*** and ***Normandy Coast***. In Wellington there was further blast damage to the north shed, and the south shed was totally destroyed by HE and fire.

A new Third Officer had arrived to take up his post on the ***Australia Star*** (11,122) in North Sandon after the ***Malakand*** went up; the taxi driver who took him to the dock and the Chief Officer on board were eager to brief him on what he'd missed, however. The ***Australia Star*** had got off lightly, though "a large piece of side stringer" from the ***Malakand*** landed on the after deck, and the cook had to be sent to hospital with a badly gashed hand from a flying rivet.

The Second Officer had a wife in Birkenhead, so the new man volunteered to relieve him of his night duty and ended up fire-watching for the rest of the week with the Bosun and six soldiers (often to be found on ships as well as in the warehouses).

"Searchlights criss-crossed the sky, occasionally picking out a plane, then tracer appeared from all round Liverpool aiming at the target, with Anti Aircraft guns opening up," but at first there was no trouble around Sandon Dock.

Now, bombs fell on Sandon immediately after the alert, fitted with the screaming whistle that was added to many German bombs – "most demoralizing."..."I had only just gone on deck when I heard one coming down directly above me, so I threw myself down on the deck, followed by three of the soldiers, and I thought this must be the end. The explosion was deafening, and the blast blew me into the scuppers against the bulwarks, rendering me completely deaf in my left ear. (I am still deaf.) However, finding myself in one piece, we discovered the bomb had landed on the warehouse alongside and this was now burning fiercely. The Bosun

Royal Daffodil II at Seacombe landing stage. A poster advertising a dance has "CANCELLED" pasted across it.

The Overhead Railway down again at the south end of Canada Dock Station. Fires are burning in the docks beyond and *Lobos* is dimly visible to the left. There are hoses across the dock road taking water inland.

ran down the gangway pulling a hosepipe, and we all assisted, but it seemed a futile gesture, endeavouring to put out the flames."

They went back aboard when a fire-bomb landed on the funnel; it was a motor ship, so the bomb fizzed on top of the funnel rather than falling down it. It proved so inaccessible that in the end they let it burn out harmlessly. "Many times that night we crashed to the deck and said our prayers", and by morning there were fires all round, but the ***Australia Star*** came through unscathed. She sailed independently for New Zealand on the 18th: "and I must say we were very pleased to be away from Liverpool."

HE landed in the avenue at South Huskisson 1 (some without exploding), and one of the west side sheds – all still more or less intact – was demolished. J. Rank Ltd's ***No. 4*** barge was reported to be making water at the west end of North 2 and sank later. At 0230 the Norwegian coaster ***Stromboli*** (1,376), in the north-west corner, was hit by an HE bomb in her starboard coal-bunker and quickly turned over to port and sank.[303] All the crew were able to get off and were given dry clothes on the ***Moena.***

At North 3, the feeling on the ***Moena*** (probably not uncommon) was that they were the centre of attention, being well-lit by fires and with bombs landing all around. The Fourth Mate thought this was all to the good: "We'll be all right tonight, Captain, they're aiming at us." In fact, they only had to deal with incendiaries, though the sheds alongside were further damaged by fire and HE. Incendiaries started a fire in bags of sugar piled over the ***Moena's*** ammunition, but the Third Mate took a party to extinguish this with hoses from the ship.[304]

Canada Dock was still a bad place to be. The ***Salland,*** now at the west end of South 1, was in trouble again with most of her crew off taking shelter; the ***Moena's*** Second Mate took a party to deal with a fire in the forecastle before it got out of hand. (She was able to sail for London on the 16th, but examination there revealed "considerable fire destruction.") The ***Waiwera,*** to the east, was hit by a delayed-action bomb in No. 6 hold – third deck down – that went off later without serious effect. Between these ships, the flat ***Rover,*** loaded with plywood, was burnt out and sank. The ***Lobos,*** on the north side, was hit by a small bomb that exploded in No. 5 hold. If the ***Elstree Grange*** was hit again, it is unlikely that anyone would have noticed. A couple more sheds on either side of this branch were demolished by HE and fire.

In South 2 the ***Baron Inchcape*** received one or two HE bombs forward, causing leakage in the first three holds that soon had her bow resting on the bottom. On the east side, the Overhead Railway was hit yet again and another span brought down. At the east end of Canada 3, by the wreck of the ***Domino,*** the steam derrick barge ***Burmah*** was burnt out and sank later with the loss of her cargo of ship's refuse. (One feels that this might have given John Masefield ideas for a fourth verse.)

To the west, incendiaries fell on the ***Tacoma Star,*** whose deck was piled high with dunnage from the holds. (This would seem to be the converse of the ***Moena's*** flooded decks.) The mass of light timber caught fire at once. As gunnery officer, Denis Foss thought of the ammunition locker for the stern gun and went with a couple of quartermasters to clear the shells out. When the quartermasters saw that the thermometer on the magazine wall showed five degrees in excess of the danger mark, they thought better of it. The position was saved by the arrival of two black West African seamen who cheerfully offered to help, and the shells were all tossed into the dock. (This practice was deprecated by the Dock Board.)[305]

With the engine-room under water, the crew were reduced to tackling the fire with stirrup-pumps and buckets, though as the ship was on the bottom already it was an easy matter to lean over the side to fill the buckets. In the end it was found more effective to heave the dunnage overboard (one suspects that the Dockmaster would not have been particularly thrilled about this either) and the fire was quelled without any further damage to the ship.

On ***Maplin,*** at the tongue, David Large was climbing up to deal with a fire in the "port for'ard cutter" on the boat deck shortly after 0100. He had just called to two men standing on the starboard side by No. 2 hatch to pass up a hose when a bomb fell through the hatch and he was blown into the cutter. He came round soon after to find his overalls in tatters and water being played on him and the cutter by a rating on ***Adventure.*** The other two men had been deafened by the explosion but were otherwise unhurt. Mr. Large was able to go down into the hold to inspect the damage; it had been filled with empty drums to provide buoyancy in the event of a torpedo hit. The bomb had made a mess of these and the ship was taking water, but otherwise she was not badly damaged. Mr. Large received a Commendation.

Outside of ***Maplin, Adventure*** suffered splinter damage from six bombs that fell in the dock off her starboard side. As before, she landed parties to help others with fire-fighting.[306] The pumping station was hit again by HE and gutted. Hartley's robust edifice survived (for a few years) but the burning of this gothick folly must have added a somewhat unreal note to the scene.

The bridge over the Canada-Brocklebank passage was hit by HE and left stuck in the 'on' position. At the south side of the Brocklebank Branch Dock, the Belgian steamer ***Gandia*** (9,626) was set alight by incendiaries. With the fire dangerously near the magazine, Inspector Skelton went aboard and removed the ammunition chests, so saving the vessel from certain destruction.[307] (He was awarded the Belgian Croix de Guerre for this action. It will come as no surprise that the remarkable Thomas Morton Skelton appears to have been the most decorated officer in the Liverpool Police Force – service medals possibly excluded. He also numbered the stopping of runaway horses among his accomplishments.) Sheds burned on either side of Carriers' Dock.

The tug ***Hornby*** was sunk at her moorings at East Langton, being found by her master next morning with only the mast and funnel above water. It appeared that she had been holed by splinters from a near miss and set on fire, but sank before the fire could do much damage. The presence in the same area of a tug, a barge, and a dock all called 'Hornby' has led to some confusion in the records.

The graving docks here were both flooded, the damage by HE to No. 2 being particularly bad. HMS ***Belmont*** in 2 upper seems to have got off lightly, but the ***Marton*** – now unmanned – was burnt out in 2 lower. She was hit by a large bomb amidships between 2400 and 0100 and her back broken; fire broke out at once, possibly assisted by incendiaries. The dock was flooded in the hope of saving her, but without success. There was oil as well as debris scattered over the dock bottom afterwards and it may be that the flooding of the dock made matters worse rather than better – always a risk when there was oil about. The ***Marton*** ended up heeled over on her side; a gutted wreck, especially forward where she was "a skeleton mass of buckled and collapsed plating."

The floating crane ***Hercules*** was moored at the crane quay, between the graving docks and the branch, when what must have been a large HE bomb landed in the water near her port bow. The whole crane jib – already loosened four nights earlier – was thrown off and landed on the quay in such a way as to obstruct the bridge over Langton Branch entrance passage, as she began to settle by the stern.

In the branch, HE bombs fell at 0108 on the ***Trentino*** – through the hatch into No. 3 hold – and on the shed alongside, blowing debris over the ship. Incendiaries followed. Cargo in the hold caught fire within a few minutes (the ***Trentino*** had brought in "1,353 tons rosin, cork and fish oil") and this spread rapidly to the other holds. The shed that her crew had saved four nights earlier was also in flames along with another of those at South Alexandra 1 across the avenue. The crew abandoned ship without casualties and remained at the scene till 0830 when she was down by the head, "the fire being visible within the holds of the ship through her side in places." No help was available from the fire service (presumably a failure of communications in this instance) and she finally sank at 1015.[308] When she was examined later, masonry from the sheds and quay wall was found on her in pieces weighing as much as several tons. It was also noted that "her sides in way of No. 2 hold are so badly set in that they are concave over the whole length of this hold."[309]

Also in the branch were ***No. 12 Pneumatic Elevator*** (743) and six barges, all of which were badly damaged – the barge ***Ivy P*** was burnt out after catching fire from the ***Trentino.*** (The others were the ***Thorneycroft, Douglas Vernon, Marjorie, Ainsdale*** and ***Attractive.***) The Dock Board's offices and stores at the east end of the branch were gutted and two bombs added craters to one of the sheds already lost on the Saturday night.

The surviving shed at West Alexandra was damaged by HE, and the open quay where the adjacent sheds had stood till December was cratered. At the south end, the ***Roxburgh Castle***, lying on the bottom since Saturday, suffered more fire damage. (Discharge of her cargo had been started on Monday.) The short quay between branches 1 and 2 was home to the floating crane ***Atlas*** (457). She suffered blast damage, had two fire-bombs through the deck aft, and started taking water. In spite of this she was sent into Gladstone Dock for use as a fire-float.

The sheds at South 2 were gutted and blasted. At the West end, the Belgian steamer ***Leopold II*** (2,902) was hit by an HE bomb and slightly damaged. What was meant by slight damage in this instance was that: "The gun platform, poop deck, main deck and starboard side were all perforated, jointing and hull plates opened up, shell plates fractured in places, funnel broken, pipes, electrical appliances in messroom and storeroom broken up, damage to rooms in poop, starboard lifeboat damaged, several doors damaged by blast and explosion, and cabin on bridge damaged,"[310] none of which, presumably, would have prevented the ship from sailing in twenty-four hours or so.

At the east end the ***Argos Hill*** (7,178) was scorched by the shed fires and the ***Empire Bronze*** (8,142) was damaged by blast and fire. The latter had been discharging grain till the power was cut off on Saturday night. It was probably in this area that the grain storage barges ***El Marine*** and ***Keswick*** suffered fire damage. Most of the sheds at North 3 were gutted, the steam derrick barge ***Rose*** and the flat ***Ida Burton***, both loaded with caustic soda, being sunk here. At the east end four more barges – ***Jolly Days, Spaniel***, and two belonging to ICI were gutted and one of them sunk. The ***Jolly Days*** (352) had been acquired by the Dock Board early in the war and fitted up as a 'water boat', with water tanks and other plant, to service the Board's vessels.

Hornby Dock got off lightly again, though there were fires in some of the sheds. At South Gladstone 1 a latex tank was blown up and the ***Talthybius*** was in trouble again at the north quay. "A large number of incendiary bombs fell on the ship setting fire to roof of wireless cabin. This fire was extinguished by the crew and fires on deck were also put out. High explosive bombs fell on quay and damage was caused by blast to the forepeak. A fire was started in the forepeak, but this was quickly put out by the crew. On examination of vessel a delayed action bomb was found in No. 1 hold. This bomb had pierced the decks and rested on the cargo of paper and metal. The bomb was later removed."[311]

It was South 1 that the ***Atlas*** was called to. Firemen ran hoses up to the top of her jib, possibly from a trailer pump on deck, and used her as a kind of floating turn-table escape for a few days.[312]

At ten minutes past midnight incendiaries fell across HMS ***Worcestershire's*** bridge and well deck and the quay alongside the graving dock. Ratings from ***Furious*** were sent to assist ***Worcestershire's*** fire party, but it was not till 0135 that all fires on the ship were put out, and by then there was more work for them to do around the dock.[313]

The destroyers and sloops clustered three deep at West Gladstone were soon in trouble.[314] A little after 0030 a bomb fell in the dock by ***Viscount*** – moored outside ***Vanquisher*** and ***Rockingham. Viscount*** and ***Vanquisher*** were both drenched and the former began to settle aft as the engine room and after boiler room flooded. Lengths of suction hose were borrowed from surrounding vessels to allow ***Vanquisher*** to assist in pumping out ***Viscount's*** engine room, while men were mustered to help transfer seventy-three depth charges and three torpedoes from her upper deck to ***Vanquisher.***

At 0100 more incendiaries were seen falling on the sheds by the graving dock and ***Vanquisher*** sent two men to help there. It was noted that locked doors led to delay in getting to the fires; these sheds contained Naval stores and one must suppose that they were not subject to the usual Dock Board rules. More alarmingly, a parachute mine splashed into the basin at 0115, about a hundred yards from the entrance.[315]

News of ***Viscount's*** troubles reached Naval Headquarters in the Liver Building and they turned again to the salvage-boat on stand-by at Prince's Stage – this time the ***Vigilant.*** She set off at 0130, but like the ***Salvor*** before her, she could not get into the dock as the power for the gates had failed.

The destroyer north of ***Viscount*** was ***Hurricane,*** moored outside ***Enchantress*** and a former US destroyer. At 0145 ***Hurricane*** was hit on the port side aft by a bomb that went straight through her and exploded underneath, breaking her back and bending the propeller shafts. The blast also tossed depth charges onto ***Enchantress*** and destroyed the after fuel tanks. Fortunately, the oil fuel did not take fire, but ***Hurricane*** was drenched in the stuff. Sand had to be laid on the deck before ratings from ***Enchantress,*** and later ***Rockingham,*** could transfer depth charges. ***Enchantress*** also assisted with her pumps.

At 0200 sticks of bombs landed on the beach to port of ***Furious,*** and at 0230 four flares were dropped over Gladstone. All round the dock, ships opened up with their light armament to shoot them down. At 0300 a bomb fell on the quay by the destroyers and a splinter exploded ready-use cordite charges on the deck of ***Ripley,*** moored behind ***Rockingham.*** The crew were able to bring it under control without assistance. Hard work by all concerned kept ***Viscount*** and ***Hurricane*** afloat through the night.

In the river, the newly-arrived ***Duchess of Bedford*** escaped a near miss without suffering any significant damage, as did the ***Alfred Jones,*** commodore ship of the convoy due to sail next day. One of the escorts, moored near the Bar Lightship overnight, was ***Campanula.*** Nicholas Monsarrat: "Occasionally a turning aircraft roared overhead, shaping up for another run over the target; but all one's attention was for the noise and the amazing display ashore – star-shells, flares, tracer from ships, the pin-point flicker of the barrage, the crash of bombs, sickening one."[316]

The ***San Emiliano*** was still tied up at South Dingle oil jetty. When the raid ended, a dock gateman, Mr. J. H. Tyler, went aboard to check the moorings and fell into the river as he returned by way of a temporary gangway. This was a common enough mishap in the blackout and it was often a dock gateman that went to the rescue, but Mr. Tyler had injured himself on the way down and could only call for help while hanging on to the jetty. He was hindered by the woodwork being slippery with oil while there was oil and petrol on the water as well, a legacy of the previous night's incident. There was also a strong ebb tide running and the fires at the north end did nothing to alleviate the darkness.

But his cries had been heard and the ship's captain lowered a rope. He was about to go down it himself when an apprentice – D. O. Clarke – came up and volunteered. Clarke shinned down the rope to one of the cross-beams under the jetty, only to find when he used his torch that the gateman was at the next one, some fifteen feet away. Clarke was unable to swim, but he called for a life-jacket and another rope and with the aid of these he was able to reach Mr. Tyler and bring him to a rope ladder let down from the ship. Mr. Clarke was awarded the silver medal of the Liverpool Shipwreck and Humane Society.[317]

By 0412 twenty-two fires were reported to be burning along the docks,[318] mostly at the north end. This raid was certainly not as bad as Saturday night's, but coming on top of the previous six it created a very serious situation. The absence of anything comparable to the worst incidents of the third night is a matter of luck as much as evacuation. It is worthy of note that, in Liverpool, Police Divisions A, B and D, covering the city centre with the districts immediately to the north and east, had each been involved in all the raids of May to date; this did not apply to any other area on the Lancashire side.

THURSDAY 8th MAY

Next morning there was another Regional Commissioner's meeting at which Firebrace reported that the situation in Liverpool was all right, but that there were many serious fires in Bootle. He noted that, quite apart from leakage into the river, the use of water from the docks for fire-fighting was leading to a significant lowering of the water level.[319]

It may be supposed that trekking now reached its height. Sir Harry Haig thought the maximum figure for Liverpool was 50,000 – Alderman Shennan thought it was more like 100,000. It is said that 25,000 people slept outside Bootle that night – half the population. The Bootle Emergency Committee was happy to see them go but would have preferred a more organised and long-term evacuation. The rest centres in neighbouring towns were soon filled and many carried their own bedding to sleep in fields and woods or at the roadsides. The Chief Constable of Lancashire reported that they were cheerful and good-humoured but determined to achieve an uninterrupted night's sleep.

The sheer number of homeless people, together with the lack of alternative accommodation in areas like Bootle, where all but one of the rest centres had been knocked out, meant that trekking had to be given official sanction. Plans were made to bring some organisation to bear, with trains being laid on from Aintree and Lime Street to Wigan, St. Helens, and other outlying towns from 1930 hours that evening.[320]

In Liverpool, 1,050 bodies had been taken to Webster Road and ninety were in various hospitals, of which 430 had been identified. An office, staffed by volunteers from the University, had been opened at Earle Road School where relatives could be interviewed and shown clothes and effects to make identification less of an ordeal.[321]

The remaining festivities in connection with Litherland's War Weapons Week were cancelled, the concluding ball in the Town Hall being one of the items lost. The selling centres had been damaged or demolished, but functions arranged by the Luftwaffe brought in the money and the final figure was in excess of the £100,000 target – so helping to ensure that: "Litherland will not become Hitlerland."[322]

From Gladstone to Sandon there were no ships moving, though the destroyers ***Hurricane*** and ***Viscount*** were extracted from Gladstone without disturbing the mine there and sent across to graving docks in Birkenhead. (They would have been demagnetised by 'wiping'.) There was no power for most cranes and dock gates. ***Worcestershire*** still had men ashore tackling fires and ***Furious*** was taking on Hurricanes – 229 Squadron from Speke. South of Salisbury Dock entrance, things were not too bad. Sixty-nine soldiers were sent from Chester during the day to restore communications along the docks.[323]

In the afternoon, a mobile canteen was heading for the bridge to West Alexandra Dock when the steering jammed. The vehicle swerved and toppled into the dock by the gate. All four WVS ladies inside were able to get out before it sank, but were still in difficulties, and a number of men rushed to their aid. Eugene Byrne was driving an electric bogey at West Langton when he heard the commotion and hurried to the scene. He jumped to a wire hawser that ran over the dock passage and proceeded hand over hand till he was above two of the women; then someone threw a rope from the bridge and Byrne slid down this, took hold of one woman by her clothes, and held the other between his legs till a boat arrived. Mr. Byrne and the three men who saved the other two were honoured by the Liverpool Shipwreck and Humane Society.[324]

This was, of course, just one more job for the salvage men.

There were 200 men clearing the fallen Overhead Railway at Canada and hoping it wouldn't keep coming down faster than they could take it away. Fifty wagons were being filled with rubble for the Breck Road crater; as the direct route was now blocked by the damage to Spellow tunnel, plans were made for getting it through either by road or through Waterloo Goods Station and Edge Hill. One line at Waterloo was expected to be clear by evening and craters in the yard were being filled. Fires and unexploded bombs still precluded a proper inspection of the damaged viaducts to Exchange and North Docks. Where the Exchange viaduct had been repaired after the December demolition at Bentinck Street, the temporary timber construction had been burnt and steel girders warped; another section a little to the north had been brought down as well.[325]

With roads blocked by debris, craters, UXBs, unsafe buildings and fallen bridges, it was increasingly difficult simply to move around Bootle and North Liverpool.

The fires were reported to be more or less in hand by 1700. Few doubted that the enemy would be back to stoke them up again.

SHIPPING MOVEMENTS – 8th MAY

Inward	*G.T.*	*From*	*Outward*	*G.T.*	*To*
EMPIRE GANNET	5672	New Orleans* to Garston	**ALFRED JONES**	5013	Bathurst ex Ellesmere Port
HOPEPEAK	5179	St. John* to Manchester	**CORILLA**	8096	Curacao
INVERSUIR	9456	Trinidad* to Stanlow	**ECLIPSE**	9767	Aruba
PACIFIC EXPORTER	6734	Baltimore* to Manchester	**EMPIRE COMET**	6914	Montreal
SALAMIS	8286	New York* to Manchester	**GRONINGEN**	1205	Belfast
SAN DARIO	1137	?	**HENRY STANLEY**	5026	Takoradi
SAN DELFINO	8072	Aruba* to Manchester	**HOEGH SCOUT**	9924	New York ex Stanlow
YSELHAVEN	4802	Barbados*	**MOBEKA**	6111	West Coast Africa
			TIBIA	10356	Curacao ex Dingle

*Convoy sailed Halifax 20th April

RECOVERY

There was a raid of sorts on the night of the 8th, but enemy activity was scattered and mostly ineffective. Although the alert lasted over four hours on Merseyside the only incidents recorded locally were two parachute mines on Bootle at 0055. Eleven houses were demolished by the one at Alt Road and Linacre Lane (quaintly reported in London as "a lane in Bootle").[326] The other landed on the gas works, destroying the experimental works and causing much damage to other buildings.[327] There appear to have been no serious casualties.

The problems caused by Wednesday night's raid continued. The ***Hercules*** sank in Langton Dock during the night, and numerous fires still burned. With immaculate timing, the rule about running wires across the docks was brought into force on this night, twenty four hours after the last occasion on which it might have been of use.

Edith Pargeter was in town on the 9th. "There are smoking ruins everywhere. Water runs down from side-streets where firemen have been at work...The coloured fronts of half the cinemas are sagging in a fashion which suggests collapse, though I think none of them have collapsed yet. The dust of fall upon fall still hangs visibly russet in the primrose-coloured sunlight."[328]

The Middleton firemen were told to go and help wherever they could. A policeman on the dock road pointed them to a dock warehouse full of oranges, salmon and tinned fruit, and when they got the fire out, they were given oranges to take home. Later in the day they were sent back to Middleton, passing lines of vans and lorries full of trekkers parked on the grass verges along the East Lancashire Road.

The mine in Gladstone Dock was set off at 1740 that evening by a minesweeper using the LL sweep devised to deal with magnetic mines – without causing any damage.[329] This suggests that: *a.* no-one was going to risk the counter-mining technique so soon after events south of the Pier Head; *b.* it would have worked if they had, as this was evidently an ordinary magnetic mine. At 0140 on the next night there was an unexplained explosion in the dock a hundred yards from ***Furious.*** (After taking on more Hurricanes and Fulmars, ***Furious*** sailed on the 11th, taking the aircraft to Malta and the Middle East where they were urgently needed.) Other delayed-action bombs exploded around the docks at odd times, adding to the damage; one went off at the Langton/Brocklebank passage on the 9th.

There was every reason to expect the bombers to return, but they had almost done with Merseyside. From the 9th to the 24th May, there were alerts on nine nights, on a few of which the guns were brought into play, but the enemy did nothing more than lay mines off the coast. On the 14th, an 'aerial minefield' was set up. This involved the dropping of small bombs on parachutes ahead of the bomber stream, intended – like AA shells – to explode before reaching the ground if they did not meet a bomber first. They had no luck on this occasion, and this rather desperate idea was abandoned soon after.[330]

With the approach of the next full moon, people looked for trouble again and were not disappointed. There were raids on four of the five nights following the 28th May. That on the night of 31st/1st June was lighter than it might have been as some of the bombers went astray and attacked neutral Dublin by mistake – killing about thirty there. There was a further scattering of raids up to January 1942, but the damage and casualties were negligible in comparison with what had gone before. By the end, there had been about ninety raids on Merseyside. (It all depends how wide the net is drawn and what you count as a raid – the figure for any single borough would be lower.) In the last year of the war, air-launched V1s came no nearer than Manchester.

It was a while before the after-effects of the May raids ceased. There were still six fires burning in Bootle on the 10th, and fresh fires continued to

Egremont landing stage adrift - the Victoria Tower and the chimneys of Clarence Dock Power Station are visible on the Liverpool bank.

Erecting the Bellman hangar at Brunswick Dock, 9th June 1941. This was ordered after the September raids and it may be just as well that it had not been delivered earlier. The buildings to the right belong to the dockyard.

break out in the smouldering ruins for weeks, some of considerable proportions.[331] 10 Bomb Disposal Company,[332] based in the Manchester area, moved three sections to Crosby to be nearer their work and were joined on the 8th by six sections of 24 Company from Chiswick, who stayed till the 24th. Between them they cleared 219 bombs (presumably HE) and 185 AA shells. On the 13th May a 250-kg bomb exploded at the rear of 432 Hawthorne Road, Bootle, killing four men of 10 Company. These seem to have been the only casualties among the Royal Engineers, the men killed at Salthouse and Toxteth Docks being Naval personnel.

On the 13th, the hopper *'F'* (496) was blown up, presumably by a mine, 350 yards south of Dingle oil jetty. Of the eleven men aboard, five were killed, the survivors mustering on the foredeck as she sank by the stern – her bow remained out of the water for a while when she touched bottom. A tanker at the jetty sent a lifeboat to take them off. The ***Hilda*** (250) was a 'balloon barrage vessel' – one of several employed to maintain the barrage across the estuary and its approaches. At 2106 on the 18th she was anchoring at her usual station in Liverpool Bay when she too set off a mine. She was kept afloat with pumps and brought safely to port without serious damage. As if the Mersey didn't have enough problems, a coaster, the ***Newlands***, ran amuck on the 13th and demolished Egremont Ferry pier, thus bringing that ferry to an untimely end. (The floating stage, which carried a searchlight post, was cut off. The equipment was recovered and the post set up again on what was left of the pier.)[333] The ***John***, burnt out in Canada 3, foundered on the 17th.

The task facing those who had to get the docks working again seemed frightful at first. During the entire blitz 91.5 acres of dock shed floor space were totally destroyed, 65.8 acres suffered major damage and 27.2 acres minor damage. Most of this (nine tenths in the case of total destruction) occurred in Liverpool and Bootle, and most of that in May. A lot of the damage inflicted in earlier raids had still to be made good.

Craters were no problem – there was plenty of rubble to fill them with – and burnt wooden sheds as at Canada 2 were soon cleared. In other places the tangled mess of cranes, railway wagons and roof girders mixed in with concrete and brickwork had to be cut up before removal for scrap, with fresh UXBs being found as the work proceeded. Oxy-acetylene cutting equipment and men trained to use it were in short supply, and when they *were* found there was a shortage of gas cylinders. Still – it got done. It took eighty days to clear a thousand-foot berth properly, and at one time thirty-three were being cleared at once. But it only took twenty days to clear a wrecked berth enough to allow the working of cargo over the rubble; even at Huskisson the ground floors of some of the wrecked sheds were in use again by the 16th.

By today's standards, the river remained busy enough throughout. During May, sixteen convoys (123 ships) arrived and fifteen (139 ships) left. Perhaps the saddest departure was that of the training ship ***Conway***, towed out to find a safer berth in the Menai Straits on the evening of the 21st May.[334] The tonnage figures quoted in ***Port at War*** tell a remarkable story:

Week ending		tonnage	
April	19th	85,187	
	26th	181,562	(exceptionally high)
May	3rd	145,596	
	10th	35,026	
	17th	85,678	
	24th	84,032	
	31st	93,283	
June	7th	108,773	
	14th	126,936	

In the week ended 26th July the port handled 140,500 tons of feed-stuffs, beating the record set in April.[335]

In Liverpool, 465 roads were closed – 196 in the city centre – and, of 205,000 houses, 113,000 were damaged. 6,000 of these were not likely to be repaired in six months. Of Bootle's 17,000 houses, 14,000 were damaged, of which 5,000 would not be repaired in six months. Out of Bootle's current population of about 50,000, 20,000 were homeless. The damage extended to the adjoining areas of Crosby, Litherland and Huyton, and billets had to be found for 42,000 people in ten days. Bootle was trying to find accommodation for its people in Crosby by the 5th; Liverpool, which was not in such a desperate state, offered 400 houses on its Woolfall Heath estate in Huyton as soon as the military contingents there could be moved out. (The Suffolk Regiment left on the 11th, to sleep under canvas in Knowsley Park.) Within weeks, four 'British Restaurants' had been set up in Bootle – three in the parks and one in Alexandra Dock Goods Station. They were large marquees, with field kitchens, and soon proved a roaring success.[336] Industry and commerce were similarly affected, and one might find the head office of a major company temporarily housed in a suburban semi. Demolition work on such premises was often held up by the need to recover safes containing irreplaceable records. The fate of L. S. Dixon & Company's records was still unknown on the 12th May as the safe was buried under smouldering debris; when it was recovered, the papers and minute books inside were found to be singed, but substantially intact. At Woodhouse's furniture shop in Lord Street, all but one of the hire-purchase ledgers were recovered from the safe; the other had been left out and was lost. The firm kept quiet about it and reconstructed the missing ledger as people came in to pay their next instalment. The difficulties faced by some firms, perhaps with suppliers' or customers' records being lost as well, must have been a book-keeper's nightmare.

Through May, six or seven thousand men were put to work clearing the rubble. Building surveyors were lent by Lancashire towns from Fleetwood to Oldham and 200 engineering students from the University volunteered for rescue and demolition work. Demolition – sometimes with explosives – was also being carried out by contractors assisted by 30 Troop of the Parachute Corps. The Liverpool Emergency Committee did not favour Sunday work except for the removal of dangerous buildings – an attitude that some found inappropriate. Through lack of equipment, debris was often manhandled back onto bombed sites to clear the streets and later loaded onto lorries in a separate operation. It was alleged that the Council failed to ask for mobile cranes that would have been available.[337]

In spite of the problems, progress was made. The Queen's Drive cordon was removed on the 14th and the others had gone by the 19th. Linacre Gas Works was functioning again by the 16th. The trams gradually moved back into the centre, while buses from Manchester, St. Helens and Southport, as well as the Ribble and Crosville companies, took the strain.

Telephone connections were restored as quickly as possible by GPO staff assisted by military reinforcements, sometimes by stringing the wires from lamp posts and convenient buildings. Two field telephone vans sent by the London Fire Brigade proved so useful that Liverpool resolved to obtain two of its own. Makeshift telephone bureaux were set up around the city centre within days of the raids for those who had been cut off, and these remained in use till the end of the year. The new Seel Street exchange was brought into use on the 5th June, and full trunk facilities were available through Lancaster House within about four months. In the long term the planned conversion to automatic exchanges was speeded up – not easy in wartime conditions.[338]

The reopening of the many blocked roads, including some major ones, was a mammoth task, complicated by the need to bury the new salt-water mains at thirty-two main crossings to allow trams to pass.[339] As late as the 25th August there were still forty-seven roads completely closed – including James Street, where some demolition was still to be done. Where Stanley Road had been brought down over the railway, tram services were not restored till January 1942.

A party from the Ministry of Information came to see how things were going 9th-12th June.[340] They found that the spirit of the people was recovering, but added to the weight of abuse heaped on the local leadership. "The members of the War Emergency Committee appear to be satisfied with the steps taken during the raids and to be confident that their planning could meet any and every emergency. We did not find this confidence among the other officials we met nor among members of the general public, who feared that plans would quickly break down if intensive raiding took place again." And it was generally thought that the war would continue with ever-heavier raids, as indeed it did elsewhere.

The MoI had its own problems as "the Town Clerk of Liverpool did not welcome co-operation and the work done by the Ministry of Information was carried out under difficulties. The blitz arrangements there appear to be run entirely by the War Emergency Committee of three headed by the Mayor (sic). This brooks no interference, appears to be completely satisfied, and resents the idea of what was described to us as Government intrusion." In Bootle on the other hand all help was welcomed by the Town Clerk and ARP Controller, Harold Partington notably 150 Lancashire miners who arrived with picks and shovels and a corn miller from outside who offered 75 vans with gangs to move furniture from damaged property.

It is in the nature of things that these reports should dwell on failure with a view to improvement. Leaving aside the Chief Constable's troubles on the 5th, no-one has a bad word to say for the police, wardens, rescue parties, doctors, nurses or ambulance drivers, all of whom were under Council control; but neither can one find reports investigating the reasons for their success in coping with everything thrown at them. The Lord Mayor received letters of appreciation from the Ministry of Food and from Sir Harry Haig[341] – it must be supposed that, whatever their differences in the stress of battle, Sir Harry meant what he said in praising the Civil Defence services and the Emergency Committee's work in reconstruction and caring for the homeless. Disagreements about the means do not signify any lack of concern. We are, after all, dealing with the same men who had impressed the Inspector General of ARP with their efficiency and sturdy independence only a few months earlier.

SALVAGE

The tailing off of the raids and mining of the approaches after May left the Marine Department free to concentrate on clearing the sunken and damaged vessels already cluttering the port and the river.

One of the first things to be tackled was the state of the Board's own plant. The ***Mammoth*** (200-ton lift) was a major salvage job in itself, requiring the complete demolition of the 500-ton jib before she could even be raised, which was done on the 19th October. She was not restored to use again till September 1942. The ***Atlas*** (100-ton lift) was seriously damaged. The ***Hercules*** (50-ton lift) was raised and taken to dry dock where she had to be cut in two

Dismantling the *Mammoth's* jib, 18th September 1941. The ship beyond has a paravane boom attached to her bow as part of the equipment to provide protection for convoys from moored mines.

The *No. 20 Hopper/Watchful* under repair in Clarence No. 2 Graving Dock with the *Ulster Star* behind. On the right No. 1 dock appears to have been blanked out and probably contains a warship.

and realigned – work completed September 1942. The ***Samson*** (30-ton lift) needed repairs. Only the ***Titan***, with her somewhat weedy 25-ton lift, was really fit for duty.[342]

In the circumstances, the ***Atlas*** and ***Samson*** had to be kept at work until they could be relieved, finally receiving attention in September 1941 and October 1942 respectively. Some relief was provided by luggage ferries equipped with 15-ton cranes; the ***Oxton***, commissioned June 1941, and the ***Bebington***, commissioned three months later. All these cranes, especially the last two, were also needed for handling heavy loads on and off ships.

Of the Board's five camels – used for raising sunken vessels – only two were available at first; the two in Huskisson were in use by the end of May. Also in Huskisson, the long-awaited salvage-boat ***Watchful*** needed to be recovered as soon as possible. The tug ***Huskisson*** may have been engaged on this task when she entered Huskisson 2 and, unsurprisingly, was damaged underwater through striking submerged wreckage on the 29th June.[343]

There were other urgent tasks. Vessels in danger of sinking, such as the ***Clan MacInnes***, were taken to dry dock for repair – when a free one could be found. The graving docks themselves needed to be cleared of wrecks and then patched up for further use – the ***Marton*** trapped HMS ***Belmont*** in Langton 2 Upper until late July and the dock had been so badly damaged by the fire that it was out of use for nine months. The log-jam was so great that some vessels were sent elsewhere; when it was decided, after some heart-searching, that the ***Nadin*** was worth repairing, she was towed to the Bristol Channel. The ***Moscha D. Kydoniefs*** was repaired in Lisbon and the ***Jean Jadot*** at Quebec (a fractured propeller shaft having been discovered on arrival there – attributed to the ***Malakand***). Floating hulks, such as the ***Elstree Grange***, had to be removed from the quays. The larger ships for which there was no hope were beached along King's Dock river wall for breaking up. Smaller vessels were made seaworthy enough for the passage to Tranmere or New Ferry beaches to await their fate. Sometimes – as with the hapless ***Kileenan*** – it was simply a matter of recovering engines and boilers for scrap.

There was hardly any such thing as a typical salvage job, each wreck presenting its own problems. The ***Bra-Kar's*** shelter deck was flooded from end to end so that a temporary bulkhead had to be built to counter leakage at the stern before anything else could be done. The ***Trentino*** was listed away from the quay, making it impossible to put pumps aboard from that side. In order to transfer the salvage plant from a vessel lying alongside, it was first necessary to build platforms on the ***Trentino's*** deck.

The ***Stromboli's*** stern was lifted with the aid of camels and swung away from the dock wall. This allowed the whole ship to be lifted by camels – still on her side – and carried into Huskisson 2 out of everyone's way. Before this could be done, a channel had to be surveyed and marked by buoys and underwater wreckage removed. Huskisson Dock was allowed to run dry for several tides so that the hole that had sunk the ***Stromboli*** could be patched by logs; only then was it possible to right her and pump the water out. When the dock was drained, two bodies were found – one recent, the other probably dating from May 1941.[344]

The ***Lyster*** was sufficiently out of the way to be a low priority job and by the time her case was taken up again in 1942 she was sunk deep in mud. Large tripods were fixed securely to her raised side and wires run from these to winches built into the floor of the shed opposite solely for this purpose. Helped by salvage boats, these were able to haul the ***Lyster*** bodily onto an even keel from which position she was relatively easy to float.[345] (This was good practice for the much larger ***Empress of Canada*** job after the war.)

Some wrecks in the river were simply blasted into smaller and smaller pieces until they no longer presented a hazard to shipping; William Clarke remembers Captain Brock in a diving suit going down to the wreck of what must have been the ***Corbet*** with a large quantity of "ammo gelatine" round his waist for this purpose.

There were also the cargoes, which had to be salved wherever possible. The ***Baron Inchcape***, with her bow on the bottom, still contained thousands of tons of grain – sixty per cent of which was recovered in good condition. The rest had been contaminated by Mersey water, which at least had the advantage of causing the grain to swell and plug the leaks. The cargo was extracted from the 9th May to 2nd July, by the end of which time the damaged grain was giving off such foul gases that the men had to wear gas masks and gold braid turned green. In the end nearly all the cargo was saved, for either human or animal consumption.

With forty such jobs to be tackled at once, the salvage men cannot have been pleased when some critics commented on the initially slow progress. In the absence of further serious raids, the mountain of work was whittled away, though some of the jobs outstanding from before May outlasted the war owing to the peculiar problems involved. The ***Ullapool*** had to be demolished gently to avoid any risk to the under-river tunnel that passed close by. After an attempt involving balloons and compressed air had failed, the ***Silvio*** was cut into twenty-three conveniently-sized portions that were all on the quayside by May 1947.[346] The ***Tacoma City***, from which the steel cargo was recovered whenever conditions were right and the Marine Department not otherwise occupied, was finally reported cleared in October 1963!

Huskisson No. 2 branch was one of the last areas to be dealt with. The end was dammed with rubble so that it could be drained – with difficulty, as the water found unsuspected ways of seeping in again. At last it was done and the awesome wreckage of the ***Malakand*** revealed, together with the other remaining wreck, the ***Ellesport.*** The first job was the removal of bombs remaining on board – 1,350 of them, presumably a hold full.[347] This was done by the Royal Navy and the bombs returned to the RAF for disposal. It is said that oil fuel was recovered as well[348] (she had taken on 215 tons on the last day of April) and there was talk of other – unspecified – cargo. The British Iron & Steel Corporation (Salvage) Ltd. then moved in to recover what they could of the ship for scrap – one of Auxiliary Fireman Charles Hughes's jobs at this period was to stand by in case of fires being started in the wreck by sparks from the cutting operations. As it was found that the branch itself had suffered serious damage, it was decided that it should be filled in to provide a useful space; there was still no shortage of rubble.[349] The lower framing of the ***Malakand*** was left on the bottom where it lies still, along with the ***Ellesport.*** The useful space is still known as the ***Malakand*** area.

RAILWAYS

On the 9th May there were no stations open for dock traffic and fires still prevented examination of the Exchange viaduct at Bentinck Street. A week later there had been considerable improvement. Lines had been opened to Waterloo, North Mersey, Park Lane, Bankfield, North Docks and Langton – the last allowing coal to be taken to Linacre Gas Works again. From North Docks it was possible to reach Sandon by the line that crossed Blackstone Street on the level – or it would have been if an auxiliary water pipe had not been laid across the track. Alexandra could be reached from North Mersey and there was talk of taking trains by this route, on to Atlantic Dock Junction, and then back to Canada (thus sparing the over-worked dock lines). The Canada Dock coal hoists were ready for use by the 15th, but were prevented from working by UXBs. The ***Domino's*** mast was also in the way – blocking one of the hoists until it was cut off on the 12th.

The High Level Coal Railway at Bramley-Moore and Wellington Docks was functioning again from the 19th. The Bootle branch was re-opened to Canada on the 18th and to Alexandra on the 19th – partly single-track at first. By this time the total of wagons forwarded daily had reached half the April figure. On the 23rd the Bootle branch was closed again by a landslip – for a week this time. A single line under Stanley Road restored the direct route to Sandon and Huskisson on the 5th June.[350]

The Overhead Railway moved its Head Office again – to a train in Seaforth Sands carriage shed – and was running from Seaforth Sands to Alexandra and Dingle to Brunswick by the 12th, the gap being filled by buses. The future of the line was in doubt, however, as there were powerful voices calling for it to be demolished – to provide useful scrap and to preserve the dock lines from further blockages. This would also have allowed the provision of a third goods line along the docks. Fortunately, it proved impossible to arrange any reasonable alternative and it was decided to go ahead with repairs. The Railway Control Officer objected strongly, claiming that goods traffic was more important, though how he expected seamen and dockers to handle the traffic without adequate transport for themselves is not clear. Since the railway was never hit again, hindsight confirms that the correct decision was reached. The line was restored in sections, until the 1st November 1941 when normal service was resumed along its whole length.[351]

Central Station was re-opened (less two platforms) on the 10th. Two days later the express passenger service from Southport was re-introduced as after the December raids, taking a route right round the south end of the city. There were two trains to Liverpool in the morning and two back in the evening – all well-filled. Plans were made for running this service via Wigan and St. Helens if necessary. (There was also the evacuation service; on Saturday the 10th four trains ran from Aintree to Wigan, Leigh and other safe havens, taking 2,048 men, women and children out – the workmen among them returning daily.) Goods trains were running over the viaduct to Great Howard Street by the 23rd June – single line – and electric passenger services resumed on the 5th July. The lines to Exchange were not fully restored till the 2nd May, 1942.[352]

The replacement of all the lost buildings could not be contemplated until after the war, and some of the smaller goods stations were never re-opened. In spite of this, Liverpool's railways would carry more traffic than ever before in the years 1943/44.

If I have not paid as much attention to the Mersey Railway as to other lines, this is because it was a purely passenger-carrying undertaking; but the restoration of its outlets in Liverpool is a saga that throws light on the multiplicity of problems involved in getting the city on its feet again.[353] On the 4th May both exits from James Street Station were blocked and the steps up to the concourse of Central Station were thought to be threatened by the tottering end wall of Lewis's. This left the passage under the Lyceum Club as the only way in or out for the thousands that used the line every day – more than in peacetime and more again when the ferry services were disrupted.

The partial re-opening of Central on the 10th did not help the Mersey, whose concourse entrance

The magnificent tower of James Street Station, previously inaccessible for photographers. Those must be the troublesome water tanks on top. Other buildings visible from left to right are the PSNC, Dock Board (one of the corner domes) and Liver Building. Comparison with the later view on p.55 is interesting remained in the roped-off section. Some relief came with the re-opening on the same day of the Water Street entrance to James Street – provided with a wooden canopy in case of falling debris from India Buildings. Inspection of the James Street building revealed that it was a dangerous ruin.

The station had a hydraulic tower to match the one that still rises above Hamilton Square Station in Birkenhead – built in connection with the three hydraulic lifts provided when the line was opened. Two of these had been replaced by four electric lifts, but the third remained and needed to be restored to use if possible. The tower was cracked from top to bottom, however, and it was decided that all but sixteen feet of this would have to be demolished together with everything else above the ground floor.

This decision was reinforced on the 11th, the day after trains resumed their James Street stop, when a large mass of debris fell down the No. 3-4 lift shaft. The roof of No. 4 lift was now buried in three feet of bricks and rubble and the clouds of dust led to the station being closed again for half an hour. Eleven days later another section of the Moor Street warehouses collapsed and more debris was unloaded down the shaft onto the remaining hydraulic lift. At least, the water seepage from the broken main was much reduced by the end of the month – it had been pouring through the bare rock and between the bricks in the subway as well as the station.

While a third of James Street's lift capacity was vested in the hydraulic lift, it was essential to salve the three water tanks from the top of the tower during demolition. On the 8th July the second of these was being swung away from the tower when the wire sling holding it broke. The tank fell a hundred feet onto the floor over the hydraulic lift shaft and large chunks of concrete from this rained down the shaft to smash through the roof of the lift cage. It was not until the 1st September that James Street Station was near enough to the ground to permit the street to be re-opened for traffic.

Meanwhile, on the 16th July, the demolition of Lewis's was far enough advanced for Central Station to be fully re-opened, including the second Mersey entrance. After being patched up in a very plain manner – with the flaked granite pillars at the front encased in reinforced concrete – the James Street building was restored to use on the 28th December. With some ingenuity even the battered hydraulic lift was reinstated soon after and the Mersey Railway was once again in full working order.

THE FIRE SERVICE

By the 10th May, 558 fire appliances had been brought in to reinforce the local brigades, coming from as far away as Norwich, Reading and London. Firebrace departed a couple of weeks later, leaving his deputy, A. P. L. Sullivan, in charge. The National Fire Service, incorporating the AFS and all the local brigades, was formed on the 17th August. Firebrace headed the new organisation as Chief of Fire Staff and Sullivan returned to being his deputy while another London man took charge of the NFS in Liverpool and Bootle – as Fire Force Commander. When he left in 1942 he was replaced by Sullivan again.

J. F. Collins of Bootle became a Divisional Officer in the Liverpool area; what of Liverpool's former chief, H. R. Owen? It was on the 26th May that the ARP Controller presented the Liverpool Emergency Committee with a letter from the Home Office containing "a Direction of the Minister of Home Security under Regulation 29A" appointing Sullivan as Acting Chief Officer of the LFB, under the Emergency Committee.[354] The relevant minute also records that Mr. Owen was to be "granted leave of absence with pay, pending further instructions." In fact, he was suspended on Home Office orders without any prior consultation and against the Emergency Committee's wishes.[355]

Regulation 29A, inserted in the Defence Regulations in 1940, stated (among other things) that the Minister of Home Security could place "any services provided by a local authority in the discharge of its civil defence functions wholly or partly under the control of...any person appointed by him" – also that he could give directions as to the appointment and dismissal of persons discharging defence functions for a local authority as appeared "to be necessary or expedient in the interests of the public safety or the defence of the realm."

G. V. Blackstone's ***History of the British Fire Service***[356] refers to these events briefly and suggests that they were the result of a report written by Firebrace that was "severely critical", particularly with regard to absence of cohesion between AFS and LFB, inadequate facilities for repair and maintenance of equipment, 'sketchy' communications and poor arrangements for receiving reinforcements.

The only information that seems to be available on what followed is contained in a series of Watch Committee minutes from November 1941 to March 1942.[357] These reveal that Owen was brought before an Inquiry in November. The Watch Committee wished to be represented at the hearing on the grounds that any criticism of Owen would reflect on all those responsible for the fire services. They were advised that the Inquiry was "limited to matters relating to Mr. Owen's personal conduct" and had no bearing on anyone else. They were, however, allowed to instruct a Mr R. S. Trotter to represent them at the adjourned hearing, held at Liverpool's Municipal Annexe in Dale Street on the 1st and 2nd January.

Trotter reported that, "The Inquiry, which was very thorough and careful, dealt in the main with the matters referred to in the part of Commander Firebrace's report of the 11th May, 1941, which related to Mr. Owen personally. The events most discussed were those of the night of the 6th/7th May, 1941." (It will be recalled that this was the night that Firebrace took an advisory role.) Owen himself was the first witness, followed, after cross-examination, by other witnesses on his behalf, including the Chairman of the Watch Committee. The Chief Constable also presented a statement, presumably in support of Owen, and Firebrace was recalled and cross-examined on the second day. Firebrace, one gathers, had earlier been the main 'prosecution' witness. (I am not sure if this word is correct in law – the proceedings certainly have all the appearance of a trial.) The hearing ended with speeches for and against Owen; the Commissioner (in charge of the Inquiry) did not allow Trotter to speak "as there was nothing in the evidence before him implicit of any criticism of the Watch Committee."

On the 17th March, the Committee noted receipt of a report from the Home Office on Owen. They heard the details "with satisfaction" and placed on record "their confidence in Mr. Owen and appreciation of the services he has rendered the City." Owen was reinstated in the NFS as a Divisional Officer in the Cardiff area as from the 17th. It is obvious that, whatever the charges against him were, Owen had been honourably acquitted. His new posting was a demotion, but this was not uncommon in the reorganisation that followed the formation of the NFS.

After the war, the Chief Constable gave a brief account of these events.[358] Firebrace, and later Sullivan, were put in charge solely because of their wider experience. The Emergency Committee received extracts from a report – evidently Firebrace's – that they thought unduly critical of Owen and the Liverpool Fire Brigade generally. In response to their objections, a Mr C. Paley Scott, KC, was appointed to hold an inquiry that completely vindicated the LFB and its Chief Officer. This account cannot be squared exactly with that in the minutes, but doubtless refers to the same inquiry.

It is most unfortunate that no further information has come to light on these transactions. Correspondence with the Home Office (who have given much help in other areas) has produced no indication that the records of the Inquiry or Firebrace's report still exist, though I hope they will surface one day. In the meantime, speculation on the nature of the charges against Owen would be improper, but it is worth pointing out that there is not the slightest hint that the failure to get reinforcements to Liverpool on the Saturday night formed any part of them. His employers were plainly sorry to lose a man who had steered the Liverpool fire service through the worst of the blitz, bearing a burden that few of us would wish to take up and none of his successors had to.

To leave Mr Owen on a happier note; in October 1942 a ship loaded with ammunition and motor vehicles caught fire off the Welsh coast. The vehicles had full petrol tanks so as to be ready for instant use, possibly in the North African landings. Owen was one of a team of South Wales firemen praised for their action in boarding the stricken vessel at sea and saving her after a long and gallant fight.[359]

There is no doubt that the fire service did exhibit some failings – the Chief Constable was notably defensive about its performance in May in his post-war report – but what were they? The "muddle" over reinforcements may have occurred outside Liverpool, but Liverpool seems to have been behind Manchester in the provision of emergency water tanks on blitzed sites. The ***Echo*** of 26th May, 1941 contains a reference to severe criticism relating to control, co-ordination and "tardiness in the use of river water", that may owe something to Firebrace's report. According to information sent to Mass-Observation: "Another man was incensed about what he termed the failure of the fire fighting services in Liverpool...Why, (he said) we had to bring the military in to lay water pipes for us; why hadn't they made proper arrangements to draw water from the Mersey for fire fighting? It's not the rank and file, they are as brave as lions; it's the direction, no cohesion, different departments fighting with each other."[360]

Such comments may or may not be fair. According to Mr Eglin, the shortage of equipment and emergency water supplies and the delay in laying salt-water mains were the fault of central government. It is only fair to say that the steel piping for salt-water mains had only recently been made available and that London, which had acquired some in April, did not have it installed when it was needed on the 10th May.[361] A rumour that Liverpool firemen were not allowed to take water from the docks seems to be a wild invention: they were doubtless advised that it was a last resort, as salt water could damage foodstuffs and machinery.

It is all too easy, when concentrating on one area, to assume that the problems and failures discovered were unique to that area. This is rarely the case. The vast expansion of the fire services as a result of the war made it difficult to provide enough competent and experienced officers, and the curious reluctance of the regular fire brigade men to co-operate with the AFS was so widespread that it must have had some more or less rational basis. Fear of having to compete with the newcomers for their jobs later is the usual explanation.

One has heard it suggested that men commonly joined the AFS to evade call-up and were thus not always the most admirable figures. This is grossly unfair, even if it was true in some cases. Many gave up their spare time to training well before the war started, while some of the critics were just hoping it would never happen – others were in reserved occupations anyway. Volunteers were publicly recruited, indeed ardently recruited when the numbers consistently fell short of establishment, and the fire service in a place like Liverpool had no use for the halt, the lame and the blind; the civilian services needed men fit for military service if the ports, and with them the country, were to survive. You can hardly beg for public-spirited volunteers only to say to those who turn up: "Oh yes – trying to get out of the army, eh?" As a matter of fact, soldiers with experience in the AFS were being encouraged to *return* to the fire service as early as October 1940.

There *were* those in the service who, left to themselves, would shelter in a doorway when they were supposed to be manning their pumps. There were others who lacked resource. On one occasion (not during a raid) a fire started in a Liverpool dock shed. A party of firemen was on hand with a pump, but the Leading Fireman was absent on business of his own and the others did not know how to start the pump, which was the Leading Fireman's job, nor did they realise that there would have been enough pressure in the mains if they had simply connected the hose to a hydrant. They were helpless. Fortunately, some dockers came and put the fire out with buckets of water.[362]

Reinforcements also fell short of the ideal at times. It was not uncommon for the brigades called on to retain their regular firemen and senior officers at home – along, needless to say, with their best equipment – and send only auxiliaries. The shortage of experienced officers on these occasions was one of the main reasons for things getting out of hand. London made a point of sending out well-balanced teams, including regulars and senior officers; another honourable exception nearer to home was the Stretford and Urmston Brigade, whose Chief Officer is said to have helped to save the Bluecoat Building. The problem of different brigades having incompatible equipment continued until after the formation of the NFS, and many of those called to Liverpool in May were faced with their first serious fires as well as their first air raids. During one of the May raids, Charles Hughes was with a party dashing from fire to fire in the Commercial Road area while the bombs fell. They were surprised to find an out-of-town pump unattended and proceeded to make use of it. Soon after the 'all-clear' sounded, some firemen came strolling up. "Hey, what are you doing with our pump?" they asked. The Liverpool men explained that they were using it to put out fires, enquired where the others had been, and were astonished when the would-be helpers explained that they were under orders to seek shelter during alerts!

Such failings were too common, but by no means universal. Had I been able to obtain more information about times and places I should have said something about Auxiliary Patrol Officer Goldston, whose action in obtaining water from the docks in spite of exploding time bombs prevented the spread of fire – also Divisional Officer Morland, who remained in his threatened headquarters until it was partly demolished by a falling wall and communications cut off. He then set up an emergency HQ, so maintaining some sort of control over the situation. There were other such stories that would make for a more balanced picture if only the details were available. It must also be remembered that the men who poured water on a burning ammunition ship for hours on end were not a specially picked team of volunteers – just a random sample of local auxiliary firemen who happened to be available and who were given the right sort of leadership. Virtually every man in the service would have done just what they did if called upon to do so.

The effects of the service's failure in May were certainly serious, but should not be exaggerated. Peacetime fires in the docks, with plenty of equipment on call, could take days to put out and fires aboard ships present very specialised problems that junior officers and the AFS could not be expected to handle effectively. Accounts of buildings gutted in spite of the efforts of the fire service may conceal valiant work in preventing the spread of fire to neighbouring property. Also, it is an easy matter to look at a map and suggest taking water from the nearest dock – a fireman faced with streets full of burning rubble might have seen things differently.

Many of the faults, locally and nationally, were dealt with by the NFS, but changes started before then – mostly under Sullivan. Liverpool's existing plans for the provision of surface pipelines and emergency water tanks were speeded up and expanded. At the end of May, Sullivan announced an interim reorganisation of the service.[363] Sector Posts would be abolished and all pumps concentrated at Auxiliary Stations instead. The separate docks divisions would be abolished. The AFS were to man District Control Rooms to free senior LFB men. (There was a tendency for experienced officers to be stuck in Control when they would have been better employed taking charge at major fires.) All stations were to have incident boards (there were none before). Consideration was to be given to the provision of bases on the outskirts of the city for reinforcements to report to, rather than in "the target area" as before. A direct telephone line should be provided between Hatton Garden and the Regional Commissioner's Office in Manchester. Instead of the officer in charge at a fire sending a message in the form "Assistance required at..." and the District Inspector deciding what to send: "I propose to trust the man at the fire to ask for what help he requires."

Blackstone clarifies this last point, saying that in London the officer at a fire would assess the situation and request whatever number of additional pumps seemed to be needed: three, ten, fifty or whatever. "In one big port there were only two standard reinforcement messages – 'Send assistance' and 'Send more assistance'!"[364] Very amusing. I don't have Liverpool's reply to this, but I can suggest one. Whether the message was sent by hand or by telephone, the District Inspector must have been given some indication of the size of the fire on which to base his decision – and it was not much use the men at the fires specifying how many pumps were needed if Control didn't have them to send. Requests for fifty pumps may have been bandied about nonchalantly in London, but Liverpool did not have 2,500 pumps to play with. As I have said before, the Liverpool men may have made mistakes, but they were not idiots.

There was more to follow. Additional telephonists were taken on to cope with the rush of calls during raids. More fire-floats, towing vehicles, staff cars and motor cycles were ordered and, later on, a great deal of new equipment for maintenance. Home Security approved all this, along with the posting of 500 conscripted men to the Liverpool AFS.[365] All this led to resentment at the sudden arrival of "masses of equipment which the deposed fire chief is said to have pleaded for in vain."[366]

There is no doubt that the fire service nationwide was much better fitted to cope with raids some months after the worst of them had passed.

BURYING THE DEAD

On the 16th May there were rescue parties still working at seventeen incidents in Liverpool, all in the north end or city centre. News of those still missing kept trickling in, so that as one closed another would have to be re-opened. Sometimes the work had to be suspended when unexploded bombs turned up. At Index Street a light party and "86 Supplementary men" were making a general search of the ruins. At Great George Square – reported clear on the morning of the 5th – the bodies of eleven Belgian seamen had been recovered since the 13th, and the final total would be over twenty.[367]

The incident at Weaver Buildings – burnt with the Corn Exchange – had been closed on the 3rd. It was re-opened on the 16th in the hope of finding a missing fireman, but the task was hopeless until the unsafe building had been demolished. The site was kept under observation until a steam crane could be moved in on the 3rd June. A heavy party then resumed the search until they were able to report on the 9th: "Charred bones, spectacles in case and cigarette case recovered in debris."[368]

At Mill Road, Pilkington's men worked till the 13th. Towards the end there was some unpleasantness with contractors' men on other sites accusing the volunteers of blacklegging. The 83rd and last victim – a baby girl – was brought out on the 17th (a few more died of their injuries) but rescue parties carried on searching until they were certain there was no-one else to be found. The incident was reported closed at 1415 on the 29th after over twenty-five days of continuous effort.[369]

Rescue parties were still active at six incidents on the 26th May. On June the 19th and 20th, men of a first aid party had to partly strip before wading through crude oil in the bottom of one of the gutted hulks beached at King's Dock to recover bodies.[370]

At Walton Gaol the search continued till the last two men were found on the 28th May, but when the ruins of I block were being tackled in 1952 a skeleton was found. It belonged to a man of about 35, and was without hands or feet. At the inquest it was agreed that he must have been a prisoner killed when I block was hit, although the man was never identified and there had been no prisoners unaccounted for at the time. An alternative version has it that one was not found and was assumed to have escaped, but this probably arises from the two who did escape briefly. The City Engineer's records clearly state that the incident was closed when the last missing bodies were recovered.[371] It is all very odd. (It is conceivable that the hands and feet had been recovered in 1941 and counted as a body – there was sometimes less to be found.)

Periodically there are claims that at some major incidents the bodies were deliberately left and the site bulldozed over them. In view of what has been said above, it would appear that such rumours are completely baseless.

The mortuary service had its problems. In Liverpool, the hapless Parks and Gardens staff had been brought in to assist, but some found it impossible to face the work and stopped turning up. "One superintendent appears to have lost his reason since after sending a number of wrong bodies for inclusion in the public funeral he left the mortuary and has not again reported for duty."[372] Medical students proved better suited, though even their enthusiasm must have wavered at times. The cemetery records of the period make sobering reading: the roll-calls of whole families, the burial of a mother with her day-old baby, the four bodies of uncertain sex buried in one coffin.

For a while after the Saturday night, arrangements for the identification of bodies were chaotic. This was mostly on account of the sheer numbers involved – on one day 5,000 people visited Webster Road for this purpose – but identification was sometimes removed before the bodies were dispatched to the mortuary, and normal standards were inevitably not always observed. On the *Tacoma Star*, Denis

Foss found a crewman dead in his bunk and already stiff – it appeared that a small piece of shrapnel had come in through the side of the ship. He was a heavy man and simply getting him up to the deck was a tricky job. "A furniture van came for him, and when we opened the canvas at the back it was some 6 feet high in dead bodies, and we had great difficulty in swinging him on top of them." (The City Engineer's Department vehicles set aside for the transport of bodies were sometimes taken for furniture vans.)

When the rush was over and only a few bodies remained, it was discovered that two of them had officially been buried already. With Home Office approval, the coffins were disinterred, opened, and found to be full of sandbags. In each case, when the hearse had arrived to take the body for a private funeral, it had proved impossible to find it. Thinking that the bodies had mistakenly been sent to the mass grave, the undertakers had coffins filled with sand handed over instead with the idea of sparing the relatives further distress. They were hauled through the courts, but only bound over as they had meant well.[373]

Rapid improvements were made in the process of identification after the first few days and the facilities were expanded to cater for up to 2,000 dead – next time.

There were three public funerals at Anfield Cemetery – for 214 bodies on the 13th, 74 on the 17th, and 126 on the 23rd. By no means all of these were unidentified. The situation was eased by the availability of "communal catacombs" in the form of red-brick tunnels. All of Liverpool's mass interments (there were also two in December) seem to have taken the same form, with sections of the vault left open so that the coffins, each draped with the Union Flag, could be seen. Representatives of the Council and the forces attended, and services were conducted by leaders of the various denominations.[374]

The ***Bootle Times*** of 16th May contained a prominent notice: "FUNERAL OF AIR RAID VICTIMS – Bootle's unidentified air raid victims will be buried at 11 o'clock this morning in Bootle Cemetery." Similar notices had appeared in relation to the dead of earlier raids on Liverpool, but the Censor now refused to allow the publication of details of the first Liverpool funeral; the ***Daily Telegraph*** was the only newspaper to break ranks and print the information. Notices were put up and relatives informed by the police "where possible", but many who would have wished to attend were left completely in the dark.[375]

After all this confusion, accounts of the first funeral were published the following day – some in the national press. The two that followed appear to have passed unrecorded.

"Saturday night's raid on Liverpool. Crowd gather round a casualty list." A *News Chronicle* picture taken on the 4th and passed by the Censor.

MORALE

It is not wise to generalise about morale, which obviously varies from one individual to another. Some areas were hardly touched while others were devastated. Some had lost home, family and friends – some had been successful in their own battle to save life or property and had found unsuspected reserves of strength and resourcefulness. Those, such as myself, brought up in the immediate post-war tradition of cheerful defiance are liable to be most impressed by the discovery that some behaved badly (in the worst cases looting the property of those bombed out of their homes) and perhaps to over-emphasise that aspect of life. A more recent generation, taught to 'knock' and doubt, will be surprised to find that much of the wartime "we can take it" propaganda was based on sober truth – it is just not the whole truth.

Having said that, it does seem that morale in the Liverpool area took a knock in May 1941. While it was noted that in one industry morale was high and absenteeism non-existent, in another men were slow to return to work. Some fire-watchers resigned or stopped volunteering. General Sir Frederick Pile, in charge of ground anti-aircraft defences, said that "In Liverpool civilian morale had touched a lower level by the last night of the raids than at any other time in any other place during the Blitz, *and I am not surprised.*" Pile spent two nights there himself "*and it was most unpleasant... But at low level or not, the morale held.*"[376] (Curiously, this has been quoted several times *without* the words that I have put in italics.) According to some, this was not entirely attributable to the enemy. The attitude of local officialdom was reported to be: "that the safety of the people matters more than their comfort"[377] – which suggests a failure to appreciate the importance of morale.

It should be borne in mind that this was one of the blackest periods of the war for Britain – so there was no cheer in the news from other parts. The initial excitement of standing alone and bravely facing up to aerial bombardment had worn off somewhat, and there was no great improvement to be looked for in the near future. It was generally thought that the raids would continue until Liverpool looked like Berlin did in 1945.

The outside observers that crowded into Liverpool at this time included one from Mass-Observation – in the city for three days around the 18th May.[378] He was most impressed by "The almost universal criticism and dissatisfaction with post-blitz administration" and "The superficially apparent atmosphere of ineptitude that seems to oppress the town" – notably in the failure to press on with reconstruction work on Sundays. There were "unprintably violent comments on local leadership", whose prestige was exceptionally low – especially among "the most responsible sections of the community." Where he might have expected to learn of heads rolling on account of "the confusions that have arisen", the talk was rather of honours being distributed. (Criticisms of this sort were universal in the wake of serious raids. If things really *were* worse in Liverpool, this may have been a reflection of the weight of the attack rather than peculiar inefficiency. Harold Partington of Bootle received the OBE in July – by all accounts well-earned. The Liverpool administration was apparently overlooked for the remainder of 1941.)

"Feeding arrangements completely collapsed as far as the majority of townspeople were concerned" (a wild exaggeration). This was put down to poor organisation, and it was also said that the offer of canteens from other places was refused in the belief that the situation was "fully under control." The use of "lorries and random vehicles" for nightly evacuation led to talk of "refugees" and comparison with "newsreels, Madrid, and so on."

In spite of such problems, this reporter found morale impressive on the whole – but doubted whether it would have held in the face of further raids without some improvement at the top.

The Mass-Observation report is most interesting when it comes to the subject of rumours. The main Liverpool rumour had it that the city was under martial law on account of riots and peace demonstrations. This was thought to be as bad as the nun-stormtrooper rumour of 1940. "It has been heard, for instance, by one person in London within three hours, from a responsible M.P., a BBC official, a senior civil servant, the editor of an important paper, and a senior officer in the Services." Having seen the crowds of sightseers in the city, the reporter could only say that, far from martial law, it seemed that no control was being exercised at all.

Apart from the soldiers on fire-watching, traffic control, and demolition duty, there were armed patrols of the Home Guard watching over damaged areas. Otherwise, the only obvious source of this one was the difficulty of getting into the city or contacting friends and relations inside – together with the lack of any official explanation of the problems.

One of Mass-Observation's volunteer observers was a WAAF in Preston. On the 10th May her friend Jean stood at the window of their bedroom and asked: "Have you heard about Liverpool?"

"*What* about Liverpool?"

"Everyone's talking about it. Surely you must have – They say" (she whispered this bit, dramatically) – "they say the people there want to give in."

"I don't blame them, judging from the reports of the raids there."

"Yes, but I don't believe it's the *people.* I think it's those wretched Irish, trying to create panic. It's very easy to. They're going around shouting 'Stop the War' and 'We've had enough'. *English* people wouldn't do that."

"It's surprising what you'll do when you've lost everything."

"I was told they have got martial law there, and that if anyone is found saying they want the war stopped, they're shot on the spot."

Later the same morning the girls hitched a lift in a lorry from Liverpool – a splendid opportunity to learn the truth of the matter.

Jean: "They're saying terrible things about Liverpool. Some of the stories are too ghastly to believe."

Driver: "However bad they are, they can't be worse than the truth, that's a fact. I've been doing what all the other lorries have – taking people out into the fields, and just leaving them there, lorry and all. The local Council *hasn't done a thing* – only given them food. That I will say." (!)

Me: "They *must* have known it was going to happen."

Driver: "You bet they did. They'd got the coffins all made out last spring – 50,000 of them – that's why we were so short of wood. But not a jot for the living. There's *50,917 dead*, and God-knows-how-many wounded, just walking the streets, with their bandages on."

Jean: "There's martial law, isn't there?"

Driver: "Well, not exactly. But there's a lot of military with bayonets – they've more or less taken it over, as you might say."

(Jean's response to this appalling catalogue was: "Well, you've relieved my mind ever so much...")

From this and other sources come stories of food riots and people (usually Irish) hanging white flags from their windows. The white-flag rumour apparently turned up in the press and was investigated by Luke Hogan who traced it to curtains fluttering from broken windows in the Scotland Road area.[379] Talk of a big *daylight* raid on the 4th was probably inspired by the unusual number of large explosions during that day, and the one about coach-trips being run from outside for sightseers doubtless arose from the use of pleasure coaches to replace trams and also to bring in helpers of various kinds (not that some people wouldn't have run such tours if it had been possible to do so). The origin of the story of train-loads of bodies sent out of the area for cremation elsewhere is a bit of a mystery.

These stories circulated widely – towns around Liverpool were reported to be seething with them – and it was a week after the last raid before anything was done to counteract them. Then Lord Derby was given the true casualty figures (not for publication) before speaking at a public meeting,[380] and efforts were made by word of mouth and through newspaper editorials to damp things down.

"Lorry lifts for Liverpool people", a fascinating *Allied Newspapers* picture, dated 5th May. This was passed by the Censor, who was doubtless influenced by the generally cheerful air. It would have been easy enough to find people who were not taking things so calmly, but a desire to sleep outsides Liverpool was not incompatible with high morale.

It is interesting that the Mass-Observation report on Liverpool's reaction to the December raids attributes the exceptionally high morale then to a number of factors – including the relative absence of transport dislocation and serious damage in the city centre (where it is keenly felt by almost everybody) as well as the fact that gas and electricity supplies, telephones and such-like had only been slightly affected. If this is so, then a fall in morale after the May raids is hardly to be wondered at.

COULD LIVERPOOL HAVE HELD OUT?

The subject of morale leads naturally into the question of whether Liverpool could have held out in the face of further heavy raids. The usual answer is "no", but this seems unduly pessimistic in view of what some continental cities endured. The same view has been expressed with regard to other heavily-bombed areas, notably London's East End. In the face of this it is curious that people should persist in arguing that it was foolish of the British Government to think that the Germans could be bombed into submission when the same technique had so obviously failed on us. In 1941 this was not obvious at all. Those in the know thought that the Luftwaffe's attacks on the ports were coming all too near to succeeding – in terms of both material damage and the effects on morale – and that the abandonment of this target ranked with the failure to persevere with attacks on the radar stations and air-fields earlier in the Battle of Britain. They most certainly did not think that the British people were prepared to put up with the bombing indefinitely. (Would one have wished them to?) This being so, it was quite rational for them to conclude that the RAF, with bigger and better bombers soon to be available, could succeed where the Luftwaffe had failed only through lack of perseverance. Yes – recovery in both morale and the physical capacity of the ports was rapid, but only after the bombing had stopped. We now know that they were wrong about the Germans – as, no doubt, they were wrong about the British. Isn't hindsight wonderful?

The effects of the May raids on the Port of Liverpool have already been detailed at some length, but one may add that 7,370 tons of oilcakes (7.3% of total UK stocks) had been destroyed along with 8,770 tons of flour, oats, oil seeds, sugar, frozen meat and other food items up to a total of 26,000 tons.[381] The Official History considers the loss of timber to have been the most damaging item without putting a figure on it. 40,000 tons of shipping had been sunk and another 22,500 tons reduced to scrap – a useful addition to the U-boat campaign. To all this must be added the damage to the ports of Belfast, Barrow, Hull and the Clyde over the same period. To keep up the pressure from the air would have meant postponing the attack on Russia for a year, but few would see that as a particularly terrible mistake.

On the other hand, the rapid recovery of the port has also been noticed; it was working at 90% of capacity by the end of July. Some of the credit must go to the work done in reducing the turn-round time of ships, but, after making due allowance for this, the figures might still be taken as showing that the raids were not as bad as had been supposed at first. This is true to a point, but paradoxically it is also an indication of just how damaging they were. Houses and churches that were destroyed or badly damaged were not restored until after the war; they were not crucial to the war effort and the bombs that fell on them were largely wasted. On the other hand it was absolutely vital to get the docks functioning again, and men and resources were taken from other important jobs to get this done as quickly as possible. (On the 6th May the Ministry of Works directed a thousand men to Liverpool from Ellesmere Port where they had been building a new refinery for Shell, though it appears that work on this had just been abandoned anyway. They stayed for three months.) To gauge the full effect of any heavy air raid one has to take into account delays in work on projects that might be many miles away from the target – usually an impossible task.

The idea that a few more raids might somehow have knocked Liverpool out for the duration is hardly sustainable, but what if the enemy had persisted in his assault on the ports over a long period? This would certainly have been trying, though it was virtually impossible to destroy a port with the bombs available in 1941 and the law of diminishing returns was already setting in. An increasing number of bombs were only adding craters to sheds already gutted or assisting with demolition that would have had to be done anyway.

And lessons were being learned even in the first week of May. Some ships would have been saved if the rule about warping them off the quaysides had been introduced a week earlier, and now steps were taken to remove inflammable goods from the dock area as far as possible; timber in particular being ordered out.[382] It would have been better if this could have been done earlier, as had been widely suggested after December. This process would be taken further by the creation of the inland sorting depot at Simonswood, near Kirkby – authorised in January 1941 and in full operation by September 1942. The value of these inland depots was disputed, though they would have greatly reduced the quantity of goods lying in the vulnerable dock areas. It had been agreed early in the war that when the worst happened, dock sheds were a luxury for many cargoes – they could simply be handled over the bare quays. (In May 1941 experiments were made in the transfer of goods to lighters in the river, but nothing seems to have come of this.)[383] There is no doubt that the Port of Liverpool would have taken a lot of closing.

There were also improvements in civil defence – first the laying of salt-water mains, and then the reorganisation of the fire service nationally, with the provision of more men and equipment for Liverpool in particular. By the end of 1941, steps had been taken to protect telephone services by the laying of a 'ring main' with an under-river section from Aigburth to Bromborough.[384] In the air, radar-equipped night-fighters were becoming effective by May 1941 and would have made further raids more expensive for the enemy than they had been in the past.

More extensive evacuation might have been necessary, along with better shelters for those who had to stay; progress was being made on both these fronts. One of the most important changes to be made was also one of the easiest. The people of London were undoubtedly sustained in their ordeal by the knowledge that the eyes of the world were on them. If Liverpool had been given the same treatment it would have done wonders for morale. It is true that the veil of secrecy that had caused so much ill-feeling earlier in the war had been lifted to some extent, but more was needed.

When all is said and done, the impression that Liverpool could have taken no more arises from *one* raid carried out in near perfect conditions – in which a ship and a train, both loaded with ammunition, exploded – in which two vital communications centres were knocked out – and in which something went wrong with the arrangements for calling in reinforcements. This combination of misfortunes, cumulative in its effects, was largely due to good luck on one side and mistakes on the other that were unlikely to be repeated on the same scale. It may be that Liverpool could not have taken many more such nights, but the chances of further German successes of this order were negligible.

Appendices

APPENDIX I

BOMB-LOADS

I have frequently quoted the weight of bombs dropped according to German records. Unfortunately, while these figures ostensibly show the actual weight of bombs delivered to the targets according to the claims of German bomber crews, they cannot be accepted as accurate. British calculations, based on a study of what bombs dropped where, suggest that on average only ten or twenty per cent of bomb-loads landed on the target cities. In extreme cases the target might escape entirely; on the other hand, Coventry was thought to have received 47% of a heavy bomb-load on the night of 14th/15th November, 1940. The success rate was not noticeably higher when easily-found targets such as Hull were attacked. This helps to explain why casualties and damage sometimes bear no relation to the alleged weight of the attack.

On the three nights from 20th to 23rd December, 1940, the bomb census team noted the fall of 576 HE bombs (84.3 metric tons) on Merseyside, made up as follows.[385]

	20/21		21/22		22/23	
TYPE OF BOMB	No.	WEIGHT (tonnes)	No.	WEIGHT (tonnes)	No.	WEIGHT (tonnes)
1000kg	1	1.0	2	2.0	0	-
500kg	15	7.5	22	11.0	3	1.5
250kg	39	9.75	120	30.0	16	4.0
50kg	90	4.5	247	12.35	14	0.7
TOTALS	145	22.75	391	55.35	33	6.2

There were also seven HE bombs of uncertain size, two 20/21 and five 21/22 – apparently UXBs not recovered at the time of the survey. There is one report of an unexploded 1800-kg 'Satan' (at Brocklebank Graving Dock) and a 1000-kg 'Hermann' was also recovered intact. It is likely that both of these were in the "uncertain" category. Thirty-five mines were recorded – 11/21/3. As no information was available as to the proportion in which the two sizes then in use – 500 and 1000 kilograms – were dropped, the total weight could have been anything from 17.5 to 35 tonnes.

It is instructive to compare what the Germans thought they had dropped on the area (see next column).[386]

There is little doubt that some mines were in fact dropped, and it is possible that there was a tendency to under-estimate the size of exploded bombs from their results. However, it is plain that the Luftwaffe was not as successful in finding the target as it liked to think.

	20/21	21/22	
TYPE	No.	No.	
1800kg	12	16	
1700kg	2	2	
1000kg	61	62	
500kg	115	144	plus three oil bombs
250kg	184	291	plus one oil bomb
50kg	320	728	
Mines	nil	nil	
TOTALS	694	1243	

There are other points worth noting. Compared with Birmingham, Liverpool was favoured with a much higher proportion of the heavier HE bombs, presumably with the intention of causing the maximum damage to dock installations. 6.6 per cent of HE bombs failed to explode (with little variation in respect of different types). Experience in other parts was similar.

Of the 576 HE bombs recorded on Merseyside, 50.2% fell on open ground, roadways, yards and gardens (often causing damage to property nearby), 24.0% on houses, and 16.1% on industrial targets. A mere 1.0% fell on churches and hospitals with their grounds and, on this occasion, none on offices. The number and size of those that fell in the river was unknown. Very substantial properties might be destroyed by fire bombs (omitted from this survey) or by fire spreading from neighbouring buildings – dangers that were greater in commercial and industrial areas.

Another report[387] gives the percentage of bombs on the target as follows: December 20/21 – 11%, 21/22 – 21%. It is not at all clear how it was decided that bombs were intended for a particular target or where the line was drawn between hits and misses, but these percentages applied to the German claims give a close approximation to the weight of HE actually recorded on Merseyside. This suggests that the missing bombs must have been scattered over the towns and open countryside surrounding the built-up area of Merseyside, so allowing the Germans to think that they had been on target and the British to guess what the target had been.

The percentage of bombs on target given for Liverpool 3rd/4th May is thirty-five. In view of the loss of bomb census records this must be a fairly rough estimate. Calculations based on casualties – normally three or four killed per ton of HE exploded – suggest that a higher figure might be nearer the mark.

APPENDIX II

CASUALTIES

There were around 4,200 fatal casualties resulting from air raids on Merseyside, distributed as on p.160.[388]

These figures, which come from various sources, seem to offer a reasonable basis for comparison within Merseyside and in relation to other areas, but unfortunately they cannot be regarded as exact.

Small errors are inevitable, and there is no satisfactory answer to the problem of victims dying days, weeks or even years after the raid in which they were injured. More surprisingly, some Home Office figures exclude certain categories: members of the armed forces whether on duty or home on leave, merchant seamen, and even police and firemen! I do not know which, if any, of these are included. The position of foreign nationals is doubtful. If a fireman from Birmingham was injured at a fire in Bootle and died shortly after in a Liverpool hospital, is he included? If so, where? Such uncertainties make it dangerous to use figures acquired from different sources for comparative purposes.

It does seem extraordinary that it is not possible to find out how many people were killed in air-raids either nationally or in particular towns, but that is the position – the number of servicemen involved especially is sometimes significant and it is hard to see why anyone should want to exclude them from these figures.

Things are even worse when we come to consider the numbers killed on each night of the May raids. Such information would have been obtainable with reasonable accuracy at the time and is freely quoted for the heavier raids on London. For Merseyside, however, we have little more than the early and incomplete figures (for Liverpool only) quoted by Major Spong of the Inspector General's Department [389]:

May 1st/2nd	20
2nd/3rd	125
3rd/4th	954
4th/5th	4
5th/6th	15
6th/7th	32
7th/8th	37
Total	**1187**

The official list of Civilian War Dead includes police, firemen and some merchant seamen (the Belgians at Great George Square among them), but it contains errors and omissions and gives the date of death or fatal injury only as – for example – 4th May. So, was it that night or the night before? Granted that many incidents – especially the larger ones – can be attributed to a particular raid, and assuming the rest to be spread in the same pattern (none of Spong's figures being overstated), we come to the following distribution:

MAY	Liverpool	Bootle	Litherland	Crosby	Huyton	Birkenhead
1/2	20	-	-	-	-	11
2/3	125	5	-	14	-	12
3/4	1050	156	19	24	13	-
4/5	86	8	-	-	-	-
5/6	15	-	-	-	-	3
6/7	62	-	-	-	-	2
7/8	95	88	4	22	-	-
TOTALS	1397	257	23	60	13	28

Add Wallasey and Bebington 6.

Given the element of guesswork one cannot be too definite, but there is little doubt that 1250, give or take a hundred, died as a result of Saturday night's raid. This is twice as bad as Coventry's worst night and can be compared only with London's three bad raids around the same time. The Official History's figures for these are: 16th/17th April – 1179, 19th/20th April – 1208, 10th/11th May – 1452.

Human nature being what it is, people in heavily bombed areas soon took a perverse pleasure in claiming that they had had it worse than anyone else; indeed, the number of places that claim to have been the worst hit shows the ingenuity of statisticians, for whom this field is wide open.

From first to last there were about 60,000 people killed in the United Kingdom by bombs and rockets; half of them in London and 4,000 on Merseyside, which had the second largest concentration of casualties. Bearing in mind the fact that London was many times bigger than any other city, how does Merseyside compare on the basis of numbers killed per thousand of the population?

The Emergency Medical Services – that part of the Official History most concerned with these matters – contains statistics that make this comparison possible.[390] Admittedly, it hops about between the Metropolitan Police area (the usual definition of Greater London) and the London Defence Region, but this is unlikely to be significant. The former comprised ninety separate local authorities plus parts of nine others on the periphery. The latter was rounded off to take in ninety-five complete authorities with no fractions. Casualties in the nine authorities involved in this swap were low.

According to ***The Emergency Medical Services*** there were 19,278 killed in the London Defence Region during the 1940-41 blitz against 3,920 in Liverpool, Birkenhead, Wallasey and Bootle. The population of the Metropolitan Police area was 7,591,600 in June 1940, falling to 6,194,000 by the end of June 1941. The equivalent figures for the Merseyside four are 1,058,620 and 914,540. (These figures are the 'ration strength' and ought to be accurate.) From here it is simple arithmetic. If we take the populations in June 1940 there were 2.54 killed per thousand in London and 3.70 per thousand on Merseyside. The June 1941 populations give 3.11 per thousand in London and 4.29 per thousand on Merseyside.

A Londoner might reasonably argue that it would be fairer to include all the local authorities mentioned below. The Official History does not contain comparable figures for the other four, but if we take what population figures are available (from 1934 to 1945) we get a further total of 158,020. If we round this up, to save argument, to the improbable figure of 200,000, and add it to the Merseyside calculations along with the casualties to May 1941 inclusive, we get revised figures for Greater Merseyside of 3.29 and 3.72 per thousand.

Various quibbles are possible, but the answer is clear and unambiguous – London was a safer place than Merseyside in which to spend the years 1940-41. This fact is not obvious from such general accounts of the blitz as have appeared, and I suspect that the suggestion will provoke raised eyebrows when it is reported in London.

Our putative Londoner might change tack and argue that the London raids were much heavier in the central area – the County of London – or in certain selected boroughs, and that this should provide the basis for comparison. Unfortunately this is not possible. Merseyside too suffered its worst casualties in a more restricted area, but in the absence of separate statistics for the different districts of Liverpool no accurate comparison can be made; though a rough comparison of London County with Liverpool and Bootle suggests that if it could the result would be unchanged.

We must not overdo the argument. London had more raids in 1940-41, including a run of fifty-seven nights without a break. They also had more raids after Merseyside's last of January 1942, culminating in the rocket bombardment of 1944-45 that went on by day and night with no real possibility of people taking shelter. Over the war as a whole, London certainly had it worse. Also, the fact that Merseyside had the misfortune to be ahead of London in 1941 does not preclude the possibility that somewhere else – Plymouth most likely - did worse still. It is often claimed that Bootle was the hardest-hit borough in the country, apparently on a bombs-per-square-mile basis, but this is certainly not the case in respect of casualties.

To maintain a sense of proportion – a neighbour of mine was a prisoner of war in Germany and witnessed the RAF raids on Hamburg and their results. On his return to Liverpool he responded to accounts of how terrible it had been there by telling people that, so far as he could see, Liverpool had not been bombed at all. He did not make himself popular, but he had a point.

		Liverpool	Bootle	Litherland	Crosby	Huyton	Birkenhead	Wallasey	Bebington
1940	August	37	-	-	8	-	4	9	-
	September	221	28	2	1	-	24	4	3
	October	106	10	-	-	1	17	3	14
	November	305	6	-	-	-	2	3	2
	December	412	108	-	10	-	63	119	1
1941	January	43	-	-	-	2	8	2	-
	February	2	-	-	-	-	-	-	-
	March	101	-	-	16	-	277	189	34
	April	36	-	17	9	-	8	-	-
	May	1453	257	25	61	13	28	3	3
June 1941 - January 1942		20	15	-	14	-	23	-	6
	TOTALS	2736	424	44	119	16	454	332	63

APPENDIX III

A NORTH-WEST PORT?

One of the most persistent myths of the Merseyside blitz has it that raids on the area were *never* mentioned in the press or on the radio except as involving an anonymous north-west port. The statement is repeated indignantly by writers on the subject; it has inspired poets; it has been made to me by about one person in four of those that I have spoken to or corresponded with in the course of researching this book.

It is totally untrue – complete and utter nonsense.

Unless there has been an Orwellian programme of deliberate tampering with newspaper files as well as the records of the BBC, it is clear that all the worst raids and many of the lesser ones were attributed to Liverpool or Merseyside quite openly. If we were talking about half-a-dozen raids it would be possible to dismiss the matter as pardonable exaggeration, but for 'never' we must read 'frequently'.

That people today should believe what they have read or heard is only natural, but one is surprised to find a writer restating the myth while, on the same page, he gives information taken directly from a newspaper – where it appeared under the headline: "MERSEYSIDE NIGHT RAID". In the face of this sort of thing we must confess that the myth is indestructible, but how on earth did it arise?

Before the raids started it was agreed in Whitehall that it would be best not to give information that would assist the enemy in judging the success of any bombing campaign. Names of towns attacked would be suppressed except for larger targets such as London *and Liverpool*. This policy was not unreasonable. When bombing by night, especially when their navigation beams were being tampered with, the Germans really could not be sure that they had dropped their bombs within fifty miles of the intended target unless somebody told them – the RAF had the same problem. Subsequent aerial reconnaissance might confirm success, but could not be expected to reveal where the many bombs that went astray had landed.

Unfortunately, the original resolution was not adhered to. Through August and up to late September only London was named with any regularity. Merseyside, which suffered about thirty raids and 300 dead in this period was mentioned as a target only once (18th/19th September) – otherwise it was "a north-west coastal town." Along with the citizens of many other towns and cities, Liverpudlians fumed as they saw the sufferings of London played up for propaganda purposes and its citizens credited with courage, resilience, and good-humoured defiance while messages of comfort and support rolled in from all sides.

Steps were taken to bring Merseyside's grievances to the notice of Whitehall. The mayors of the area joined in expressing the public disquiet at the sight of enemy aircraft flying across in daylight untroubled by the RAF, and Lord Derby took up the question of Liverpool's anonymity with Sir Archibald Sinclair, the Secretary of State for Air. There were limits to the improvements that could be made in the defences, but Sir Archibald wrote to the Lord Mayor of Liverpool on the 24th, telling him that he had given instructions that Liverpool should be anonymous no longer.[391] On the 27th September newspapers ascribed the previous night's raid to Liverpool and from that date official communiqués regularly referred to the area by name.

A survey of ***The Times*** from then to the 30th November 1940 reveals forty-eight official references to London, fifteen to Merseyside, and four to other places, one of them Coventry. The press was able to expand on these brief communiqués, naming Liverpool where relevant but not other places on Merseyside; the local press also mentioned slight raids not referred to in the communiqués. The national papers naturally said less, but ***The Times*** contains occasional articles including one on the 23rd October referring to Liverpool's 200th raid – presumably the *200th* alert, which is not quite the same thing.

The Coventry raid of 14th/15th November was the first of a series of heavy attacks on provincial targets – Bristol, Birmingham, Sheffield and Southampton followed. Being heavier raids than Liverpool had been getting, they received fuller coverage – unfairly so in the eyes of Liverpudlians. Liverpool's raid of 28th/29th November was reported as the heaviest on Merseyside to date: "but casualties are described as remarkably light." The reader could have been forgiven for not recognising in a reference to people trapped under a school what proved to be the worst single incident of the 1940-41 blitz anywhere in the country.

The pre-Christmas raids received an honourable mention – "HEAVY RAIDS ON MERSEYSIDE" – while the big raid on Manchester that followed was at first attributed to "a city in the North West." This was spoiled for Liverpool when Manchester was named almost immediately after and made the subject of special treatment by the BBC.

While references to Liverpool were no longer suppressed, a further public relations disaster occurred with the raid of 12th/13th March. The first big raid on Merseyside for several months was duly noted, although – "the damage and casualties bore no relation to the scale of the attack." Casualties on Clydeside at the same time were also reported as light. Since it was soon clear locally that the casualties in both places had in fact been decidedly heavy, this did not go down well. The Ministry of Home Security was understandably indignant at having got into trouble through relying on early reports from the places concerned, but on the 18th March a communiqué was released for publication stating that about 500 had been killed in each place.

In May, the local press gave extensive coverage to the raids; indeed, to anyone brought up on stories of strict censorship – all "We can take it" and vague references to north-west ports – the ***Bootle Times*** of the 9th May is an eye-opener. The leader endorsed Alderman Mahon's call for the evacuation of women and children: "The worst calamity in the history of Merseyside has come upon us...Bootle as a town is in ruins." There was a call for proper organisation of evacuation – "to afford shelter for the people who are aimlessly trekking from the stricken port night by night to find safety under hedges and in ditches and fields."

References in the national press were on a more modest scale, but it was plainly stated that Liverpool had suffered a series of heavy raids – the ***Daily Sketch*** of 5th May for instance: "Merseyside, and particularly Liverpool, the most frequently raided area outside London, had its biggest hammering of the war during Saturday night." Within a fortnight, photographs of the damage to Lewis's and the Museum had appeared and in September even the devastation around Lord Street was revealed.

Yet still people felt that events on Merseyside were being played down relative to other places. The Ministry of Information report prepared after a visit to the area in June noted that: "There is still a considerable feeling of neglect because these raids were not at first given sufficient publicity. Liverpool dislikes being disguised as a 'North West town', while London raids are described in detail, and the suppression of casualty figures and the extent of the damage is resented."[392]

It is fascinating to see that the "North West town" legend was flourishing at a time when Liverpool had been regularly in the news for over seven months. Apparently as a result of the March unpleasantness, it had been decided to give civilian casualties only as a monthly figure for the country as a whole, which prevented the true scale of Merseyside's worst raid from being published.

It is not possible to say if the general impression of neglect was justified without spending a lot of time going through newspaper files with a tape-measure, but there is one reason for thinking that it was. It seems that no Liverpool raids were ever featured in the cinema newsreels, film of royal visits at a later date being no substitute. When one learns that the Manchester raids of December 1940 *were* covered, the case becomes convincing.

Subsequent events have not helped. At the time, the obvious answer to the critics was that it would all be put right after the war. It has not been. Films and television documentaries are heavily dependent on newsreel film from the period – which is nearly all devoted to London, with a nod in the direction of Coventry. On more than one occasion one has heard the rest of the country dismissed with a list of blitzed provincial cities *excluding* Liverpool, and the casualty figures for Merseyside's worst raid seem never to have been published. Londoners naturally attributed their city's prominence in the news to their own hardships and noble qualities, and tend to have little patience with people who seem to be belatedly trying to steal their thunder; one writer lavishing praise on the capital even states that no other town suffered more than eight raids! (He may have *meant* on successive nights, but that is not what he *says*.)

So, there is no denying that Liverpool did not get the credit it deserved during the war and has not caught up since. That, however, is no reason for Liverpudlians to make false claims that they were never mentioned – especially when they are surrounded by places like Birkenhead, Wallasey and Bootle that, in the national press at least, *really* weren't.

The Censor at work. "The Rotunda Theatre after last night's raid" was the *News Chronicle's* idea of a suitable caption for this picture. The Censor passed it for publication so long as it was called "a recent raid." He also wanted the right-hand side omitted to "eliminate indications of burning." Only the back wall survives; the rounded end with a dome above that gave the building its name was on the right.

APPENDIX IV

EXPLOSIVE CARGOES

After the events of 3rd/4th May there was a strong feeling that better ways of handling the import and export of high explosives should be found.[393] The LMS promised never again to stable ammunition trains overnight at Breck Road sidings, only to be caught doing it again within three months.[394]

The Port Emergency Committee took the view that a repetition of the ***Malakand*** explosion ought to be made impossible, at least in the Port of Liverpool. Loading such ships from barges in the river was considered, but proved impractical in the strong Mersey currents – especially as up to fourteen ships at a time were involved. (It was done at Holyhead and in the Clyde.)

The Port Emergency Committee then argued that large, dangerous cargoes should go to other ports, but all available ports were being used to capacity and Liverpool was the biggest of them all with London not fully operational. Ellesmere Port and Bowater's Wharf on the Manchester Ship Canal were less populous, but the Canal could not be risked. In the middle of June it was reported in London that Sir Lionel Warner of the MDHB was refusing to accept "any incoming vessel with explosives on board."[395] This must have concentrated minds wonderfully in Whitehall and caused alarm in the ports that had to take up the slack – notably Holyhead.

By the 8th May it was agreed that the Liverpool docks could be limited to ships carrying up to 500 tons of dangerous cargo, those with more going to Birkenhead. This was not, as Liverpudlians will instantly assume, because Birkenhead was considered expendable; there were simply better facilities on that side of the river for rapid discharge from railway to ship and vice versa. To have such cargoes in the docks for a shorter period was at least something. It was also recommended that the most dangerous materials should not all be piled into one ship, but should be mixed with those considered less dangerous – such as incendiaries and small-arms ammunition.[396]

By July 1941, in order to speed their passage through the port, explosives were being loaded overnight with a locomotive on hand to haul the railway wagons to safety at the first sign of impending attack.

At the end of December 1941, Bowater's Wharf was made available for cargoes up to 500 tons, which it was thought would not imperil the Canal though an explosion there would have been bad for the paper mills.

With the build-up to the Normandy invasion, the quantities of explosives crossing the Atlantic were such that peacetime prudence in such matters had to go by the board. Except for certain high-risk areas (which by then did not include the Mersey), the limit was raised to 2,000 tons net of explosives per ship. 1,000 tons gross of bulk explosive were reckoned at 900 tons net, 1,000 tons of bombs being 500 tons net (the upper limit for the Ship Canal). When the ***Malakand*** went up she was loaded only to a quarter of the new limit.

All things considered, Liverpool could have done a lot worse. Quite a number of ammunition ships blew up during the course of the war, and where this happened in harbour, the results were usually more destructive than appears to have been the case here. In April 1941, for example, an air raid on the Greek port of Piraeus left three ships on fire – each with explosives aboard. All three went up in the next few hours, along with lighters full of TNT, and the resultant devastation of the port, together with the loss of eight or nine other ships and many small craft, had a damaging effect on the progress of the Greek campaign.

The disaster at Bari in December 1943 had a similar effect on the Italian campaign, though there, the Allies were on the offensive and better able to cope. Over thirty ships were unloading when a surprise air raid scored hits on two ammunition ships and a tanker full of petrol. The fires and explosions that followed led to the destruction of nineteen transporters and severe damage to several more. The presence of mustard gas on one of the ships added to the horror and over a thousand people died.

At Bombay in April 1944 there was a ship – the ***Fort Stikine*** – that had sailed from Birkenhead with a cargo that included 1,400 tons (gross) of mixed explosives – shells, torpedoes, mines, signal rockets, magnesium flares, and incendiaries. Shortly after she started unloading, a fire started in cotton picked up on the voyage. The first of two explosions came three and a half hours later. The incendiaries – not 'dangerous' – were scattered over a wide area of the city and caused many fires. At least 233 people were killed, including 64 firemen. The destruction was widespread and not, as in Liverpool, obscured by air raid damage.

The most noticeable difference from the ***Malakand*** explosion, however, is that this one was followed by a full inquiry, the findings of which were published during the war.

APPENDIX V

The details given are as follows: ***name*; *gross tonnage (or displacement)*; *type*; *whether damaged, sunk, etc.*; *place*; *date (all May 1941)*; *additional notes, ownership, subsequent fate, etc.*** The abbreviations used are:

B .... barge or flat	FC........ floating crane	HMS..... warship
ML........ motor launch	MV .... motor vessel (cargo)	P .... passenger
SDB ...... steam derrick barge	SHB ...... steam hopper barge	SS.......... steamship (cargo)

This list is not complete and some of the details are uncertain – it includes a few vessels not mentioned in the text for this reason or because there was little more to be said about them. Some vessels that suffered trivial damage are omitted.

ADDA	7816	MV	Damaged	NE Queen's 1	6/7	1
ADVENTURE	(7260)	HMS	Damaged	Canada Tongue	3/4 & 7/8	2
A E BURTON	77	B	Badly damaged	N Huskisson	3/4	3
AID	209	B	Lost – fire	?	4/5	4
AINSDALE	-	B	Badly damaged	N Langton Branch	7/8	5
ANNEBERG	2537	SS	Damaged	S Bramley-Moore	6/7	6
ARGOS HILL	7178	SS	Damaged	S Alexandra 2	7/8	7
ASIATIC	3741	SS	Damaged	E Harrington	6/7	8
ATLAS	457	FC	Slight damage	Alexandra	7/8	9
ATTRACTIVE	41	B	Badly damaged	N Langton Branch	7/8	10
BARBELL	-	B	Damaged	West Float	6/7	11
BARNACLE	138	B	Lost – fire	Canada	3/4	12
BARONESA	8663	SS	Damaged	In river	3/4	13
BARON INCHCAPE	7005	SS	Damaged	S Canada 2	3/4 & 7/8	14
BEBINGTON	732	P	Damaged	Wallasey Stage	6/7	15
BISON	274	Tug	Sunk	NW Gladstone 1	3/4	16
BONGO	(net) 46	B	Sunk	N Huskisson 3	3/4	17
BONITA	65	Tug	Sunk	W Waterloo	3/4	18
BRA-KAR	3778	MV	Sunk	S Canada 2	3/4	19
BRILL	106	B	Lost	?	3/4	20
BURMAH	127	SDB	Sunk	E Canada 3	7/8	21
BUSIRIS	943	SS	Damaged	W Huskisson	3/4	22
CANTAL	3178	SS	Damaged	N Alexandra 2	3/4	23
CHANTILLY	10065	SS	Damaged	Sandon	3/4	24
CLAM	159	B	Damaged	Huskisson 3	3/4	25
CLAN MACINNES	4672	SS	Badly damaged	N King's 2	3/4 & 6/7	26
CORBET	468	SS	Sunk	In River	3	27
CRAGDALE	168	B	Badly damaged	E Harrington	6/7	28
CROSSHOUSE	-	B	Damaged	W Waterloo	3/4	29
DACE	143	B	Lost – fire	?	3/4	30
DOMINO	1453	SS	Sunk	S Canada 3	3/4	31
DOUGLAS VERNON	-	B	Badly damaged	N Langton Branch	7/8	32
ELLESBANK	43	B	Sunk	S Stanley	6/7	33
ELLESPORT	55	B	Sunk	E Huskisson 2	3/4	34
EL MARINE	158	B	Damaged	Hornby - Langton	7/8	35
ELSTREE GRANGE	6598	SS	Gutted	N Canada 1	3/4	36
EMILY BURTON	58	B	Sunk	N Huskisson 3	3/4	37
EMPIRE BRONZE	8142	-	Damaged	S Alexandra 2	7/8	38
ENID BLANCHE	99	Tug	Sunk	E B'bank Branch	3/4	39
ERIC BURTON	(net) 56	B	Badly damaged	N Huskisson	3/4	40
EUROPA	10224	P	Gutted	B'bank Graving	3/4	41

SHIPS SUNK & DAMAGED

The following vessels were still awaiting salvage at the beginning of May 1941:

INNISFALLEN	in river	broken up after April 1943
LYSTER	Brunswick Dock	raised April 1943 and repaired
MAMMOTH	West Float	raised and to Gladstone Graving Dock 31.10.41 - 9.1.42
OVERDALE	Huskisson 2	raised 13.11.41 – to Tranmere Beach
SILVIO	S. Alexandra 1	cut up in situ 1946/47
TACOMA CITY	in river	finally cleared 1963
ULLAPOOL	in river	broken up – still working 1947

1 Elder Dempster
2 Minelayer
3 Burton & Son Ltd. – motor barge
4 John R. Nicholson
5
6 Rederi A/B (Finland)
7 Ernels Shipping Co.
8 W. H. Cockerline & Co.
9 MDHB
10 H. E. R. Ainscough
11
12 Rea Ltd. – sailing barge – to Tranmere Beach July
13 Furness Houlder Argentine Line
14 Hogarth Shipping Co. – to Canada Graving Dock July and repaired
15 Birkenhead Ferry
16 Mersey Towing Co. – raised and repaired – Canning 1 Gvg Dk 27.6 - 8.9.41
17 Burton – sailing barge – raised and to Tranmere Beach August – repaired
18 Liverpool Lighterage Co. – raised and to Tranmere Beach Sept. – broken up
19 Fred Olsen & Co. (Norway) – to Tranmere Beach 2.7.41 and broken up
20 Rea Ltd. – to Tranmere Beach for breaking up
21 Michael Halligan – engines and boilers saved
22 Moss Hutchison
23 CGT (France) – to Cammell Laird for repair June
24 Messageries Maritimes (France) – to B'bank Gvg Dock 12.6 - 11.7.41
25 Rea Ltd. – sailing barge
26 Clan Line – to dry dock May and repaired
27 Alexander King – dispersed with explosives
28 Richard Abel – apparently broken up
29
30 Rea Ltd.
31 Ellerman's Wilson Line – raised August – to New Ferry Beach & broken up
32
33 J. G. Pugh Ltd. – raised and broken up
34 Wolverhampton Corrugated Iron Co. Ltd. – left when dock filled in
35
36 Houlder Line – to King's Dock river wall 14.5 and broken up
37 Motor barge – raised and to Tranmere Beach August – broken up
38 Ministry of Shipping
39 Thames Steam Tug & Lighterage Co. – to Tranmere Beach Sept. – to owners
40 Burton & Son Ltd.
41 Det Östasiatiske Kompagni (Denmark) – to New Ferry Beach June – broken up

EUTHALIA	3553	SS	Damaged	Brunswick	4/5	42
F (sic)	496	SHB	Sunk	In River	13	43
GANDIA	9626	SS	Damaged	SE B'bank Branch	7/8	44
GLITTO	166	SDB	Sunk	N Alexandra 3	3/4	45
GROSVENOR	43	B	Sunk	S Stanley	6/7	46
HERCULES	652	FC	Sunk	E Langton	7/8	47
HILDA	250	-	Damaged	Liverpool Bay	18	48
HORNBY	201	Tug	Sunk	E Langton	7/8	49
HORNBY	50	B	Sunk	E Alexandra 3	3/4	50
HURRICANE	(1340)	HMS	Damaged	W Gladstone	7/8	51
IDA BURTON	46	B	Sunk	N Alexandra 3	7/8	52
INDUSTRIA	4861	SS	Damaged	N Queen's 2	6/7	53
IVY P	79	B	Lost – fire	Langton Branch	7/8	54
JOHN	(net) 67	B	Sunk	E Canada 3	3/4	55
JOLLY DAYS	352	B	Gutted	E Alexandra 3	7/8	56
JOSIAH/JOSHUA	-	B	Sunk	Canada 2	3?	57
JUNE BURTON	(net) 65	B	Badly damaged	N Huskisson	3/4	58
KENFINCH	113	SS	Damaged	N Huskisson 2	3/4	59
KESWICK	-	B	Damaged	Hornby - Langton	7/8	60
KILEENAN	72	SDB	Sunk	Salthouse	7	61
LEOPOLD II	2902	SS	Damaged	S Alexandra 2	7/8	62
LIMPET	(net) 164	B	Damaged	Huskisson	3/4	63
LING	164	B	Burnt & Sunk	Huskisson?	3/4	64
LOBOS	6479	MV	Damaged	N Canada 1	3/4 & 7/8	65
LUCE	143	B	Sunk	E Canada 2	3/4	66
MAHOUT	7921	SS	Damaged	S Huskisson 3	3/4	67
MALAKAND	7649	SS	Blown up	S Huskisson 2	3/4	68
MAPLIN	5780	HMS	Damaged	Canada Tongue	7/8	69
MARJORIE	-	B	Badly damaged	N Langton Branch	7/8	70
MARLOW	606	P	Damaged	Wallasey Stage	6/7	71
MARTON	4969	SS	Gutted	Langton Graving 2	3/4 & 7/8	72
MIMOSA	3071	SS	Damaged	N King's 2	3/4	73
MOBEKA	6111	MV	Slight damage	NE Queen's	7/8	74
MOENA	9286	SS	Slight damage	N Huskisson 3	3/4	75
MOOSE	208	Tug	Damaged	N Gladstone 1	3/4	76
MORAG	-	ML	Sunk	Huskisson	3/4	77
MOSCHA D. KYDONIEFS	3874	SS	Damaged	E Harrington	6/7	78
MOSDALE	3022	MV	Damaged	E Sandon	3/4	79
MUS	81	B	Badly damaged	?	3/4	80
NADIN	3852	SS	Damaged	E Alexandra 3	3/4	81
NORMANDY COAST	1428	SS	Slight damage	Salisbury	7/8	82
ORRELL	50	B	Sunk	E Alexandra 3	3/4	83
OYSTER	(net) 133	B	Sunk	E Canada 2	3/4	84
PANAGHIS	5187	SS	Slight damage	Ilchester Wharf	6/7	85
PIKE	168	B	Lost – fire	Canada	3/4	86
RAY	91	B	Badly damaged	?	3/4	87
RICHARD ABEL	-	B	Damaged	E Wapping Basin	3/4	88
ROACH	108	B	Badly damaged	?	3/4	89
ROSE	143	SDB	Sunk	N Alexandra 3	7/8	90
ROSE	-	B	Slight damage	Queen's 2	6/7	91
ROUMANIE	3563	SS	Damaged	E Toxteth	3/4	92
ROVER	40	B	Sunk	S Canada 1	7/8	93
ROXBURGH CASTLE	7801	MV	Sunk	W Alexandra	3/4 & 7/8	94
ROYAL DAFFODIL II	591	P	Sunk	Seacombe Stage	7/8	95
SALLAND	6447	SS	Badly damaged	Canada	3/4 & 7/8	96
SAMSON	522	FC	Slight damage	Huskisson	3/4	97
SAN EMILIANO	8071	MV	Slight damage	In river	6/7	98
SAN FABIAN	13031	SS	Badly damaged	Stanlow	3/4	99

42 C. D. Coumarianos (Greece)
43 LMS Railway – dispersed with explosives
44 Cie Maritime Belge (Lloyd Royal) SA (Belgium)
45 Raised and repaired
46 Raised and broken up
47 MDHB – raised and repaired – B'bank Graving Dock 10.6 - 4.12.41
48 Balloon barrage vessel
49 Alexandra Towing Co. – raised May and repaired
50 Elevator barge – raised and to Tranmere Beach June – broken up
51 'Havant' class destroyer – to Birkenhead 2 Gvg Dock 9.5 - 13.6.41
52 Burton – sailing barge – raised and to Tranmere Beach July – broken up
53 Metcalfe Shipping Co.
54 Liverpool Derricking & Carrying Co. Ltd.
55 John Marmion – raised and broken up
56 MDHB
57
58 Burton & Son Ltd.
59 B. I. Transport Co.
60 Grain storage barge
61 Wadsworth Lighterage & Coaling Co. Ltd. – part recovered as scrap
62 Cie. Royale Belgo-Argentine (Belgium)
63 Rea Ltd. – sailing barge
64 Rea Ltd. – sailing barge – lost (Sunk Sept. 1940 and repaired)
65 PSNC
66 Rea Ltd. – raised October and broken up
67 T. & J. Brocklebank
68 T. & J. Brocklebank – part salvaged for scrap – rest left when dock filled
69 Fighter catapult ship
70
71 Wallasey ferry
72 'K' Steamship Co. – to New Ferry Beach July and broken up
73 Society Commerciale et d'Armement SA (Greece)
74 Cie. Maritime Belge (Belgium)
75 Nederland Line (Holland)
76 Mersey Towing Co. – to Clarence 2 Graving Dock 14.5 - 23.6.41
77 Salvage reported unlikely 31.7.41
78 D. A. Kydoniefs (Greece)
79 A/S Mosvold Shipping Co. (Norway)
80 Rea Ltd. – to Tranmere Beach May – broken up (dated from 1865)
81 Soc. Commerciale et d'Armement SA (Greece)
82 Coast Lines
83 Elevator barge – raised and to Tranmere Beach July – broken up
84 Rea Ltd. – sailing barge – raised and to Tranmere Beach October – repaired
85 N. D. Lykiardopulo (Greece)
86 Rea Ltd. – sailing barge
87 Rea Ltd. – to Tranmere Beach – broken up
88 Richard Abel
89 Rea Ltd. – broken up
90 ICI – raised and to Tranmere Beach in two parts July/Aug – broken up
91 Duke's Grain Warehousing Co. Ltd.
92 Cie. Nationale Belge de Transports Maritimes (Belgium)
93 Raised and to Tranmere Beach September – broken up
94 Union Castle – raised May and repaired
95 Wallasey ferry – raised July 1942 – in service by June 1943
96 Royal Dutch Lloyd
97 MDHB
98 Eagle Oil & Shipping Co. – tanker
99 Eagle Oil & Shipping Co. – tanker

SANTIAGO	3864	SS	Damaged	In river?	7/8?	100
SILVERDALE	176	B	Gutted	Canada	3/4	101
SILVERSANDAL	6770	MV	Damaged	In river	3/4 & 4/5	102
SIRIUS	174	-	Sunk	Albert	3	103
SKIRMISHER	582	P	Damaged	Huskisson	3/4	104
SPANIEL	-	B	Gutted	E Alexandra 3	7/8	105
STORMONT	1031	SS	Slight damage	Salisbury	7/8	106
STROMBOLI	1376	SS	Sunk	NW Huskisson	7/8	107
STYLUS	100	B	Damaged	Langton	?	108
TACOMA STAR	7924	SS	Sunk	W Canada	3/4	109
TALTHYBIUS	10254	SS	Damaged	N Gladstone 1	3/4 & 7/8	110
THORNEYCROFT	-	B	Badly damaged	N Langton Branch	7/8	111
TRAFFIC	155	B	Sunk	E Canada 2	3/4	112
TRENTINO	3079	SS	Sunk	N Langton Branch	7/8	113
VAN ORLEY	352	HMS	Badly damaged	E Huskisson 2	3/4	114
VISCOUNT	(1120)	HMS	Damaged	W Gladstone	7/8	115
WAIWERA	12435	MV	Slight damage	S Canada 1	3/4 & 7/8	116
WALTON	82	B	Gutted	Huskisson 2	3/4	117
WAPITI	208	Tug	Damaged	N Gladstone 1	3/4	118
No. 2 SURVEYOR	7	ML	Sunk	Albert	3	119
No. 2 CAMEL	863	-	Damaged	N Huskisson 2	3/4	120
No. 3 CAMEL	-	-	Damaged	N Huskisson 2	3/4	121
No. 4 CAMEL	310	-	Damaged	Albert	3	122
No. 4 BARGE	110	B	Sunk	NW Huskisson 2	7/8	123
No. 11 ELEVATOR	295	-	Sunk	N Huskisson 2	3/4	124
No. 12 ELEVATOR	743	-	Badly damaged	N Langton Branch	7/8	125
No. 20 HOPPER	703	-	Sunk	N Huskisson 2	3/4	126
No. 33 HOPPER	718	SHB	Sunk	W Waterloo	3/4	127

100	Santiago Steamship Co. (Panama)
101	Rea Ltd. – sailing barge – to Tranmere Beach July – broken up
102	Silver Line
103	MDHB – Lightship – raised December and to Tranmere Beach – broken up 1943
104	Cunard White Star – tender
105	
106	Belfast, Mersey & Manchester Steamship Co.
107	Den Norske Middelhavslinje A/S (Norway) – to Tranmere Beach 14.4.42 - broken up
108	W.T. Scales – Pumping flat – beached and repaired
109	Blue Star Line – raised June and repaired
110	Ocean Steamship Co.
111	
112	Liverpool Lighterage Co. – steam barge – raised October and broken up
113	Ellerman's Wilson Line – raised May – to King's Wall – broken up Tranmere
114	Anti-Submarine trawler – to King's wall June and broken up
115	'V' class destroyer – to Birkenhead 2 Graving Dock for repair 9.5 - 7.6.41
116	Shaw Savill & Albion Co.
117	United Grain Elevators Ltd. – steam barge – lost
118	To Clarence 2 Graving Dock 14.5 - 23.6.41
119	MDHB – raised November and broken up
120	MDHB
121	MDHB
122	MDHB – to Canning 2 Graving Dock 9.5 - 25.6.41
123	J. Rank – raised and repaired after November
124	United Grain Elevators Ltd. – lost
125	MDHB
126	MDHB – SHB converting to salvage boat WATCHFUL – raised June and repaired
127	MDHB – raised circa September and repaired

NOTES

Where not specified, the sources noted are to be found in the following archives.

Public Record Office, Kew. Refs: ADM, AIR, AN, HO, INF, MT, PREM, RAIL and WO.

Liverpool Record Office. Liverpool Council Committee minutes, ref 352 MIN. Liverpool Shipwreck and Humane Society reports. Report on the Police Establishment. Items noted as Liverpool RO.

Merseyside Maritime Museum Record Centre. MDHB records and items noted as NMGM.

Lancashire County Record Office. Items noted as Preston RO.

To keep the notes within reasonable bounds, the following sources are not generally given specific references.

Major Salt's ***History of Bootle ARP***, Bootle Public Library, ref B 14/1.

War Damage Records for the Borough of Crosby, Crosby Public Library, ref C 940.6.

Huyton-with-Roby Incident Book, Preston RO.

Lancashire Incident Report Book, Preston RO.

Engineer's Department, Liverpool RO, Acc 3323. (Liverpool incidents 1st/2nd to 6th/7th May.)

Report on the Police Establishment for the Seven years Ending 31st December 1945 (Liverpool, 1946). (A brief list of Liverpool incidents in each raid.)

MDHB PEC 11/3. Covers docks, shipping and railways – good on salvage.

MDHB dock registers, for details of which ship was where.

MT 63/140. Brief details re ships in May.

Lloyd's ***Weekly Casualty Reports*** and Loss Cards, the Guildhall Library, London. A mine of information on shipping casualties.

The Blitz Then and Now, vol. 2 (London, 1988). Details of bomb-loads etc. from German records.

ADDITIONAL BIBLIOGRAPHY

Earl of Derby et al., ***Bombers over Merseyside***, Liverpool Daily Post and Echo Ltd., Liverpool, 1943.

Anon, ***The Civilian War Dead of the United Kingdom and the Commonwealth***, Imperial War Graves Commissio, Londonn, 1975.

Richard Whittington-Egan, ***The Great Liverpool Blitz***, The Gallery Press, Neston, Wirral, 1987.

Kelly's Liverpool Directory, 1940, 1941 and 1943, London.

Rodney Whitworth, ***Merseyside at War***, Scouse Press, Liverpool, 1988.

T. J. Buckley, ***Port at War***, MD&HB, Liverpool, 1946.

G. Proudman, ***Wallasey Warden Service, 1938-1944***, Wallasey, 1945

1 The ***Report on the Police Establishment*** includes a list of Liverpool policemen awarded medals with dates and places. This ensures that the police play a larger part in this book than is strictly fair.
2 352 MIN/DEF 26 February 1940.
3 J. W. de Roever, ***De Nederland in Wereldoorlog II*** (Netherland Line, 1951) p. 115.
4 352 MIN/DEF 2 September 1939.
5 ***The Liverpolitan***, October 1939 p. 5.
6 ***Liverpool Echo***, 22 January 1940. 352 MIN/WAT 19 March 1940.
7 MDHB ***Port at War*** correspondence.
8 352 MIN/WAT 16 April 1940.
9 Ibid. 29 August 1939.
10 Ibid. 15 April 1941.
11 352 MIN/DEF 1 & 22 September 1939. 12. Ibid. 7 December 1939.
13 Gen. Sir Frederick Pile, ***Ack, Ack*** (London, 1949) p. 135.
14 HO 186/2316.
15 Liverpool Shipwreck and Humane Society, 102nd Annual Report p.26.
16 352 MIN/DEF 27 September - 2 October 1940.
17 ***Liverpool Echo***, 25 January 1941 and 28 May 1956. ***London Gazette***, 24 January and 14 February 1941.
18 ADM 199/110.
19 ***Liverpool Daily Post***, 2 October 1940.
20 HO 186/557.
21 S. A. Harris, ***The Development of Gas Supply on North Merseyside*** (Liverpool, 1956) p. 151-2.
22 352 MIN/DEF 2 December 1940.
23 352 MIN/WAT 17 September 1940.
24 B/LWC, Liverpool Warehousing Co., Directors' Minute Book, 31 December 1940, NMGM.
25 MT 63/140.
26 352 MIN/WAT 14 January 1941. AN 2/54, HO 198/197, HO 203, MT 63/140.
27 MDHB ***Port at War*** correspondence (***Elax*** and ***Innisfallen***).
28 ADM 199/111.
29 Ibid.
30 Ocean Archive 8.89/5. NMGM.
31 T. J. Buckley, ***Port at War*** (Liverpool, 1946) p. 19.
32 HO 192/953.
33 352 MIN/WAT 14 January 1941.
34 352 MIN/DEF 14 March 1941.
35 Mass-Observation Archive, File Report 538, 'Report on Liverpool and Manchester', 6 January 1941.
36 MT 63/213 (quotation) and ***Liverpool Daily Post***, 11 January 1941.
37 HO 186/625.
38 That is to say the dockers. In spite of some laudatory comments printed since the war it is actually difficult to find anyone with a good word to say for them at the time. There are of course two sides to this, but the subject is a large one and of no great relevance to events in May 1941.
39 Alex Aiken, ***In Time of War*** (Glasgow, 1980) p. 55.
40 352 MIN/WAT 14 January 1941.
41 352 MIN/DEF 4 February 1941.
42 Ibid. 7 March 1941.
43 HO 186/1604.
44 Post Office Archives.
45 HO 192/1153/77.
46 MT 9/3587.
47 ***Liverpool Echo***, 11 January 1958.
48 Ocean Archive 915.1, NMGM.
49 HO 192/1152/74.
50 352 MIN/WAT 18 March 1941.
51 Ibid.
52 HO 186/2316.
53 352 MIN/WAT 15 April 1941.

54 ADM 199/111.
55 HO 192/1153/80.
56 *Liverpool Daily Post*, 29 April 1941.
57 WO 166/2259.
58 HO 203.
59 LFB Incident Reports – Merseyside Fire Brigade LV 085.
60 *Liverpool Echo*, 2 May 1941.
61 HO 186/557 and HO 203.
62 LFB Incident Reports, op. cit.
63 *Bootle Times*, 30 May 1941.
64 352 MIN/DEF 5 May 1941.
65 HO 203.
66 352 MIN/DEF 9 May 1941.
67 Quoted in *The Blitz Then and Now*, vol. 2 p. 580.
68 J. F. Gibson, *Brocklebanks 1770-1950* (Liverpool, 1953) vol.II p. 97.
69 WO 166/2259.
70 Ibid.
71 HO 198/197. War Damage Records for the Borough of Crosby.
72 Liverpool Police Incident Officers' record sheets, Imperial War Museum.
73 *Liverpool Daily Post*, 27 September 1941.
74 *Liverpool Echo*, 3 May 1941. HO 186/625. HO 198/197.
75 *From Peace to War* (Littlewood's, Liverpool, 1946) p. 276.
76 Edith Pargeter, *She Goes to War* (London, 1942) p. 143.
77 ADM 199/110.
78 *London Gazette*, 1 August 1941. *Liverpool Daily Post*, 2 August 1941.
79 HO 192/1152/33. C. E. Box, *Liverpool Overhead Railway* (London, 1959) p. 53.
80 J. Millar, *William Heap and His Company* (1976) p. 144.
81 *Liverpool Echo*, 3 May 1941.
82 Nicholas Monsarrat, *Life is a Four-Letter Word. Vol.2: Breaking Out*, © The Estate of Nicholas Monsarrat, (London, 1970) p. 87.
83 Edith Pargeter, op. cit., p. 144
84 *Liverpool Echo*, 3 May 1941.
85 Incident Officers' record sheets, op. cit.
86 Blackpool Air Raid Incidents – CBBL/12, Preston RO.
87 Quoted in *The Blitz Then and Now*, op. cit.
88 ADM 199/658.
89 MT 9/3587.
90 *London Gazette*, 2 May 1941.
91 WO 166/2259.
92 AIR 24/140.
93 Engineer's Department, Acc 3323, Liverpool RO.
94 WO 166/2259.
95 HO 186/625.
96 Richard Collier, *The City That Wouldn't Die* (London, 1959). Some say this practice of setting up the beams early in the afternoon was abandoned in January 1941. The pumps in Birmingham were covering for those sent to Liverpool.
97 Incident officers' record sheets, op. cit.
98 *Liverpool Daily Post* supplement, 4 May 1981.
99 *Liverpool Echo*, 13 May 1971.
100 *Liverpool Daily Post*, 30 August 1941.
101 Incident Officers' record sheets, op. cit.
102 *Liverpool Echo*, 16 May 1956.
103 Ibid. 15 & 17 December 1943.
104 See also *Liverpool Daily Post*, 6 September 1941; *London Gazette*, 29 August and 5 September 1941; 352 MIN/HOS 16 May 1941.
105 *London Gazette*, 26 August 1941. *Liverpool Echo* and *Daily Post*, 27 August 1941. WO 166/5620.
106 D. Murray, *The Story of Holy Cross* (1948) p. 69.
107 *Liverpool Daily Post*, 15 April 1942.
108 HO 186/557.
109 352 MIN/MAR 20 May 1941.
110 352 MIN/EDU II 19 May 1941.
111 HO 198/197. *Liverpool Echo*, 2 December 1957. *Liverpool Daily Post*, 27 September 1941. *London Gazette*, 26 September and 28 November 1941.
112 *Bootle Times*, 9 May 1941.
113 W. S. MacCunn, *Bluecoat Chambers* (Liverpool, 1956) p.42.
114 HO 198/197. LFB Incident Reports – Merseyside Fire Brigade LV 085. Asa Briggs, *Friends of the People* (London, 1956) p. 197. *Liverpool Echo*, 29 September 1944. *Search Pack 8* (Liverpool, 1979) – Hq 942.721084 SEA, Liverpool RO.
115 352 MIN/MAR 20 May 1941. Ben Wicks, *Waiting for the All Clear* (London, 1990).
116 The Civil Defence Cadets were a Liverpool organisation inspired by the Lord Mayor, ostensibly to engage the youth of Liverpool in ARP work but apparently intended more to combat communism.
117 352 MIN/LIB 16 May 1941.
118 *Search Pack 8*, op. cit.
119 *Liverpool Daily Post*, 2 August 1941.
120 Mr. Howe's report, private collection. *Liverpool Daily Post*, 31 July 1943. Post Office Archives.
121 Ocean Archive 11.1124, NMGM.
122 *Liverpool Echo*, 24 May 1941.
123 A. R. L. Bush, *A History of the Rockliff Family of Liverpool* (Liverpool, 1984) p. 56.
124 Records of the Mersey Railway, NMGM.
125 Mr. C. A. Neil, records of L. S. Dixon Group Ltd.
126 *Liverpool Daily Post*, 27 September 1941.
127 Post Office Archives.
128 352 MIN/DEF 12 May 1941.
129 *Bootle Times*, 9 May 1941 and 8 May 1942.
130 HO 192/1153/81.
131 RAIL 421/90.
132 *Search Pack 8*, op. cit.
133 Grayson Rollo and Howson's, HO 198/207. Sandon station, AN 2/53 (Appendix F). Cold store, HO 192/1153/81.
134 Cold store, HO 192/1153/81. Tillotson's, F. Singleton, *Tillotsons, 1850-1950* (Tillotson & Son Ltd., 1950) p. 82. Silcock, HO 192/1153/80.
135 AN 2/53 (Appendix F).
136 C. D. Hughes and HO 198/197.
137 HO 192/951 and HO 192/1153/80.
138 HO 192/1153/79.
139 S. A. Harris, op. cit., p. 152.
140 HO 192/1153/83.
141 HO 192/1153/80.
142 AN 2/53 (Appendix F).
143 Central Oil and Crean – HO 192/1153/79, Calthrop's – HO 192/951.
144 HO 192/1153/78.
145 HO 192/1153/79.
146 *From Peace to War*, op. cit., p. 276. LFB Incident Reports, op. cit.
147 *The Story of Evans Medical* (1962, 2nd edition).
148 LFB Incident Reports, op. cit. *Liverpool Echo*, 23 November 1957, 5 May 1966, 27 May 1971. *The People*, 19 May 1957. George C. Nash, *The LMS at War* (London, 1946) p. 43. *Transport Goes to War* (London, 1942) p. 4.
149 352 MIN/WAT 1 April 1941.
150 352 MIN/DEF 4 October 1940.
151 ADM 53/115222.
152 T. A. Bushell, *Eight Bells* (London, 1950) p. 33.
153 *London Gazette*, 10 October 1941. *Liverpool Daily Post*, 11 October 1941.
154 Ellerman's Wilson Line documents in private collection.
155 Lloyd's *Weekly Casualty Reports*, 6-12 June 1941.
156 Some information supplied by the East Asiatic Co. Ltd. A/S.
157 Ellerman's Wilson Line documents in private collection.
158 Some information supplied by Fred Olsen & Co.
159 Lloyd's *Weekly Casualty Reports*, 16-22 May 1941.
160 *London Gazette*, 10 October 1941. *Liverpool Daily Post*, 11 October 1941. *Sea Hazard* (Houlder Bros & Co. Ltd., 1947) p. 45.
161 ADM 53/113518.
162 MDHB WUP 112/3 23 May 1941.
163 J. W. de Roever, op. cit., p. 112-116.
164 *London Gazette*, 8 August 1941. D. L. Campbell. Reports in Brocklebank's records, NMGM – not yet catalogued.
165 MT 63/140.
166 There are three prime sources for events surrounding the *Malakand*. Brocklebank's records (NMGM) include a report dated 6th May, apparently drawn up from an interview with Mr. Allan and Mr. Exley – the two senior deck officers in the absence of the captain, who was

then in hospital. The NMGM's MDHB collection includes a box of correspondence relating to the Dock Board's publication *Port at War*, together with material collected for this (op. cit.). It contains a report by Captain Kinley – also dated 6th May – that tells much the same story with some slight differences. This is filed with a copy of the report in the Brocklebank collection and appears to be addressed to the owners. Lastly, there is Kinley's report to the fire service, which appears in censored form in *Bombers Over Merseyside* (Liverpool Daily Post and Echo, 1943). (I have been unable to trace the original, or indeed any other fire service reports.) Compared with Captain Kinley's first report, his second has differences of emphasis deriving from its intended readership as well as some downright inconsistencies. It also contains some information that was apparently not known to Kinley at the time of the first report. It is just possible that the censor has inserted disinformation as well as omitting material, though the account is frank enough to have prompted these researches. There are many other documentary sources, as noted below, but this account would be sadly incomplete were it not for the information supplied by Messrs. H. G. Allan, James Burke, D.L. Campbell and William Clarke.

167 *Liverpool Daily Post*, 10 September 1941.
168 MT 63/140.
169 Lloyd's *Weekly Casualty Reports*, 16-22 May 1941.
170 Ibid. 23-29 May 1941.
171 *Liverpool Echo*, 26 November 1943.
172 352 MIN/DEF 31 July 1941.
173 *Liverpool Echo*, 22 May 1956 (letter from Samuel Cohen).
174 Ibid. 4 May 1966.
175 Local tram experts deny that any tram came to grief in this area.
176 Mr. H. G. Allan.
177 Mr. H. G. Allan.
178 Mr. D. L. Campbell.
179 Captain Kinley: 6th May, "I asked if I could get a car to take me to the AFS HQ and one of the members drove me there"; to fire service, "Around 3 a.m., Lappin decided to go personally...I accompanied him..."
180 *Liverpool Echo*, 20 December 1941. *Liverpool Jewish Gazette*, 17 June 1955, p. 11.
181 Lloyd's *Weekly Casualty Reports*, 18-24 July 1941.
182 Ibid. 6-12 June 1941.
183 LFB Incident Reports, op. cit.
184 MDHB PEC 8/3.
185 *Sea Hazard*, op. cit., p. 44.
186 MDHB PEC 11/3.
187 HO 203.
188 352 MIN/DEF 8 May 1941.
189 BBC, Written Archives Centre, Caversham.
190 Nicholas Monsarrat, *Three Corvettes*, © The Estate of Nicholas Monsarrat, 1945, Published by Pan Books, p. 55.
191 352 MIN/LIB 16 May 1941.
192 Records of L. S. Dixon Group Ltd.
193 *Search Pack 8*, op. cit.
194 *The Cathedral Record*, Vol. XVIII, p. 221.
195 Mr. Campbell, who spoke to the *Malakand's* officers a few minutes after the first blast, is the source for Kinley calling his men off at the last minute. This is not mentioned in any other source, but it is clear from Kinley's account in *Bombers Over Merseyside* that he had wanted to get his men away for some time. Mr. Allan was not called off, but it is possible that the message did not have time to reach him at the far end of the ship from the captain.
196 J. W. de Roever, op. cit., p. 113.
197 Lloyd's *Weekly Casualty Reports*, 16-22 May 1941.
198 *Liverpool Echo*, 29 May 1956.
199 *London Gazette*, 12 September 1941. Liverpool Shipwreck and Humane Society; 103rd Annual Report p. 16.
200 *Liverpool Echo*, 14 May 1971.
201 Ibid. 22 May 1956.
202 *London Gazette*, 19 December 1941.
203 D. L. Campbell.
204 MDHB PEC 11/3.
205 *Liverpool Echo*, 2 June 1956.
206 Derby Rd – HO 192/955. Athol St – S. A. Harris, op. cit., p. 153. United Molasses – HO 192/1152/48. UXB – HO 203, 7 May 1941.
207 Lloyd's *Weekly Casualty Reports*, 23-29 May 1941.
208 HO 191/179. HO 192/1152-3.
209 HO 192/1152/71.
210 MDHB Legal, H 148(quotation). Cunard Archive, ASC 6/2. Liverpool University.
211 MDHB PEC 11/3.
212 *London Gazette*, Scoins and Mohamed 8 August 1941, Kinley 9 September 1941, White 12 September 1941, the firemen 19 December 1941, Exley 1 January 1942, Allan 1 January 1943. Lappin's comment – *Liverpool Echo*, 26 November 1943.
213 *Liverpool Echo*, 28 May 1956.
214 Ivan Southall, *Softly Tread the Brave* (London, 1960).
215 ADM 199/658.
216 *Liverpool Echo*, 15 May 1956.
217 352 MIN/DEF 23 May 1941.
218 HO 203.
219 HO 186/625.
220 Meeting – MDHB PEC 11/3. MoI - INF 1/292/1.
221 *Bootle Times*, 9 May 1941.
222 INF 1/292/1.
223 HO 203.
224 HO 199/195.
225 HO 203.
226 Suffolk Regt – WO 166/4708. RE - WO 166/3798.
227 Official History: C.L. Dunn, *The Emergency Medical Services – vol. 2* (London, 1953) p. 326.
228 Engineer's Department, Acc 3323.
229 *Liverpool Daily Post*, 6 May 1941. *Bootle Times*, 9 May 1941. Blackpool Air Raid Incidents, CBBL/12, Preston RO.
230 Birmingham Fire Services, Air Raid Summaries, Birmingham Reference Library.
231 S. A. Harris, op. cit., p. 153. Likewise, Athol St below.
232 HO 192/1153/81.
233 RAIL 421/90.
234 *Bootle Times*, 9 May 1941.
235 ADM 53/113518.
236 N. Monsarrat, *Three Corvettes*, op. cit., p. 57.
237 Ship's papers, General Register and Record Office of Shipping and Seamen.
238 Lloyd's *Weekly Casualty Reports*, 23-29 May 1941.
239 WO 166/2259.
240 WO 166/2393.
241 ADM 199/658.
242 MDHB PEC 8/1.
243 MDHB PEC 11/3.
244 HO 186/625.
245 *Report on the Police Establishment*, op. cit., p. 13.
246 ADM 199/658.
247 HO 203.
248 HO 199/195.
249 352 MIN/DEF 5 May 1941.
250 INF 1/292/1.
251 LFB Incident Reports, op. cit.
252 Ibid.
253 AN 2/54.
254 LFB Incident Reports, op. cit.
255 HO 186/538.
256 Commander Sir Aylmer Firebrace, *Fire Service Memories* (London, 1949), p. 198 et seq.
257 352 MIN/DEF 6 May 1941.
258 MDHB PEC 11/3. J. W. de Roever, op. cit., p. 115. Lloyd's *Weekly Casualty Reports*, 6-12 June 1941.
259 LFB Incident Reports, op. cit.
260 352 MIN/DEF 6 May 1941.
261 *Report on the Police Establishment*, op. cit., p. 13.
262 AN 2/740.
263 B/LWC, United Warehouse Keepers' Conference, NMGM.
264 352 MIN/DEF 8 May 1941.
265 MDHB PEC 11/3.
266 INF 1/292/1.
267 ADM 199/658. ADM 53/114290.
268 HO 203.
269 HO 186/538.

270 *Liverpool Daily Post*, 2 August 1941.
271 AN 2/54.
272 LFB Incident Reports, op. cit.
273 MT 63/140.
274 AIR 24/140.
275 LFB Incident Reports, op. cit.
276 *Lloyd's List Law Reports*, vol. 73, p. 66.
277 HO 186/538.
278 Sir Aylmer Firebrace, loc. cit.
279 HO 186/538.
280 *Liverpool Daily Post*, 5 June 1941.
281 HO 186/2316.
282 Ivan Southall, op. cit. *Liverpool Echo*, 11 January 1958 (*Restrivo*). ADM 199/658.
283 MT 9/3587.
284 Sir Aylmer Firebrace, loc. cit.
285 Engineer's Department, Acc 3323.
286 HO 203.
287 *Bootle Times*, 9 May 1941.
288 ADM 199/1186.
289 *The Blitz Then and Now*, op. cit.
290 HO 198/197. *Liverpool Echo*, 25 May 1971, p. 6.
291 C. L. Dunn, op. cit., p. 334. See also *Bootle Times*, 30 May 1941.
292 Food Products, HO 192/1153/79. Rolph, HO 192/951.
293 *Bootle Times*, 16 May 1941.
294 Bootle Fire Brigade Committee Report Book, 17 May 1941 – Bootle Library. *Liverpool Daily Post*, 14 June 1941.
295 HO 198/207.
296 Major Salt, op. cit. *Bootle Times*, 18 July 1941. *Liverpool Echo*, 17 May 1971.
297 HO 198/197. *Liverpool Echo*, 2 December 1957.
298 *The Cathedral Record*, vol. XVIII, p. 222.
299 AN 2/54.
300 Ibid.
301 352 MIN/MAR 20 May 1941.
302 LFB Incident Reports, op. cit.
303 Some information supplied by Fred Olsen & Co.
304 J. W. de Roever, op. cit., pp. 115 & 116.
305 ADM 199/658, 24 March 1941.
306 ADM 53/113518.
307 Belgian citation, courtesy of Belgian Embassy.
308 Ellerman's Wilson Line documents in private collection.
309 Lloyd's *Weekly Casualty Reports*, 23-29 May 1941.
310 Ibid. 16-22 May 1941.
311 Ibid. 23-29 May 1941.
312 MDHB *Port at War* correspondence.
313 ADM 53/115222.
314 ADM 53/114290. ADM 199/1186. ADM 199/2065.
315 WO 166/2259.
316 N. Monsarrat, *Three Corvettes*, op. cit., p. 57.
317 Liverpool Shipwreck and Humane Society; 102nd Annual Report, p. 59.
318 HO 198/197.
319 MDHB PEC 11/3.
320 Ibid. and RAIL 421/90.
321 352 MIN/DEF 8 May 1941.
322 *Bootle Times*, 16 May 1941.
323 WO 166/109.
324 *Bootle Times*, 3 October 1941.
325 MDHB PEC 11/3.
326 HO 203.
327 S. A. Harris, op. cit., p. 153.
328 Edith Pargeter, op. cit., p. 147.
329 ADM 53/114290. ADM 199/658.
330 WO 166/3057.
331 LFB Incident Reports, op. cit.
332 WO 166/4002.
333 ADM 199/658. WO 166/3057.
334 ADM 199/658.
335 HO 192/1153/80.
336 Roads, 352 MIN/WAT 20 May 1941. Houses, HO 199/195. Woolfall Heath, 352 MIN/DEF 12 May 1941. Suffolk Regiment, WO 166/4708. Restaurants, *Bootle Times*, 30 May 1941.
337 30 Troop and lack of cranes, HO 199/195. Sunday work, 352 MIN/DEF 23 May 1941.
338 352 MIN/DEF 12 May 1941 (telephone vans). Post Office Archives. Stan Roberts, *The First Hundred years of the Telephone Service in the Liverpool Telephone Area* (Liverpool, 1980) pp. 77/86.
339 352 MIN/DEF 10 June 1941.
340 HO 199/195.
341 352 MIN/DEF 3 June 1941.
342 HO 192/1152/71.
343 MDHB Docks and Quays Committee Minutes, 29 October 1941.
344 *Stromboli*, MDHB *Port at War* correspondence. Bodies, *Liverpool Echo*, 1 May 1942.
345 MDHB *Port at War* correspondence.
346 MDHB WUP W.38.
347 *Liverpool Echo*, 17 December 1957. This would seem to dispose of a document in Brocklebank's records that refers to a total of 1,866 bombs, weighing 350 tons, with no more than 875 in any one hold.
348 *Liverpool Echo*, 12 January 1945.
349 MDHB WUP W.95c.
350 AN 2/54.
351 MDHB PEC 11/3. AN 2/53 (Appendix F). AN 2/54.
352 RAIL 421/90.
353 Records of the Mersey Railway, NMGM.
354 352 MIN/DEF 26 May 1941. *Liverpool Echo*, 27 May 1941.
355 352 MIN/WAT 20 January 1942.
356 G. V. Blackstone, *History of the British Fire Service* (London, 1957) p. 420.
357 352 MIN/WAT 18 November and 16 December 1941, 20 January and 17 March 1942.
358 *Report on the Police Establishment*, op. cit., pp. 14-15.
359 *Liverpool Daily Post* and *Echo*, 22 January 1943.
360 Mass-Observation Archive: Topic Collection 'Air Raids', Box 9 File M. 361. Richard Collier, op. cit.
362 C. D. Hughes.
363 352 MIN/DEF 28 May 1941.
364 G. V. Blackstone, op. cit., p. 423.
365 352 MIN/DEF 3, 11, 26 & 27 June 1941.

INDEX

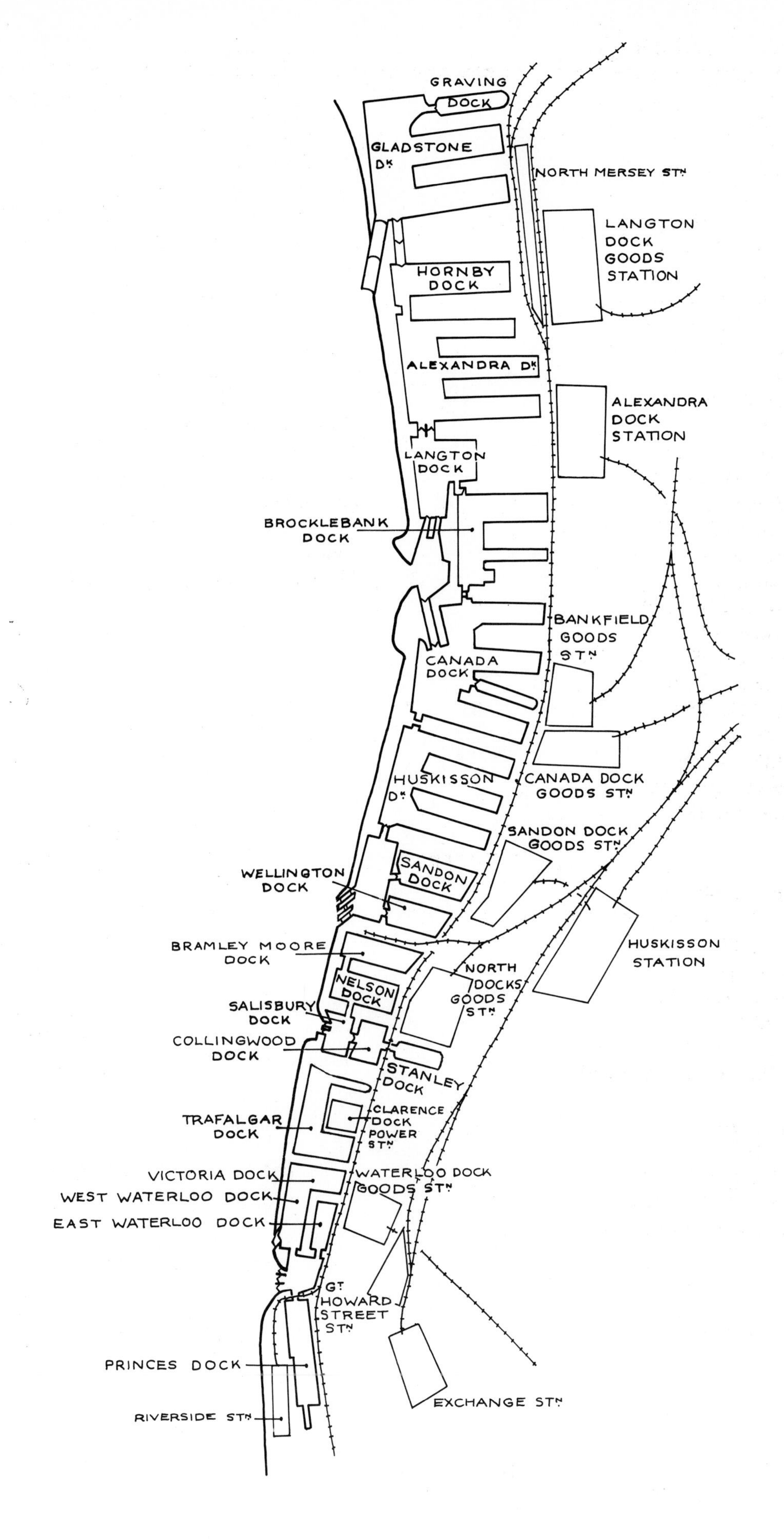

Liverpool – the North Docks

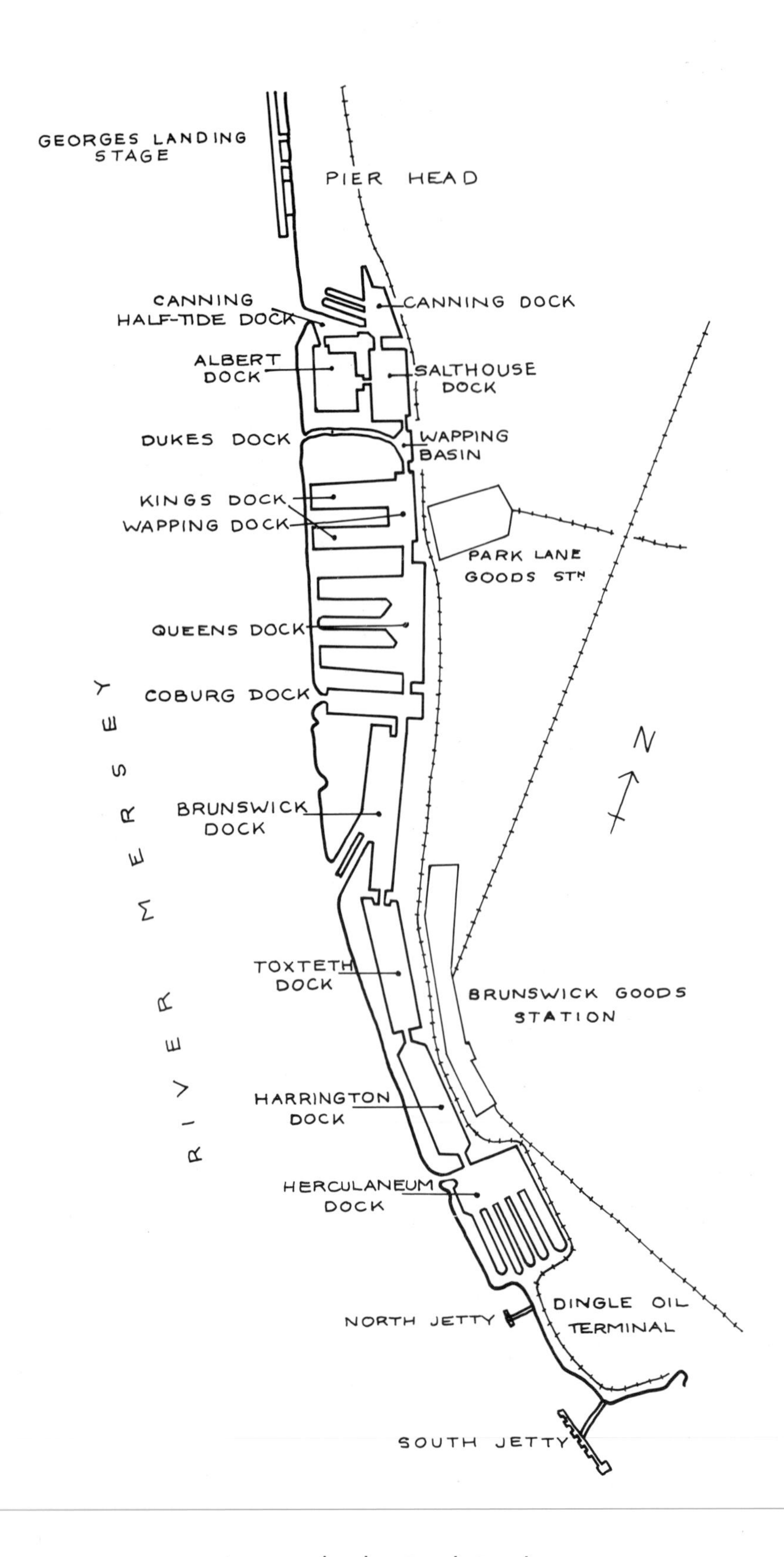

Liverpool – the South Docks

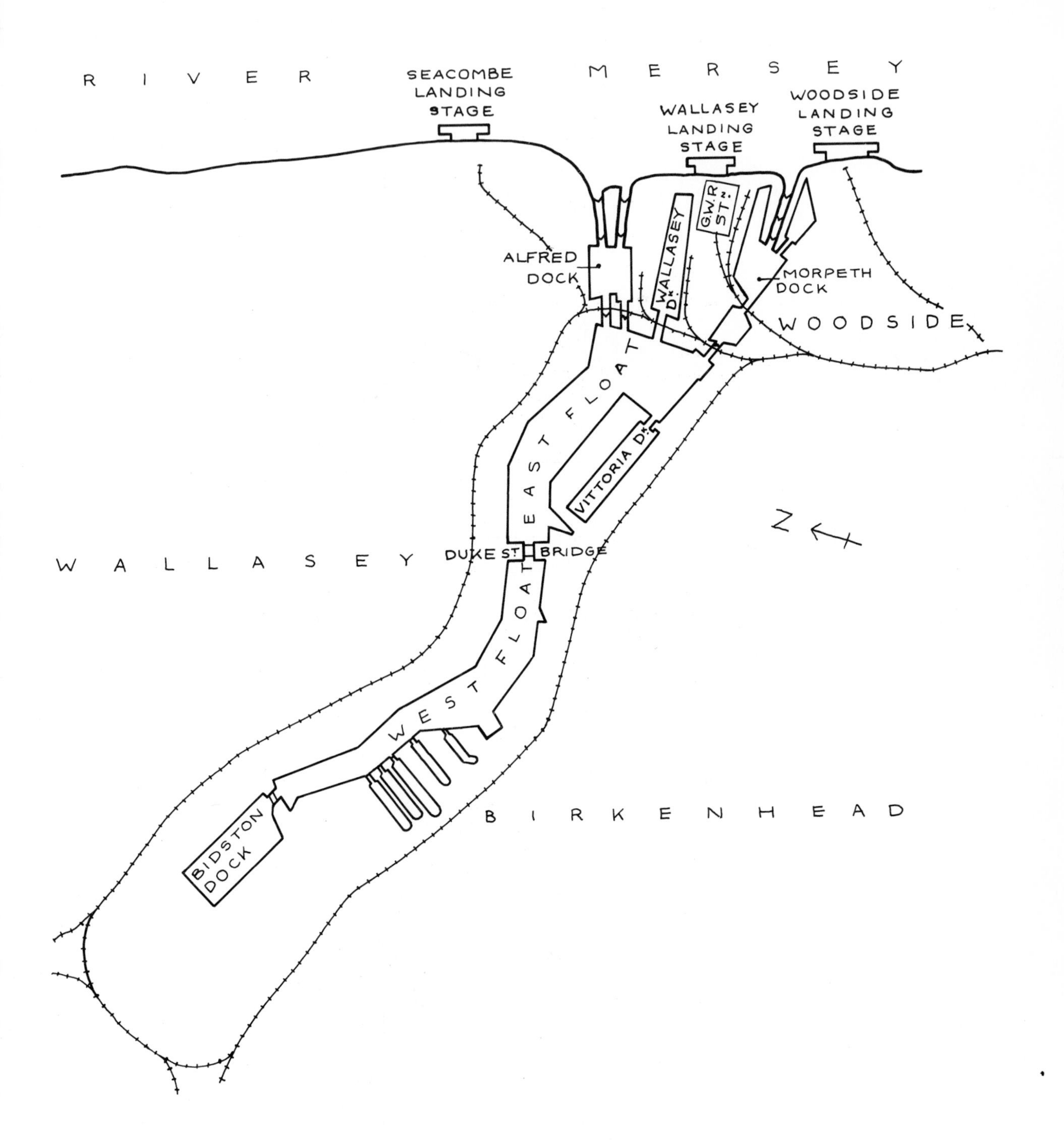

Birkenhead Docks